INTERNATIONAL DEVELOPMENT IN FOCUS

A Triple Win

Fiscal and Welfare Benefits of Economic Participation by Syrian Refugees in Jordan

JOHANNES HOOGEVEEN AND CHINEDU OBI, EDITORS

WORLD BANK GROUP

Contents

Boxes

Figures

Figures

Tables

Foreword

Seventy-six percent of Syrians of working age living in Jordan are unemployed or inactive in the labor market. Meanwhile, despite massive amounts of humanitarian aid for over a decade, more than half the Syrian refugees in the country live in extreme poverty. These facts do not undervalue the immense solidarity and generosity Jordanians and the government of Jordan have extended, and continue to extend, to their less fortunate neighbors. Instead, they point toward a need for change.

This book presents a joint effort by the United Nations High Commissioner for Refugees and the World Bank to explore the welfare of Syrian refugees in Jordan and to review the assistance they receive and their participation in the economy. The volume is timely, as a rapid rise in the global number of refugees and the emergence of new development priorities such as climate change are increasingly exposing the financial vulnerability of the humanitarian system.

As the world seeks to resolve the dilemma of how to care for more refugees with ever more limited budgets, financial donors and other actors involved will progressively give preference to approaches that limit refugee dependence and that expect refugees to contribute economically. Not only does work restore refugees' financial independence, it facilitates their productive contribution to society upon return to their home countries. Moreover, it helps ensure that financial assistance remains available for those who need it most: the vulnerable. And it frees up resources that can then be invested in the development of the host country—to the benefit of hosts and refugees alike.

This volume demonstrates that Jordan has done a remarkable job in hosting Syrian refugees, gracefully offering a safe haven to hundreds of thousands and integrating them into public-services provision and the country's economy. Doing so has already significantly reduced the financial burden of caring for refugees. This reality is widely recognized and appreciated, as financial donors' continued support to the government of Jordan reflects.

The book also shows that more can be done to increase Syrian refugees' economic participation in the economy of Jordan. It points out that a mutually beneficial bargain exists from which refugees, the people of Jordan, and financial donors all stand to gain.

How to realize this bargain is far from obvious, as experiences with the Jordan Compact, which pursued a comparable objective, have demonstrated. But with persistence, hard work, and above all, an open dialogue between the government of Jordan and its humanitarian and development partners, progress toward its realization is feasible. This is the ambition that motivated the United Nations High Commissioner for Refugees and the World Bank to prepare this volume, and this is the vision to which we are committed.

Jean-Christophe Carret
World Bank Country Director
Middle East Department

Acknowledgments

This volume would not have come about without the trust, support, and contributions of many people. At the risk of omitting someone, we thank Maria Eugenia Genoni, Maria Lagourou, and Matthew Wai-Poi, who stood at the basis of this volume when they set out to include a full-fledged consumption module in the 2021 Vulnerability Assessment Framework survey, which would make it possible to estimate, for the first time, poverty among refugees living in and outside of refugee camps in Jordan. Data from the successfully completed survey were used not only to estimate poverty, but also to calculate a new proxy means test and to inform the costing of the Jordan Response Plan.

In addition to the authors of the various chapters, we would like to thank Marguerite Duponchel and Sara Granlund for careful review of the manuscript and insightful feedback; Kareem Ur Rehman for helping us access and understand data from the Refugee Assistance Information System; Aimee Foong for closely reading the manuscript and coordinating feedback from the Jordan office of the United Nations High Commissioner for Refugees; Xavier Devictor, Ola Hisou, Takaaki Masaki, and Jeffrey Tanner for their excellent peer review; Suhair Al-Zubairi and Lanto Ramanankasina for their support throughout the process; and Holly Benner, Jean-Christophe Carret, Norbert Fiess, Alan Fuchs, and Salman Zaidi for their guidance and patience.

Finally, a special word of thanks to our sponsors, the Joint Data Center on Forced Displacement and the PROSPECTS Partnership Programme, funded through the World Bank–administered Multi-Donor Trust Fund for Forced Displacement, without whom this volume would not have seen the light of day.

About the Authors

Céline Ferré is a development economist specializing in social protection and labor, with a particular focus on forced migration and the transition to a low-carbon economy. Her current work involves measuring labor market participation among vulnerable populations, understanding their preferences, and identifying optimal job transition pathways (among coal-dependent workers in Europe; displaced populations, including Syrians and Ukrainians; and Roma). She has previous experience as an economist with the World Bank, where she worked within the Social Protection and Jobs Group.

Johannes (Hans) Hoogeveen is a senior economist and global lead for Poverty and Fragility at the World Bank. When data collection for this volume started, he was practice manager for the Poverty and Equity Global Practice in the Equitable Growth, Finance, and Institutions Vice Presidency, allowing him to closely follow the initial steps leading to this volume. Currently, his attention is focused on the Sahel region and Central Africa while increasingly working on aspects related to refugee economic participation.

Erwin Knippenberg is an economist in the Poverty and Equity Global Practice at the World Bank. He dedicates his work to conducting and leveraging data-driven analysis to inform policies affecting the poorest and most vulnerable, including refugees. He has published work on countries across the Middle East and Africa, including Afghanistan, Ethiopia, and the Islamic Republic of Iran. Previously, Erwin was an Overseas Development Institute Fellow at the Liberian Ministry of Finance. He holds a PhD in applied economics from Cornell University, where he wrote his dissertation on resilience and food security in the context of climate change.

Maria Lagourou is a humanitarian specialist, and during the time the research for this volume was conducted, she was the vulnerability assessment framework coordinator at the United Nations High Commissioner for Refugees' office in Jordan. Her work across various nongovernmental organizations and United Nations' agencies centers on connecting data to real-world needs and creating solutions that protect and empower marginalized groups. Presently, her focus is on gender-based violence and women's empowerment in Syria. She holds a master's of public administration degree from Columbia University with a focus on international economic development.

Chinedu Obi is an economist at the World Bank, where he started as a fellow focusing on forced displacement in 2020. He was seconded to the United Nations High Commissioner for Refugees in 2022 to co-lead and serve as the key liaison on the project on which this book is based. He is also a senior research fellow with the Center for Climate Change and Development in Nigeria. He is passionate about leveraging data-driven insights to address complex challenges and make a positive impact on the lives of vulnerable people. He holds a joint PhD in socioeconomics and agricultural economics from Ghent University and the University of Pisa.

Silvia Redaelli is a senior economist in the World Bank's Poverty and Equity Global Practice, where she has primarily focused on poverty, labor market, and displacement issues in fragile and conflict-affected countries. During her time in the Middle East and North Africa region, she worked on deepening the understanding of poverty and displacement dynamics in Syria. She is currently leading work on the World Bank's poverty and data agenda in Afghanistan.

Alexander Tyler is a senior liaison adviser with the United Nations High Commissioner for Refugees (UNHCR), in the regional bureau for the Middle East and North Africa. He has covered Jordan and the Syrian crisis since 2013, during which time he has contributed to a number of collaborations between the World Bank and UNHCR examining refugee welfare and protection in the region.

Executive Summary

INTRODUCTION

Since the beginning of the Syrian crisis in 2011, hundreds of thousands of Syrians have fled to Jordan. In 2023, an estimated 660,000 Syrians lived as registered refugees in the country. In response to the crisis, the government of Jordan and its people have demonstrated immense solidarity and generosity. All the while, the Jordanian authorities have had to face tough choices, balancing their policies regarding refugees against their responsibilities toward their own citizens. Throughout, the international community has continued to provide substantial funding and supported Jordan's efforts to incorporate refugees into the broader development dialogue.

Over time, Jordan's response to the arrival of Syrian refugees has evolved, as have the modalities for international assistance. Significant innovations, such as the adoption of cash assistance, have enabled refugees in camps and urban areas to receive aid quickly and safely, while empowering them to make decisions regarding expenditure priorities. The 2016 Jordan Compact sought to be a "new paradigm," promoting economic development and opportunities in Jordan to the benefit of both Jordanian hosts and Syrian refugees. It refocused efforts on realizing development opportunities by attracting new private sector investments and creating jobs for both Jordanians and Syrian refugees by capitalizing on the preferential access granted, under the compact, to the European Union market through simplified rules of origin. Additional grants and concessional financing to support Jordan's macroeconomic framework and financing needs, as outlined in the Jordan Response Plan, accompanied this refocusing.

More than 7 years after the signing of the Jordan Compact and 13 years after the start of the Syrian crisis, conditions inside Syria continue to limit refugees' ability to return, while aid for support to refugees is under pressure. Against this backdrop, this volume sets out to do three things:

- ***Shed light on the welfare of Syrian refugees in Jordan through deep dives into poverty, aid, and the labor market.***
  The analysis leverages a newly available database that includes detailed information on refugees' welfare. A collaboration between the United Nations High Commissioner for Refugees (UNHCR) and the World Bank added a

detailed consumption module to the monitoring survey UNHCR regularly implements in Jordan, the Vulnerability Assessment Framework. Information gathered through implementation of this module generated a unique database unparalleled in the humanitarian world that has made it possible to explore many new aspects of refugee welfare, including the prevalence of monetary poverty among refugees living in and outside of refugee camps and the targeting of assistance, as well as the benefits of refugees' economic participation. This volume exploits this exceptional data set, complementing it with findings from Jordan's Labor Force Survey.

The results show that despite all the goodwill toward Syrian refugees in Jordan and all the resources, innovations, and initiatives for their support, poverty among them remains pervasive and their dependency on aid considerable. Despite opportunities to work, refugee incomes are low and insufficient to attain financial autonomy. A combination of low levels of productive and human capital and labor market regulations that relegate them to less remunerative occupations, is constraining refugees in this regard.

- *Shift the discussion on burden sharing between Jordan and the international community from one about principles to one about numbers.*
  By showing how much income refugees earn under different scenarios regarding labor market participation and applying Jordan's fiscal incidence analysis to refugees, this volume estimates the costs of hosting refugees and the savings associated with refugee economic participation.

  The results show that hosting refugees involves substantial ongoing costs: $465 million annually for basic needs and $444 million for including refugees in public-services provision. Had refugees not been allowed to work at all, the cost of hosting them would have been almost twice as high: $1.77 billion per year.

  Assigning dollar figures to the cost of hosting refugees under different scenarios of economic participation establishes clear parameters that can inform conversations regarding burden sharing. It also monetizes the benefits of participation, labeled "participation savings": $860 million per year.

- *Explore how a triple win can be realized.*
  The savings associated with refugee economic participation create scope for a triple win in which Jordan is recognized for its contribution to hosting refugees, donors save on aid needed, and Syrian refugees gain in autonomy.

  The idea of a triple win is not new: the Jordan Compact also promoted the notion that economic participation brings benefits to refugees, hosts, and the international community alike. Yet conversations along these lines must also account for the potential for short-term economic disruption that hosting refugees entails.

  On top of the $860 million per year in participation savings already identified, aid organizations can save an additional $400 million per year on international assistance for refugees, money that they could reprioritize for targeted humanitarian support or reallocate to other development activities benefiting both host communities and refugees. This suggests scope for a mutually beneficial bargain.

MAIN FINDINGS

After two introductory chapters that set the stage for the volume and present a socioeconomic profile of Syrian refugees living in and outside of camps in Jordan, chapter 3 focuses on measuring poverty among refugees, a discipline that remains in its infancy, as few studies exist that calculate poverty for refugees from consumption modules. By including a consumption module in the Vulnerability Assessment Framework survey, UNHCR Jordan has unlocked new possibilities for monitoring refugees' welfare, assessing the targeting efficiency of its programs, and approximating the income refugees earn. The module can be used to assess the fiscal cost of hosting refugees and to meet reporting obligations for the 2023 UNHCR's "Global Compact on Refugees Indicator Report" (UNHCR 2023). As such, the UNHCR's innovation in Jordan is worth replicating elsewhere, particularly where including refugees in national surveys is not (yet) feasible.

Using data from 2021, chapter 3 estimates, for the first time, monetary poverty among Syrian refugees living inside camps and among host communities in Jordan, finding a much higher incidence of poverty among refugees, 58 percent, than that among members of the host community, estimated at 16 percent by Jordan's Department of Statistics. Poverty rates are lower for those living in camps (45 percent) and higher for those living in host communities (62 percent), driven by higher expenses for housing and utilities and less assistance from humanitarian agencies. This finding is puzzling, because the decision to live outside a camp is to a certain degree voluntary.[1] More than 80 percent of Syrian refugees choose to live outside of camps, accepting not only a greater likelihood of poverty, but also a greater intensity (as measured by the poverty gap, which is the difference between the poverty line and household consumption). Why would refugees expose themselves to an increased risk of becoming destitute?

Using a multidimensional poverty measure, which in addition to monetary poverty also captures education and access to services, reduces the welfare gap between refugees living in and outside of camps. Yet it still finds refugees in camps to be better off.

Chapter 3 then explores whether freedom might be an overlooked dimension of welfare, one that seems obviously critical for populations who, like refugees, can face restrictions. Compared with refugees living among Jordan's host population, those living in refugee camps have less freedom, as they face restrictions in their movements outside of the camps and fewer employment opportunities. It seems plausible that like anyone, refugees value their autonomy and experience dignity as a result of their ability to sustain themselves from their own earnings, and that they appreciate possibilities for economic advancement in their own lives and those of their children. Those who choose to live outside Jordan's refugee camps are essentially willing to forgo part of their consumption and to endure a greater risk of monetary poverty for the sake of this economic and personal autonomy.

The chapter finishes with a plea for an extended multidimensional welfare measure for refugees that includes a measure of freedom. It concludes that even though Syrian refugees in Jordan continue to remain economically vulnerable and worthy of humanitarian assistance, they should not be considered passive recipients of aid. Rather, they seek autonomy and are ready to work.

Chapter 4 shifts the focus to the realm of aid extended to Syrian refugees, emphasizing cash assistance programs offered by two of the largest humanitarian agencies: UNHCR and the World Food Programme. The chapter finds that the significant amounts of cash assistance that have been and continue to be provided play a major role in decreasing poverty among Syrian refugees in Jordan, reducing it by as much as 20 percentage points, from 78 to 58 percent. It also uncovers limitations in the way assistance is provided: inequities in who receives assistance (blanket coverage for those living in camps versus targeted availability among refugees living outside camps, who also receive less, even though they have higher estimated levels of deprivation), overlaps (a multitude of assistance programs often reach the same refugee families), and analytical constraints (the minimum expenditure basket does not reflect refugees' revealed preferences).

There appears scope to improve the delivery of humanitarian assistance in Jordan, including through a more coordinated effort to track cash assistance in UNHCR's Refugee Assistance Information System. Still, at available funding levels, expected to decrease from current amounts, even the best-targeted program will have only a limited impact on poverty among refugees. More realistic avenues for reducing poverty lie with increasing refugees' financial autonomy.

This reality, along with the revealed preference of refugees for financial autonomy, argues for a transformative change, with programs focusing less on unconditional handouts and in-kind benefits and more on aligning assistance with, and providing incentives for, refugee self-reliance.

Chapter 5 delves into labor market outcomes and explores how Syrian refugees fare relative to other participants in the Jordanian labor market. Syrian refugees have different characteristics than Jordanians and economic immigrants. They tend to be younger and less educated, to have higher dependency ratios, and to have been in Jordan for a shorter period. These differences carry over into their labor market outcomes: (lower) labor market participation, sector of employment, (higher) degree of informality, type of occupation, and (lower) pay.

Policy regulations also play a role in explaining labor market outcomes. Syrian refugees can work only in a limited number of sectors in the Jordanian economy—mainly manufacturing, construction, agriculture, and the hospitality sector, with other sectors closed to non-Jordanians—and need to obtain work permits to do so. Higher-skilled employment requires costly and highly regulated specialized work permits.

The chapter finds that personal characteristics only partly explain Syrian refugees' high propensity to earn low wages (JD 300 per month or less); restrictive labor market policies, unequal treatment, and refugees' (and employers') opting for informality account for a larger part. Increasing refugees' earnings will require investments in human capital formation as well as in measures to facilitate labor market participation, including transport and childcare. Yet most important will be a reduction in regulatory constraints and the facilitation of additional employment opportunities, creating a playing field for refugees that is level with that for other workers, and sustainable growth of Jordan's economy.

Chapter 6 estimates the monetary value that the economic participation of refugees represents. Building on the preceding chapters on poverty, cash assistance, and labor market access, it estimates the fiscal cost of hosting refugees under different scenarios of economic participation. This exercise not only quantifies costs but puts a monetary value on the savings made possible when refugees earn their own income by working.

The estimate starts by determining how much is needed for a dignified life in terms of both private goods (the cost of basic needs) and public services (the cost of service provision). The cost of basic needs is then compared with how much Syrian refugees in Jordan are currently earning. Calculating income directly is difficult, but it can be approximated by deducting assistance received from consumption (referred to as "preassistance consumption"). The difference between the poverty line and preassistance consumption then reflects refugees' need for humanitarian assistance.

Figure ES.1 illustrates how the need for assistance declines the more income refugees earn.

Using this methodology, chapter 6 presents three participation scenarios: in the baseline scenario, refugees earn no income and are fully dependent on humanitarian assistance. In the status quo scenario, with restricted income earning opportunities, refugees earn income that, in turn, reduces their need for humanitarian assistance relative to the baseline. A scenario with further economic participation leads to additional savings by increasing refugee income.

The chapter then extends the analysis in regard to the cost of service provision. Using fiscal incidence analysis and the cost of providing in-kind education and health services, as well as subsidized utilities, the analysis assigns to refugee households, in accordance with their income deciles, amounts paid in direct and indirect taxes. These amounts are then compared across the three participation scenarios.

Jordan's contribution to the burden of caring for Syrian refugees is found to be as large as that of the international community. Were Syrian refugees in Jordan not allowed to work, $1,948 per year would be needed per refugee to bring their consumption up to the poverty line level and an additional $730 per refugee to cover expenses for health, education, and other public services. By working and contributing to revenue collection, Syrian refugees reduce the amount required for assistance to $704 per refugee for basic needs and $672 per refugee for public services.

FIGURE ES.1

Using the poverty line and poverty gap to identify requirements for basic-needs assistance

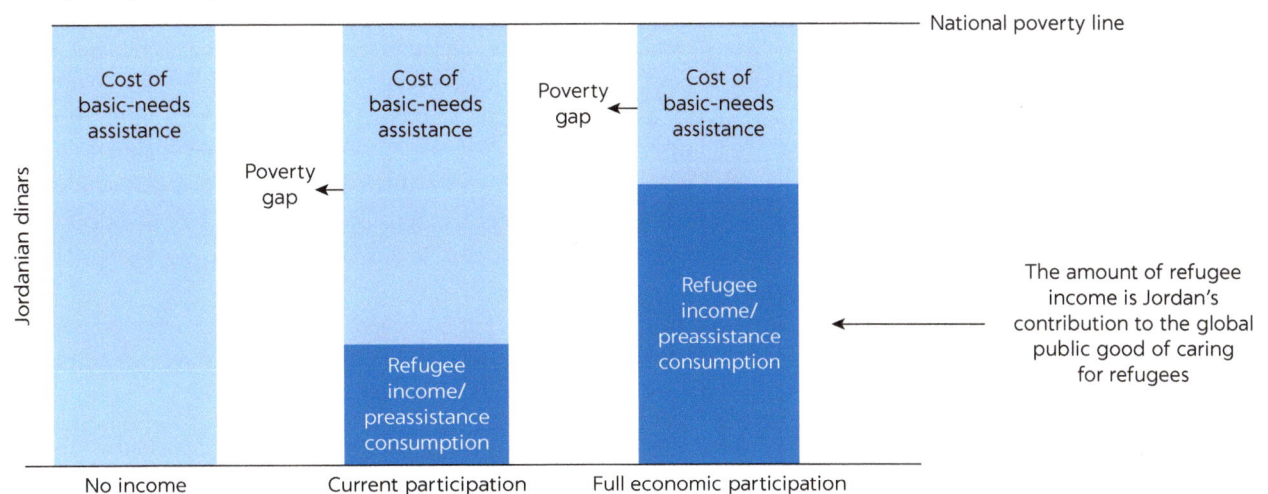

Source: Original figure for this publication.

Evaluated against 660,000 registered Syrian refugees in 2023, this implies that instead of $1.77 billion per year if they were not accessing economic opportunities, refugees require $465 million for basic needs and $444 million for public-services provision: $909 million in total. Thus, the savings achieved through refugees' economic participation amount to $860 million every year.

Chapter 6 also finds that removing employment restrictions on Syrian refugees in Jordan would increase annual savings on the cost of hosting refugees by $400 million, bringing the total savings to $1.3 billion per year and reducing the total aid needed to $500 million per year.

REALIZING THE TRIPLE WIN

It is broadly recognized that caring for refugees is a responsibility shared between donors and host countries. The Global Compact on Refugees is premised on more predictable and equitable sharing of responsibility for refugees that requires international collaboration to reach sustainable solutions. A United Nations resolution of December 2017 invites UNHCR, for instance, "to measure the impact arising from hosting, protecting and assisting refugees, with a view to assessing gaps in international cooperation and promoting burden- and responsibility-sharing that is more equitable, predictable and sustainable, and to begin reporting on the results to Member States in 2018" (United Nations 2017).

The analysis in this volume illustrates how such measurement can inform policy dialogue around a triple win. Promoting the economic participation of refugees increases their financial autonomy (win 1) and saves on aid (win 2); in the case of Syrian refugees in Jordan, these savings are the government of Jordan's contribution to the global burden of caring for refugees. Explicit recognition of this contribution is important and enhances transparency. It also facilitates a mutually beneficial bargain between international donors and host countries in which the former recognize the savings on aid achieved and make additional investments to offset any negative side effects associated with refugee economic participation and to support host country economic development, which would create jobs for Jordanians and refugees alike (win 3).

The participation savings that are already being realized, as well as the amount that could still be achieved, are sufficiently large to make a mutually beneficial bargain attractive. The Jordan Compact elaborated a first such bargain, but Syrian refugees' continued dependence on aid, their limited job opportunities (as well as those for their Jordanian hosts), and their high levels of poverty suggest the compact has not met all expectations. This reality does not mean that a bargain is not possible, or even that the Jordan Compact was not a success (after all, no counterfactual has been established). But it does mean that more ambitious refugee participation in Jordan's economy may be harder to achieve than was initially envisaged.

The possibility of a renewed bargain should motivate further discussions among the donor community, humanitarian agencies, and the government of Jordan. What would such a bargain comprise?

- *Consolidating existing achievements.* Much has been accomplished since the first Syrian refugees arrived in Jordan. Currently, 80 percent of Syrians in Jordan live outside of refugee camps among the host population; Syrian refugees make use of public services in health and education; 22 percent are fully financial autonomous and require no assistance to attain an acceptable standard of living; and their economic participation, at current levels, reduces the cost of humanitarian assistance for Syrian refugees by as much as $860 million per year.

Unfortunately, tensions threaten these achievements. Jordan has largely withdrawn electricity subsidies for refugees, the waiver of the fee for work permits is renewed annually and subject to negotiation, and recent significant increases in mandatory social security contributions for refugees may push refugees to abandon their work permits and retreat to the informal labor market. The noteworthy achievements in respect to refugee economic participation need to be consolidated, with clear commitments from the government of Jordan to continue its support for refugee participation *and* from international donors to provide predictable funding to cover the recurrent costs of refugee economic participation.

- *Expanding the economic participation of refugees.* Less restricted participation of refugees in Jordan's economy will give the 78 percent of refugees who remain dependent on assistance a shot at financial autonomy. It will also bring additional savings on humanitarian assistance, which the international community ideally would invest in development priorities benefiting both hosts and refugees. Additional participation requires a more dynamic Jordanian economy, easing of labor market restrictions on refugees, support to refugees in finding work, and investment in restoring human capital to allow refugees to meet their economic potential.

- *Aligning humanitarian assistance with the promotion of financial self-reliance.* The crisis in Syria is already prolonged, with no clear end in sight. Humanitarian assistance is most effective during emergencies, a phase that the Syrian crisis has long since passed. Rather than maintaining a parallel refugee system within Jordan, it is worth considering how refugee camps can be better integrated into the country's economy; equally worth considering is what it would take to scale down humanitarian assistance to what is needed to ensure protection to the most vulnerable only and to facilitate refugees' voluntary return to Syria in safety and dignity, once the conditions inside the country are conducive. Greater involvement of refugees in Jordan's labor market and public service provision will eventually open a pathway toward the transformation and even closure of refugee camps. Refugees who remain dependent on assistance then need to be transferred to national social protection systems, with international donors providing credible long-term commitments to bearing the cost.

To help realize these aspirational objectives, the volume proposes five concrete steps:

- *Strengthening the evidence base for refugee participation.* The discussion on burden sharing for refugees deserves to move from deliberations about principles to discussions about numbers. This volume puts a monetary value on the cost of hosting refugees and the savings attributable to refugee participation. More research could further inform the debate.[2] Preferably researchers familiar with Jordan will carry out the necessary research using Jordanian data, requiring investments in data collection and local research capacity.

- *Developing a strategy for investing in Jordan's economy.* Absorbing additional refugee labor in Jordan's economy will require an investment strategy that identifies opportunities and addresses bottlenecks. The Jordan Compact, which has been a political success but has had limited economic impact (Betts 2021), underscores the importance of a well-developed strategy. The investment strategy should build on the evidence mentioned in the first bullet and will help assure financial donors that reallocating humanitarian savings toward development activities is smart economics.

- *Creating an active dialogue based on evidence.* The objectives of the triple win can be realized only in conjunction with dialogue between the international community and Jordanian authorities. This dialogue can take many shapes. One option is to create an annual moment of reflection, for instance, through a high-level conference regarding the results of policy research on Jordan's economic progress and refugee participation. As this is not the first time that there has been a focus on realizing a triple win—the Jordan Compact also aimed to do so—the first conference might want to assess the successes and failures of the compact, the main obstacles to further refugee participation, and the gains to be realized if these obstacles were removed.

- *Aligning the delivery of humanitarian assistance with the promotion of refugee financial self-reliance.* As refugees transition to fuller economic participation, the existing provision of humanitarian aid should be made more conducive to their financial autonomy. Currently, assistance is unconditional, and the continuation of camps far away from economic opportunities is an obstacle to economic integration, as is the privileging of assistance to refugees residing in camps. With aid budgets under strain and allocations for support to refugees split across ever-increasing refugee numbers, scrutiny of the aid delivery model is needed to identify ways to increase the cost-effectiveness and targeting efficiency of delivery models and to align assistance better with refugee self-reliance. The adoption of measurable targets with respect to cost-effectiveness, efficiency, and self-reliance would be welcome, and a program of research to develop and test different approaches could support it.

- *Committing to transparency.* Any collaboration is strengthened by trust and understanding, requiring a commitment to transparency and information sharing. Trust and understanding are strengthened when there is a common appreciation of the facts. Yet, to date, much information relevant to collaboration remains inaccessible. Data from critical surveys collected by Jordan's Department of Statistics are unavailable for public analysis. While some aid organizations make information available on overhead and the share of funding that reaches beneficiaries, not all do, rendering it extremely difficult to assess the efficiency of service provision by humanitarian agencies. Donors and development partners also need to be more transparent about the financing they make available for refugees, along with the conditions attached to it. All institutional partners with a stake in realizing the triple win face challenges only they can address. Improving transparency does not require collaboration; each institution can accomplish it independent of the others, providing the government of Jordan, donors, development partners, and humanitarian agencies active in Jordan with an opportunity to demonstrate their commitment to realizing the triple win.

NOTES

1. Camps were set up only after refugees had been arriving in Jordan for some time. After the influx had saturated host communities, later arrivals were directed to the camps. Today, a government procedure permits refugees to request to officially move out of camps. See chapter 2.

2. What can be learned from the implementation of the Jordan Compact, how large the negative spillovers associated with additional refugee participation are, what options are available to address negative spillovers, how much these solutions would cost, how much financing is made available for refugees and hosts, what the regulatory and other barriers to further refugee participation are, and how humanitarian assistance can be aligned with refugee participation are just some of the issues that research could address.

REFERENCES

Betts, Alexander. 2021. *The Wealth of Refugees: How Displaced People Can Build Economies*. Oxford, UK: Oxford University Press.

UNHCR (United Nations High Commissioner for Refugees). 2023. "Global Compact on Refugees Indicator Report." UNHCR, Geneva.

United Nations. 2017. General Assembly Resolution A/RES/72/150, "Resolution Adopted by the General Assembly on 19 December 2017," (https://www.un.org/en/ga/72/resolutions .shtml).

Abbreviations

CEQ	Commitment to Equity Institute
CI	confidence interval
EU	European Union
GDP	gross domestic product
HIES	Household Income and Expenditure Survey
IHRC	International Human Rights Clinic
ILO	International Labour Organization
JD	Jordanian dinar
JDC	Joint Data Center on Forced Displacement
kcal	kilocalorie
MEB	minimum expenditure basket
MPCA	multipurpose cash assistance
NRC	Norwegian Refugee Council
RAIS	Refugee Assistance Information System
SMEB	survival minimum expenditure basket
UN	United Nations
UNHCR	United Nations High Commissioner for Refugees
WASH	water, sanitation, and hygiene
WFP	World Food Programme

All dollar amounts are US dollars unless otherwise indicated.

1 Time to Renew the Partnership

ALEXANDER TYLER

MAIN MESSAGES

In response to the Syrian refugee crisis, Jordan has demonstrated impressive solidarity and generosity in hosting a large number of Syrian refugees. It has also had to make tough choices in balancing its policies regarding refugees against its responsibilities to its own citizens. The international community has shown Jordan remarkable support, surpassing that provided in regard to all previous humanitarian emergencies in terms of the levels of funding over a sustained period. Thirteen years on, conditions inside the Syrian Arab Republic limit refugees' ability to voluntarily return, making it crucial to recognize that the refugee response is a partnership between international donors and Jordan requiring a long-term commitment.

RENEWING THE PARTNERSHIP

They came at night. Women, men, pushing out of the dark undergrowth, drawn toward the car beams of the Jordanian border guards' vehicles. Families, elderly, children, each carrying an assortment of belongings: anything of value, anything of use, anything they could save from their homes inside Syria. The border guards called out, moving forward to receive them, shouldering their bags, helping them toward makeshift, low-strung tents. The guards shared their rations and water before guiding the refugees onto trucks and buses that would take them further into Jordan, to safety.

This was a typical night in early 2013 near Tal Shihab, one of the many crossings between the southern Daraa province of Syria and northern Jordan. At the peak of the crisis, 6,000 refugees were crossing each day (Boswall and Al Akash 2015). The same scenes were playing out on the Syrian borders with Iraq, Lebanon, and Türkiye.

The conflict in Syria began in 2011 and quickly became brutal and violent, directly affecting millions of Syrians. More than 13 million have been forced to flee their homes; over half of these crossed into neighboring countries and beyond. The conflict has also become protracted. Thirteen years later, more than

6.8 million Syrians remain registered as refugees in the Arab Republic of Egypt, Iraq, Jordan, Lebanon, and Türkiye. Many have taken refuge in Jordan.

The story of the Syrian refugee crisis in Jordan has many facets. It is one of openness, compassion, and generosity on the part of the Jordanian government and people; of resilience of the refugees who have rebuilt their lives, despite their trauma and loss. It is one of international solidarity, as donor countries have provided political and financial support at levels and with a consistency over the years rarely seen in responses to other humanitarian emergencies.

It is also one of a quiet transformation in the way international aid is designed and delivered. United Nations (UN) agencies and nongovernmental organizations (NGOs), enabled by Jordan's banking infrastructure, have made significant innovations in cash programming, for instance, to distribute aid quickly and safely to refugees in camps and urban areas and empower them to make decisions about their expenditure priorities. The Jordan Compact has inspired global initiatives such as the Global Compact on Refugees, catalyzing the engagement of major developmental institutions such as the World Bank and demonstrating new ways the international community and countries hosting refugees can share the burden of supporting them.

This volume focuses on two interrelated facets: how policy choices influence the welfare of Syrian refugee families residing in Jordan and the fiscal cost of hosting them. It presents the results of the latest study in a series of collaborations between the World Bank Poverty and Equity Practice and the United Nations High Commissioner for Refugees (UNHCR) in Jordan and the wider Middle East and North Africa region (see, for instance, Joint Data Center on Forced Displacement, World Bank, and UNHCR 2020; Obi 2023; Verme et al. 2016; and World Bank Group et al. 2021). These collaborations have been financed by the two institutions' Joint Data Center on Forced Displacement and supported by the PROSPECTS Partnership Programme, which in turn is funded through the World Bank–administered Multi-Donor Trust Fund for Forced Displacement. They have represented a major step forward in improving the UNHCR's understanding of the challenges refugees face and how poverty affects and limits their choices (Verme et al. 2016). This improved understanding has in turn enabled the aid community as a whole to better target assistance and measure its impact. It has also helped the World Bank better understand the complexities of delivering aid to some of the most vulnerable groups and recognize the urgency of shifting the balance of refugee support from humanitarian assistance to economic participation.

Although the volume focuses on refugee welfare in particular, it is important to place this focus within an understanding of how the refugee response in Jordan has evolved since 2011. Over the last decade, there has been a close and dynamic interplay among the policies of Jordan's government toward refugees, Jordanian public perception, shocks such as COVID-19, and the international community's financial support to Jordan. The government's ability to implement policies that enable refugees to live in dignity, with access to public education and health care, and to work legally, as well as its confidence in implementing them, is tied to the notion that financing the refugee response is a shared, global responsibility. As domestic priorities and global events and trends have influenced the international community's financial support to Jordan, so in turn Jordan's policies toward Syrian refugees have adapted and evolved. Betts (2021) portrays well the importance of this interplay and the challenges it represents to "sustainable sanctuary" (6).

A core consideration for Jordan is its fundamental responsibility toward its own citizens—their security and welfare—and the country's economic and development trajectory, all while protecting its future demographic and cultural identity. Within this core framework, Jordan has sought to fulfill its international responsibilities by welcoming and protecting refugees. The resulting balancing act is not unique to Jordan; indeed, many larger countries and countries with better resources have struggled with it and continue to do so (Betts 2021). But as it has for many front-line countries in the global South, the sheer number of refugees arriving, not least relative to Jordan's own population and capacity to respond, has dramatically compounded the risks and consequences. Against this backdrop, chapter 2 elaborates on the evolution of Jordan's policies toward receiving and hosting large numbers of Syrian refugees, including border management and whether to limit the number of Syrian refugees accepted; the settlement of refugees in camps or in urban areas; and the extent of refugee access to public services, including health and education; as well as the legal issues involved.

The refugees themselves are not passive objects within this dynamic exchange. Just as we all do, refugees assess options and make decisions: on where they should settle, how they can provide for their families, and how to best ensure a future for their children. They develop strategies and make choices with short-, medium-, and long-term goals in mind (Betts 2021; World Bank 2020). However, the policies of the host country constrain their options and choices. Whether refugees arrive with some capital and assets, have connections with Jordanian or existing Syrian communities on which they can rely, can draw on remittances from family abroad, or arrive with nothing further defines the choices available.

Within their communities, refugees often have very different experiences based on their gender. Women and girls often face gender-related constraints in accessing education, health services, and opportunities for livelihoods and can be exposed to more acute risks, including gender-based violence and exploitation, requiring protection and further limiting their choices.

Expectations as to when they might be able to return home to Syria also particularly affect refugee families' strategies. Should they plan to simply cope for the short term or pursue longer-term goals? Initially many Syrian refugees expected that the fighting in Syria would end quickly and they would be able to return home within months. As the conflict intensified and the prospects of returning home diminished, these expectations changed (Dunmore 2015; UNHCR 2023). But by then, more and more refugees had sold their assets to cover living costs and entered into debt. Poverty among refugee households spiraled, leaving most dependent on a humanitarian aid program facing a funding crisis (Awamleh and Doraï 2023).

Though it shouldered the largest burden, Jordan did not face the Syrian crisis alone. From the beginning of the crisis, donor countries stepped up and provided significant financial, technical, and political support, building on decades of bilateral and multilateral development partnerships and humanitarian aid programs delivered by international financial institutions, UN agencies, and international and national NGOs. At the First and Second International Humanitarian Pledging Conferences for Syria in 2013 and 2014, donors pledged more than $3.9 billion to support refugee responses in the region and the humanitarian response inside Syria. When actual contributions outstripped the pledges, more than $750 million was channeled in each of those two years to aid programs in

Jordan, through UN-led Refugee Response Plan appeals. The World Food Programme put in place a massive and almost blanket feeding program through vouchers, gradually establishing a network of shops and supermarkets that refugees could access in urban areas and camps. Building on its past investments in national education systems, the United Nation's Children's Fund expanded the capacity of schools and classrooms, the number of teachers, and funding for education costs among refugee households, such as school materials and transport (Arnot and Seeger 2021). The UNHCR and many NGOs expanded cash programming, taking advantage of advanced banking systems and automated teller machine networks. Aid programs were designed to support not only refugees, but also the Jordanian communities hosting them, investing in public services and building capacity of government institutions in a manner that would benefit all (Awamleh and Doraï 2023; UNHCR 2014).

Following a familiar trend in humanitarian operations worldwide, however, international funding for the refugee response eventually began to falter. In March 2015, the Third International Humanitarian Pledging Conference, held in Kuwait, generated the lowest level of pledges by donors since the beginning of the crisis. By mid-2015, the UNHCR and World Food Programme were issuing dramatic calls for urgent funding to avert massive cuts in their programs in Jordan, on which so many refugees relied (Francis 2015; *The Guardian* 2015).

A similar story played out in Egypt, Iraq, Lebanon, and Türkiye. Refugees faced a heart-wrenching choice: stay and watch their family descend into poverty[1] and their children miss their education and their future or, using the few resources they had left, risk the dangerous and uncertain journey to Europe. Many took that risk. Between June 2015 and March 2016, millions of refugees and migrants crossed into the Balkans, Greece, and Türkiye, with many reaching other parts of Europe. Syrian refugees made up a significant portion of these movements and by 2016 had become the largest group of asylum seekers in Germany and many other European countries.

The movements catapulted the management of refugee crises to near the top of European domestic political concerns. A swell of support among Europeans expressing goodwill toward and support for refugees made engagement a major foreign policy priority in host countries neighboring Syria. Self-interest was also at work: European governments wanted to prevent future large, uncontrolled movements of refugees to Europe by addressing refugees' needs so they would stay in countries such as Jordan, Lebanon, and Türkiye (Betts 2021).

The result was transformational. In Jordan, the shift in global attention toward the management of refugee movements also had an immediate impact. Funding for the response in countries neighboring Syria skyrocketed. In February 2016, the Supporting Syria and the Region conference in London reinvigorated the international community's engagement in supporting Syrian refugees in neighboring countries (Huang and Gough 2019). Pledges reached $6.1 billion for 2016 and $6 billion from 2017–20.[2]

The London conference also heralded a new emphasis on programs that promoted inclusion in hosting countries, including access to education and the labor market, as reflected in innovative compacts between the European Union (EU) and host countries in the region. The 2016 Jordan Compact, for instance, sought to be a "new paradigm," promoting economic development and opportunities in Jordan to the benefit of Jordanians and Syrian refugees (Huang and Gough 2019). The compact included nonmonetary agreements, including one—tied to employment of Syrian refugees in Jordan—that the EU would simplify rules of origin for Jordanian exporters. The government of Jordan established a mechanism, including the Jordan Response Plan, that coordinated humanitarian and development programs, many of which sought development opportunities by attracting new investments and creating jobs for Jordanians and Syrian refugees. Sufficient grants and concessionary financing to support Jordan's macroeconomic framework and financing needs came with this new approach.

Now, in 2024, just past the 13-year anniversary of the onset of the Syrian crisis, the question remains how the partnership between the international community and Jordan will evolve. In many respects Jordan currently faces a situation similar to that in early 2015. Levels of international funding for refugee assistance have decreased dramatically across the refugee-hosting countries in the region, resulting in cuts in a number of key aid programs (Chehayeb 2023). The main UN-led regional response plan received $3.1 billion in funding in 2018, which had dropped to $1.8 billion by 2023 (3RP 2024). The economic participation of Syrian refugees has increased but remains limited, and without humanitarian assistance, almost 80 percent would be living in poverty. Meanwhile, Jordanian authorities rely on international financing to pay for refugee inclusion in public health care and education and to continue to subsidize food and water for refugees.[3]

The lack of opportunity for sustainable voluntary and safe refugee return to Syria requires a renewed commitment—with respect to both financing and policies that promote inclusion of refugees—on the part of all actors involved. Indeed, enhancing economic participation of refugees would be a key part of this commitment, but doing so would require popular support and predictable international funding over multiple years. In the short term, enhanced economic participation should aim not only to restore refugees' productive capacity, but also to invest in host communities. A new multiyear bargain is needed that enables refugees to live in dignity and recognizes and supports Jordan's contributions to hosting refugees.

This volume aims to catalyze a process of compact renewal by emphasizing, first of all, in chapter 3 of the volume, the precarious situation in which the majority of Syrian refugees in Jordan find themselves. Not only are levels of poverty among refugees extremely high, but the majority of refugees also have limited autonomy, as they either live in camps or are exposed to enormously high levels of financial stress, with dire consequences for their mental health. Either additional humanitarian assistance or earning more income in the labor market could relieve this stress. Chapter 4, on humanitarian assistance, confirms the inadequacy of the resources available for aid; chapter 5, on labor market participation among refugees, points out the constraints Syrians face in becoming productively engaged. Chapter 6 identifies the recurrent costs entertained, along with the savings that could be achieved through allowing refugees greater economic opportunities. These savings, close to $860 million per year and possibly as high as $1.3 billion, will be forgone if commitments to inclusion are not sustained; they might be sufficient to entice the international community and Jordanian authorities to renew their partnership and to strike a bargain from which all parties involved—refugees, Jordanian authorities, and international donors—would stand to gain. The volume ends, in chapter 7, with a set of recommendations for actions humanitarian agencies, development partners, and the government of Jordan could take to help realize the bargain.

NOTES

1. During the same period, refugees in Jordan increasingly moved from urban areas back to refugee camps.
2. This is as compared with the Kuwait pledging conference in March 2015, which raised $3.8 billion in pledges.
3. Until 2020, refugees also got electricity subsidies, but this benefit is no longer available. Hopper (2024) analyzes aid flows in support of refugee education and finds that Jordan is one of three countries whose official development assistance exceeds or meets the amount of resources required to finance inclusive refugee education.

REFERENCES

3RP (Regional Refugee and Resilience Plan). 2024. "2024 Regional Strategic Overview: Summary Document." United Nations Development Programme, New York, and United Nations High Commissioner for Refugees, Geneva. https://www.3rpsyriacrisis.org/wp-content/uploads/2024/04/3RP_Summary_2024.pdf.

Arnot, Tyler, and Anna Seeger. 2021. "The Jordan Ministry of Education's Response to the Syria Refugee Crisis: Case Study." United Nations Educational, Scientific and Cultural Organization International Institute for Educational Planning, Paris. https://unesdoc.unesco.org/ark:/48223/pf0000380459.

Awamleh, Zaid, and Kamel Doraï. 2023. "The Spatial Governance of the Syrian Refugee Crisis in Jordan: Refugees between Urban Settlements and Encampment Policies." CMI Report 23:3, Chr. Michelsen Institute, Bergen, Norway. https://www.cmi.no/publications/8909-the-spatial-governance-of-the-syrian-refugee-crisis-in-jordan#pdf.

Betts, Alexander. 2021. *The Wealth of Refugees: How Displaced People Can Build Economies.* Oxford: Oxford University Press.

Boswall, Karen, and Ruba Al Akash. 2015. "Personal Perspectives of Protracted Displacement: An Ethnographic Insight into the Isolation and Coping Mechanisms of Syrian Women and Girls Living as Urban Refugees in Northern Jordan." *Intervention* 13: 203–15.

Chehayeb, Kareem. 2023. "UN Agency Slashes Cash Aid to Syrian Refugees in Jordan, Raising the Alarm on Its Funding Crunch." *Associated Press*, July 18, 2023. https://apnews.com/article/jordan-syrian-refugees-aid-un-52f9fde0a559775a995c903c2dca8643.

Dunmore, Charlie. 2015. "Hope Gone in Jordan, Syrian Refugees Eye Risky Onward Journey." December 14, 2015. https://www.unhcr.org/news/stories/hope-gone-jordan-syrian-refugees-eye-risky-onward-journey.

Francis, Alexandra. 2015. "Jordan's Refugee Crisis." Carnegie Endowment for International Peace, Washington, DC. https://carnegieendowment.org/files/CP_247_Francis_Jordan_final.pdf.

Guardian, The. 2015. "WFP to Cut Food Vouchers for Syrian Refugees in Jordan and Lebanon." *The Guardian,* July 1, 2015. https://www.theguardian.com/global-development/2015/jul/01/syria-refugees-food-vouchers-cut-lebanon-jordan-wfp-un.

Hopper, Robert. 2024. "Refugee Education Financing: Key Facts and Findings; Insights into the Costs and Financing of Refugee Education in Low- and Middle-Income Countries." Policy Research Working Paper No. 10752, World Bank, Washington, DC.

Huang, Cindy, and Kate Gough. 2019. "The Jordan Compact: Three Years On, Where Do We Stand?" Blog post: https://www.cgdev.org/blog/jordan-compact-three-years-on.

Joint Data Center on Forced Displacement, World Bank, and UNHCR (United Nations High Commissioner for Refugees). 2020. *Compounding Misfortunes: Changes in Poverty since the Onset of COVID-19 on Syrian Refugees and Host Communities in Jordan, the Kurdistan Region of Iraq and Lebanon.* Washington, DC: World Bank Group. http://documents.worldbank.org/curated/en/878321608148278305/Compounding-Misfortunes-Changes-in-Poverty-Since-the-Onset-of-COVID-19-on-Syrian-Refugees-and-Host-Communities-in-Jordan-the-Kurdistan-Region-of-Iraq-and-Lebanon.

Obi, Chinedu Temple. 2023. "Poverty Measurement for Refugees in Jordan." UNHCR (United Nations High Commissioner for Refugees) and World Bank, Washington, DC. https://data.unhcr.org/en/documents/details/99518.

UNHCR (United Nations High Commissioner for Refugees). 2014. "Jordan Refugee Response 2014: Regional Response Plan 6; Support to Jordanian Communities and Institutions." Factsheet, UNHCR and United Nations Children's Fund, Geneva. https://data.unhcr.org/en/documents/details/42529.

UNHCR (United Nations High Commissioner for Refugees). 2023. "Eighth Regional Survey on Syrian Refugees' Perceptions and Intentions on Return to Syria: Egypt, Iraq, Lebanon, Jordan." UNHCR, Geneva. https://reporting.unhcr.org/syria-regional-survey-syrian-refugees%E2%80%99-perceptions-and-intentions-return-syria.

Verme, Paolo, Chiara Gigliarano, Christina Wieser, Kerren Hedlund, Marc Petzoldt, and Marco Santacroce. 2016. *The Welfare of Syrian Refugees: Evidence from Jordan and Lebanon.* Washington, DC: World Bank. doi:10.1596/978-1-4648-0770-1.

World Bank. 2020. *The Mobility of Displaced Syrians: An Economic and Social Analysis.* Washington, DC: World Bank. doi:10.1596/978-1-4648-1401-3.

World Bank Group, UNHCR (United Nations High Commissioner for Refugees), World Food Programme, and Joint Data Center on Forced Displacement. 2021. *2021 Compounding Misfortunes: An Update to the Study.* Washington, DC: World Bank.

2 Syrian Refugees in Jordan

JOHANNES HOOGEVEEN, MARIA LAGOUROU, AND CHINEDU OBI

MAIN MESSAGES

This chapter constructs a socioeconomic profile of Syrian refugees living in and outside of refugee camps in Jordan. Syrian refugees decide to live in a camp for various reasons, including prevailing policies at the time of their arrival; their own preferences; the Jordanian authorities; and access to services, jobs, and assistance. This chapter shows how the demographic characteristics of households living in and outside of camps vary, considers economic opportunities in each setting, and suggests that households with in-demand human capital and motivation for self-reliance often choose to live outside of camps, where they have more chances for employment and integration.

INTRODUCTION

Jordan has a long history of providing safety to those forced to flee their homes. Over time, about 3 million persons of Iraqi, Palestinian, and Syrian descent have arrived and settled in Jordan, which also hosts a sizable number of refugees of other nationalities.

The arrival of refugees in Jordan brought significant demographic changes. Twenty years ago, some 38,000 Syrians lived in the country: less than 1 percent of the country's population (table 2.1). At the time, non-Jordanians represented only 8 percent of the total population.[1] Between 2004 and 2015, however, the number of foreign-national residents in Jordan increased sevenfold, as the number of Syrian nationals increased to more than 33 times its previous number and the number of residents with other foreign nationalities saw a fourfold increase. By 2015, foreign nationals accounted for about 31 percent of Jordan's population, and Syrians represented 13 percent of Jordan's total resident population.

The arrival of many new residents, including refugees, in a short period of time may present both humanitarian and political challenges in any context. Jordan is no different. The international support Jordan has received and the country's policy responses with respect to settlement and economic opportunities, in turn, have had an effect on refugee welfare. At the beginning of the Syrian

TABLE 2.1 **Share of Syrians and other foreigners in Jordan, 2004 versus 2015**

	2004		2015	
	TOTAL	PERCENT OF TOTAL POPULATION	TOTAL	PERCENT OF TOTAL POPULATION
Syrians	38,130	0.7	1,265,514	13.3
Other foreigners	354,143	6.9	1,652,611	17.3
Total non-Jordanians	392,273	7.6	2,918,125	30.6

Source: Original table for this publication using data from Jordan Department of Statistics 2004 and 2015.

refugees' influx into Jordan, their presence was largely considered temporary, and they were perceived as not needing formal status or livelihood options. Beginning in 2016 with the Jordan Compact,[2] however, Syrians' participation in Jordan's labor market increased, but restrictions still confined Syrians to sectors dominated by immigrant labor (see chapter 5).

This chapter explores the socioeconomic characteristics of Syrian refugees living in Jordan. To this end it relies almost exclusively on the 2021 Vulnerability Assessment Framework survey, collected from a sample of refugees registered with the United Nations High Commissioner for Refugees (UNHCR). The chapter explores how policies influence where refugees reside, in or outside of refugee camps; how place of residence is associated with differences in living conditions; and whether refugees living in and outside of camps have different characteristics.

The first section of the chapter describes the arrival and registration of Syrian refugees in Jordan. The second section discusses the profiles of refugees living in camps and outside. The third section highlights policies in Jordan that have influenced where refugees reside (in or outside of camps). The fourth section examines changes in living conditions among Syrian refugee households over time. The last section concludes.

ARRIVAL AND REGISTRATION

The first group of Syrian refugees arrived in Jordan in late 2011. UNHCR records show that some 20,000 had arrived by December of that year. One year later, by December 2012, UNHCR had registered as many as 200,000 Syrian refugees in Jordan; many more, particularly unmarried young men and people without legal documents who could not enter Jordan officially, entered the country illegally (Yahya, Kassir, and el-Hariri 2018). The flow of refugees increased in 2013, and by the end of that year, as many as 520,000 Syrians had registered with UNHCR as refugees in Jordan.

After 2013, the arrival of refugees from the Syrian Arab Republic slowed. Between 2014 and 2015, another 112,000 Syrians registered as refugees in Jordan, but since 2016, newborns, rather than new arrivals from Syria, have mostly accounted for the increase in registered Syrian refugees in Jordan (figure 2.1).

The number of Syrian refugees in Jordan is substantial, but estimates of their precise numbers vary from source to source. According to Jordan's 2015 Population and Housing Census (Jordan Department of Statistics 2015), by early

FIGURE 2.1

Syrian refugees by date of arrival, before 2011–23

(percent)

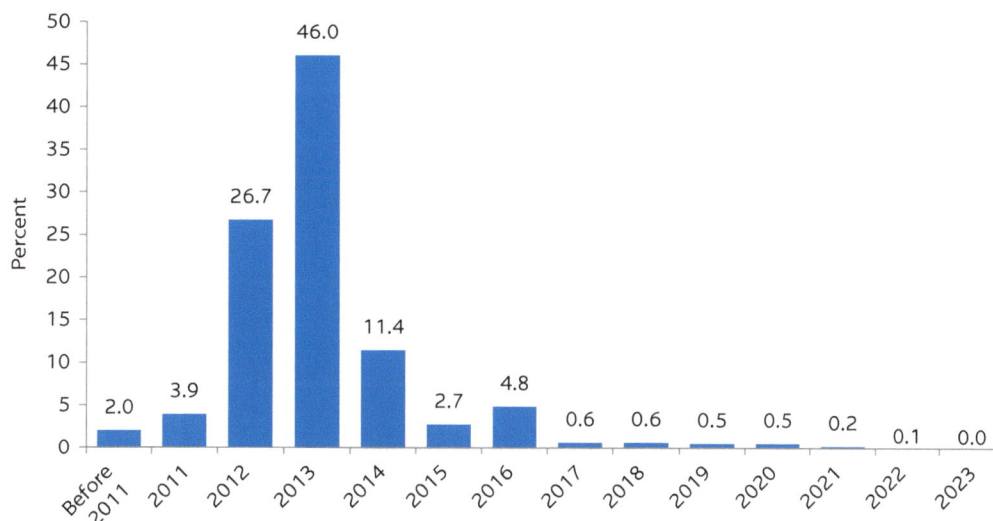

Source: Original figure for this publication using data from UNHCR 2023.

December 2015, as many as 1,265,514 Syrians lived in Jordan, of which 919,051 were registered as refugees with Jordan's Ministry of the Interior. Only 647,397 Syrian refugees were registered in UNHCR's proGres database, however. Thus, the discrepancy between these sources of data is large, and though they do overlap, they do so only partly.[3]

Policy and place of residence

Jordan has revised its policies in regard to the arrival and settlement of Syrians regularly. Before the conflict in Syria started, Syrians were allowed to move freely across the border between the two neighboring countries, with tribal, family, and trade ties playing a major role in determining patterns of cross-border mobility—either permanent or temporary migration—between southern Syria and northern Jordan.

As the number of Syrians arriving steadily increased after the start of the conflict, Jordan progressively tightened its entry and settlement policies. The opening of Za'atari camp in the northern Jordanian governorate of Mafraq in July 2012 marked Jordan's first policy shift to regulate the settlement of Syrian refugees. From its opening, Syrian refugees lacking passports, who were not allowed to settle freely within Jordan (Achilli 2015), were given a home in Za'atari camp. Built to host 80,000 people, the camp quickly became overcrowded, housing more than 120,000 UNHCR-registered refugees just a few months after its opening, even though Jordan's government allowed refugees who had a Jordanian sponsor (*kafil*) to move out of the camp and settle elsewhere in the country to avoid congestion in the camp.

Two additional camps were later established in Zarqa governorate: Mrajeeb Al Fhood camp opened in 2013 to accommodate approximately 4,000 refugees, and Azraq camp opened in 2014. The latter, built to accommodate as many as 130,000 people, never operated at full capacity, with numbers reaching 54,000 at their highest point. In parallel with the gradual sealing of crossings from Syria, two additional transit camps (Ruqban and Hadalat) opened in Mafraq, close to the Syrian border.[4] By the end of 2023, about 136,000 registered refugees lived in one of four refugee camps located in Irbid, Mafraq, and Zarqa governorates. The largest, Za'atari, hosted 84,000 Syrian refugees; Azraq and Mrajeeb Al Fhood (also known as "Emirati Jordanian camp") hosted 45,000 and 7,000 refugees, respectively; and in Irbid, Garden camp (previously known as "King Abdullah Park") hosted 300 refugees.

Government of Jordan data show that in 2015, 9 in 10 Syrians in Jordan lived in just four Jordanian governorates: Amman, Irbid, Mafraq, and Zarqa (table 2.2). The majority of Syrians in Jordan lived in host communities in the northeastern governorates, closest to the Syrian border. According to Jordan's 2015 Population and Housing Census (Jordan Department of Statistics 2015), 436,000 Syrians were living in Amman governorate and 344,00 in Irbid—34 and 27 percent of Syrians enumerated in the census, respectively—even though neither governorate had a refugee camp. Mafraq governorate was home to 208,000 Syrians (16 percent of the total), more than double the number of inhabitants of Za'atari camp at the time, and Zarqa governorate hosted 175,000 Syrians (14 percent of the total), five to six times as many as those living in

TABLE 2.2 **Distribution of non-Jordanians by governorate, 2015**
(percent)

	SYRIANS		OTHER FOREIGNERS		TOTAL NON-JORDANIANS	
	SHARE OF ALL SYRIANS IN JORDAN	SHARE OF TOTAL POPULATION IN GOVERNORATE	SHARE OF ALL OTHER FOREIGNERS IN JORDAN	SHARE OF TOTAL POPULATION IN GOVERNORATE	SHARE OF ALL NON-JORDANIANS IN JORDAN	SHARE OF TOTAL POPULATION IN GOVERNORATE
Amman	34	11	62	25	50	36
Balqa	2	6	4	14	3	19
Zarqa	14	13	16	19	15	32
Madaba	1	8	1	9	1	17
Irbid	27	19	7	6	16	26
Mafraq	16	38	2	5	8	43
Jerash	1	5	4	25	2	29
Ajloun	1	8	0	3	1	11
Karak	1	5	2	9	2	14
Tafela	0	2	0	4	0	6
Ma'an	1	6	0	5	1	11
Aqaba	1	4	3	24	2	28
Total	**100**	**13**	**100**	**17**	**100**	**31**

Source: Original table for this publication using data from Jordan Department of Statistics 2015.

Azraq and Mrajeeb Al Fhood camps combined. According to December 2023 UNHCR data, about 80 percent of Syrians in Jordan who were registered as refugees lived in host communities outside of refugee camps.[5] As of late 2023, the governorates with the highest percentages of registered Syrian refugees remained the same as in 2015.

Life within a Syrian refugee camp in Jordan can be quite different from that outside. Camp residents benefit from a breadth of services, including housing, primary health care, and education, offered free of charge inside the camps. They receive food assistance and are provided with free water and electricity. Their movement is, however, restricted. Refugees who want to go outside their camps must present a work or leave permit. Authorities may grant the latter for a variety of reasons, including for medical treatment and educational and work opportunities outside of the camp.

Refugees who live outside of camps typically live in urban areas. They can send their children to public schools free of charge and make use of public health facilities for a fee. They are free to move around, but humanitarian aid agencies provide them with only limited services. Only the most vulnerable—about a quarter of Syrian refugees registered with UNHCR—are eligible for the limited available cash assistance.

Refugees who live outside of refugee camps provide their own housing and pay for their own utilities. In fact, as chapter 3 demonstrates, refugees living outside of camps spend the most on rent and utilities (38 percent of their total consumption), even more than they do for food (33 percent).

Refugees can apply, through established procedures, to be allowed to live outside or inside the camps. Their leeway to live in or outside a camp has varied, however, over time. Early on in the Syrian crisis, the government of Jordan facilitated a process that allowed refugees to be "sponsored" by a guarantor, typically a Jordanian relative aged 35 or older. These refugees were issued service cards giving them access to various public services, including health care and education. Enforcement of the sponsorship requirement was relaxed, however, and the Ministry of the Interior still issued service cards to many registered refugees who stayed outside the camps without a sponsor.

In 2016, prior to the Jordan Compact, Jordanian authorities began enforcing the sponsorship process more rigorously, before canceling it altogether. In its place, the government initiated an "urban verification exercise" that required all Syrian refugees to reregister and obtain biometric service cards from the Ministry of the Interior. In addition to conferring legal status, facilitating freedom of movement, and providing access to services, the new card served as an identity card for Syrians born in Jordan, which can support eventual voluntary repatriation. Strict enforcement regarding who could obtain the new service cards meant that some people who had the previous cards could not get the new ones, and some refugees, such as those who had left refugee camps without authorization, were under pressure to return to them (NRC and IHRC 2016). As mentioned, however, procedures do exist through which refugees can apply to regularize their status as living outside of camps.

Through 2017, Syrian refugees had to apply for the same work permits as labor migrants. The high fees and administration involved, including official documentation that refugees often did not have, meant that only about 3,000 permits were issued to Syrians annually (Kelberer and Sullivan 2017). The permits were employer specific and did not allow refugees to switch jobs, even within the same field.

Refugee policies became less restrictive in 2017 following the signing of the Jordan Compact, an agreement to operationalize responsibility sharing for refugees between the European Union, World Bank, and various European governments and the Jordanian government. In return for integrating Syrian refugees into Jordanian health and education systems as well as the labor market, Jordan received grants and concessional loans, in addition to European Union trade concessions to help Jordan strengthen its manufacturing sector and offset any labor market effects of increased refugee participation. As part of the compact, Jordan agreed to issue 200,000 work permits for Syrian refugees in particular sectors and enroll 130,000 Syrian refugee children in formal education at all levels by the end of 2019, as well as to provide vocational training opportunities.[6]

After the compact was signed, the government introduced a flexible work permit that is not tied to a specific employer but allows Syrian refugees to move between similar jobs, employers, and governorates. For camp dwellers, the permit can also be used as a leave permit for one month, facilitating movement within and outside the camps.

Figure 2.2 shows, by arrival date, the share of current registered and active Syrian refugees who settled in camps, as well as the number who arrived each year and the stringency of the refugee policies that were in place at the time. As the figure makes clear, the proportion of Syrian refugees opting to reside in camps has varied over time depending on the type of policy in place. During periods with more restrictive refugee policies, a larger fraction of refugee arrivals have opted to remain in camps. Between 2012 and 2015, for example, when sponsorship was not strictly enforced, only about 20 percent of refugees who arrived settled in a camp. But in the first six months of 2016, when the Jordanian authorities began rigorously enforcing the sponsorship process

FIGURE 2.2

Number of Syrian refugees in camps by arrival date, 2012–23

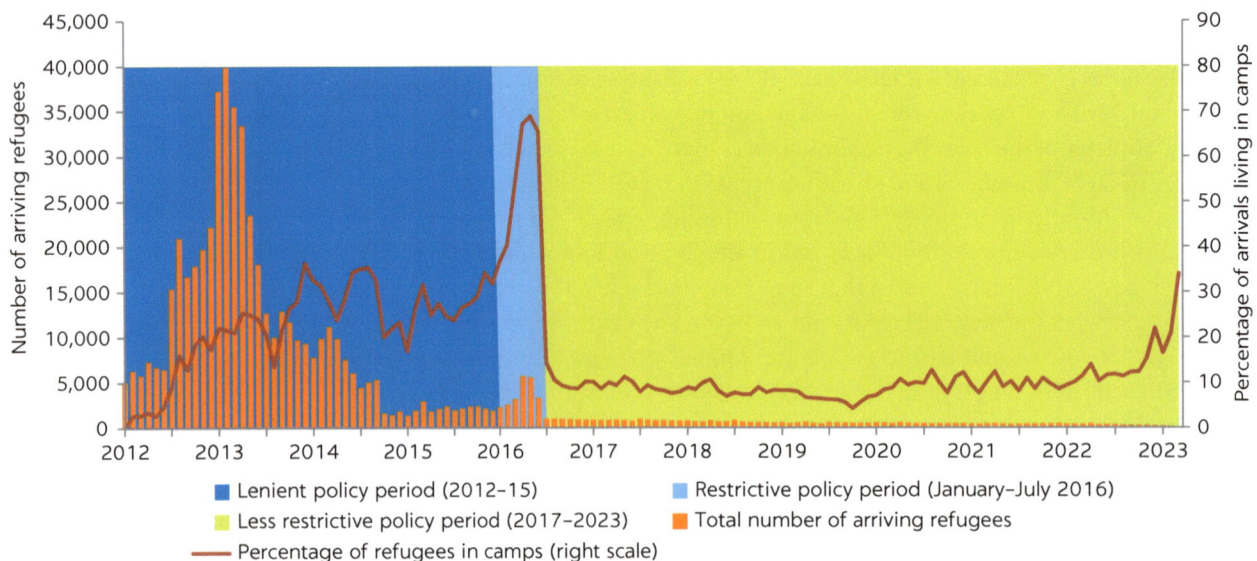

Source: Original figure for this publication using data from UNHCR 2023.

BOX 2.1

Other refugee groups in Jordan

Jordan hosts many refugees other than Syrians. Thanks to its peace and stability, it has emerged as a safe haven for refugees fleeing conflict in neighboring countries.

Palestinians are the largest refugee group in Jordan. They first arrived in Jordan during the 1948 Arab-Israeli War, with a second wave coming in the wake of the 1967 war. With the exception of persons from Gaza, the vast majority of refugees of Palestinian origin have been given Jordanian citizenship. All Palestinian refugees, including those who have been granted citizenship, maintain their refugee status and thus their right of return to their countries of origin. Jordan also hosts more than 10,000 Palestinian refugees from the Syrian Arab Republic, who face numerous challenges regarding their refugee and legal status. As of 2022, more than 2.35 million registered Palestinian refugees lived in Jordan. In addition to the 10 official refugee camps for Palestinians throughout the country, there are also 3 unofficial camps; about 18 percent of Palestinian refugees lived in the 10 recognized camps as of 2022. Since its establishment in 1949, the United Nations Relief and Works Agency for Palestine Refugees has been responsible for direct relief and work programs for Palestine refugees, both in Jordan and elsewhere.

Iraqis are another major refugee group in Jordan. They arrived in two main waves of migration. The first occurred in the 1990s following the Gulf War and Iraqi President Saddam Hussein's repression of Iraqi Shi'a and Kurds, as well as economic sanctions imposed on Iraq. Many upper-middle-class Iraqis, including professionals such as doctors, intellectuals, and teachers, sought refuge in Jordan, either settling there or using it as a transit point to other countries. After the 2003 US-led conflict in Iraq, a similar demographic profile emerged among Iraqi refugees fleeing to Jordan. Most were businessmen and former government officials, who brought potential for investment, contributing to the Jordanian economy. As many Iraqis are relatively well-off financially, most have not registered with the United Nations High Commissioner for Refugees (UNHCR) and are primarily living in host communities. The 2015 Population and Housing Census (Jordan Department of Statistics 2015) estimated that there were about 130,911 Iraqi nationals in the country, of which 42,941 were registered or had applied for refugee status with the Ministry of the Interior. As of October 2023, the UNHCR database showed 57,889 active registered refugees from Iraq, most of whom (60 percent) were of working age (ages 18 to 64) and living in the urban center of Amman (72 percent).

There are also active *refugees of other nationalities* in Jordan, including Somalis, Sudanese, Yemenis, and individuals of other countries who are registered with UNHCR. About 15,500 of the total registered 20,000 live in Amman.

In total, there were 730,000 refugees registered with UNHCR in Jordan as of October 2023, of which almost 90 percent were Syrians.

(closing the border in June 2016), about 60 percent of arriving refugees settled in camps.

Once the Jordan Compact was signed, the share of arrivals opting to stay in camps declined—to as low as 4 percent in 2019—only to increase again in 2020 during the COVID-19 pandemic. Since late 2022, the proportion of refugees opting to stay in camps has been gradually increasing.

PROFILE OF SYRIAN REFUGEES

Age and gender distribution

In comparison with the Jordanian population, the Syrian refugee population in Jordan is relatively young: 48 percent of the Syrian refugee population living outside of camps and 54 percent of those in camps are younger than 15, compared with 31 percent of Jordanians (figure 2.3).[7] The median age is also significantly lower for Syrian refugees than Jordanians: 13 for the camp population and 15 for those living outside camps, against 26 for the Jordanian population. Relative to the Jordanian population, the Syrian refugee population lacks elderly. About 8 percent of the Jordanian population is composed of adults ages 64 and older, whereas this group accounts for only about 1 percent of the Syrian refugee population.

FIGURE 2.3

Demographics of Jordanian and Syrian populations, 2021–22

(percent)

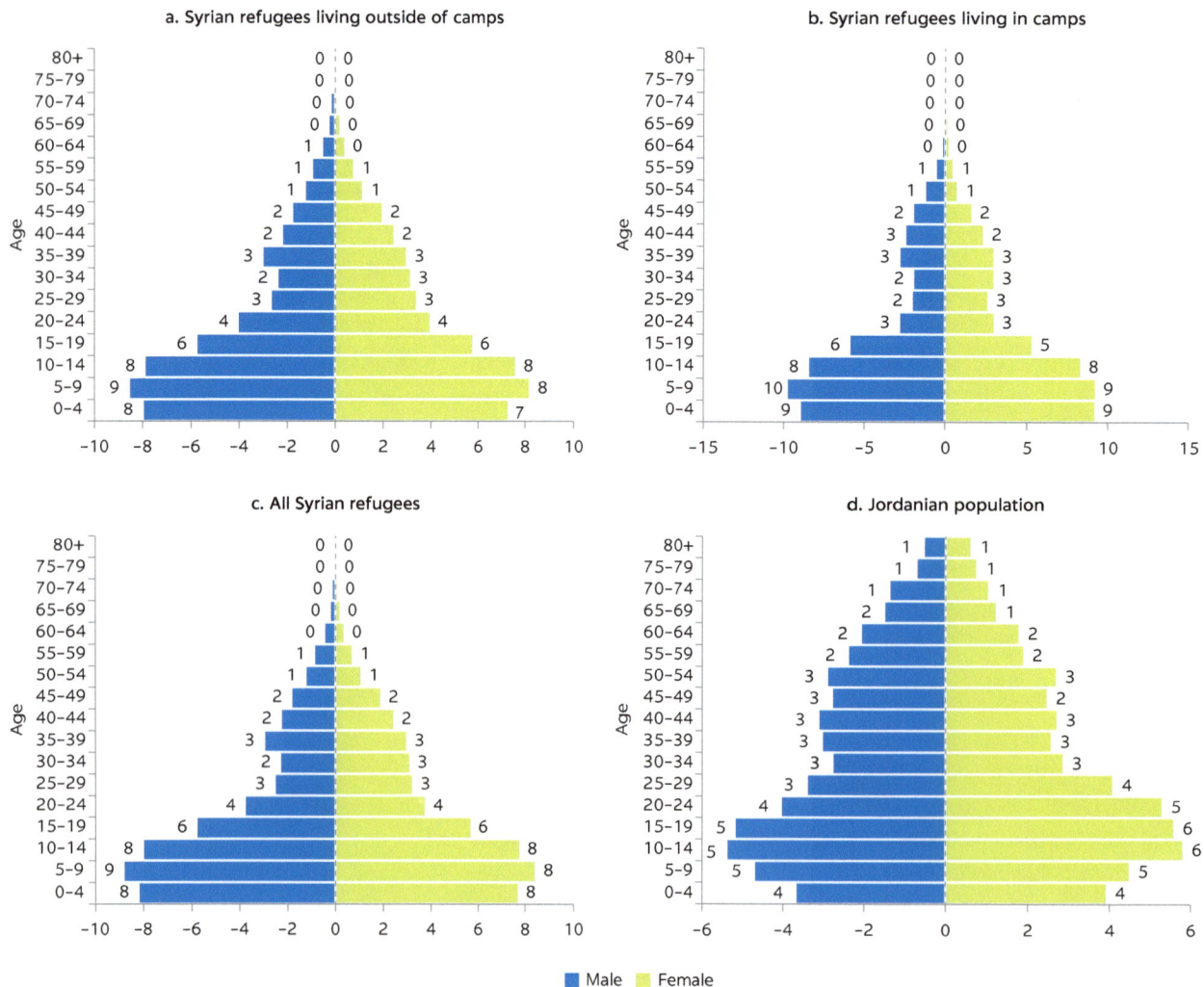

Source: Original figure for this publication using data from UNHCR 2021 and Jordan Department of Statistics 2022.

Both the Syrian refugee population and the host Jordanian population show a substantial male deficit, particularly in the 25- to 35-year-old age group. This deficit could be the result of different migration choices among prime-aged men, an excess of conflict-induced mortality in this age group, or a combination of the two (World Bank 2022).

Household types

Most Syrian refugee families are married couples with children. Figure 2.4 shows the distribution of refugee households by type. Approximately 82 percent of those living in camps are married with children, a considerably higher proportion than for those living outside (69 percent). Refugees living outside of camps have higher proportions of single-person households, couples without children, and households with divorced or widowed heads and no children.

Table 2.3 compares household structures in the two groups. Although the age of the heads of the households is similar, averaging about 44 years for both groups, refugee households living in camps are larger (about seven members, on average) and have more children (3.26) and a higher dependency ratio (1.23). Outside the camps, households have about six members, on average, and 2.38 children, with a statistically significant lower dependency ratio (0.96).[8]

A number of Syrian households share accommodations with other families, and some live with Jordanian nationals. Vulnerability Assessment Framework survey data from 2021 show that 41 percent of households in the refugee camps at that time were composed of multiple nuclear families living together, compared with 35 percent outside.

FIGURE 2.4

Syrian refugee household type by place of residence, 2021
(percent)

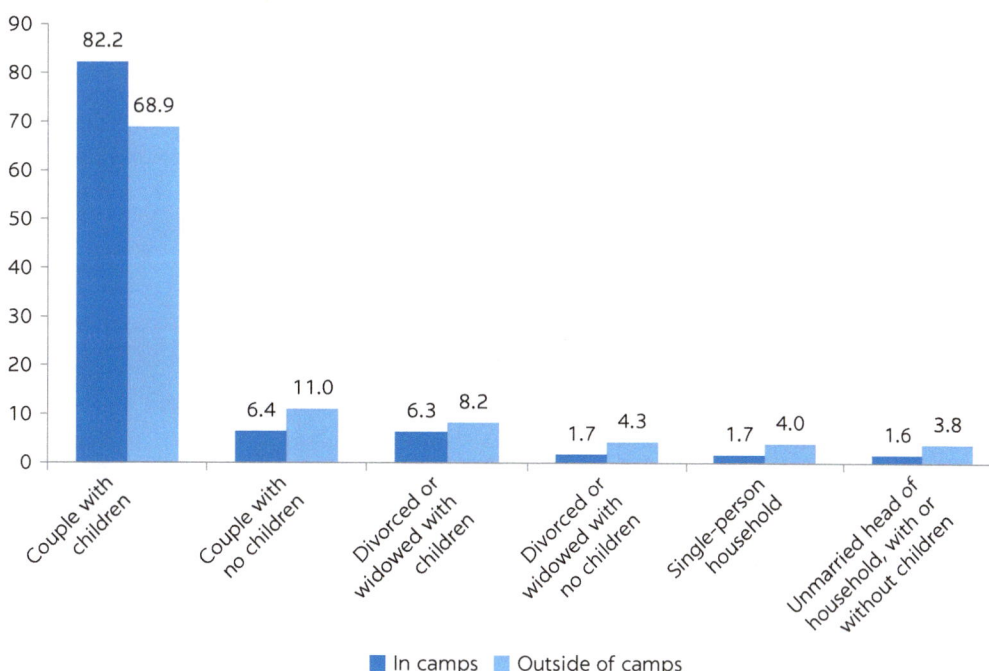

Source: Original figure for this publication using data from UNHCR 2021.

TABLE 2.3 **Household structure of Syrian refugees in Jordan, 2021**

	LIVING IN CAMPS	LIVING OUTSIDE OF CAMPS
Age of head of household (years)	43.8	44.4
Female-headed household (percent)	21.0	2.0
Household size (number of persons)	6.9	5.9
Number of children	3.3	2.4
Dependency ratio	1.2	1.0

Source: Original table for this publication using data from UNHCR 2021.

Although most Syrian refugee households in 2021 were headed by men, more outside the camps had female heads (27 percent) than in the camps (21 percent). In most cases, female headship followed divorce or widowhood. About 46 percent of female heads living outside camps and 39 percent living in camps were divorced or widowed. Other reasons refugee families might have had female heads included their spouses not living with them, family disputes, and inability to locate spouses. Many married female heads living both in and outside of camps without their spouses indicated that their spouses worked outside of Jordan or in another governorate within Jordan.

Education and health

Unlike family composition, the educational attainment of Syrian refugee adults shows little difference between those living in and outside of camps. Figure 2.5 shows the distribution of education levels among adults ages 18 and older in the two groups in 2021. As the figure reveals, among the working-age members of both groups, irrespective of gender, the share of individuals who had completed secondary school decreased with age.[9]

School enrollment for school-age children inside the camps is higher than that outside (figure 2.6). As of 2021, 85 percent of Syrian refugee children ages 6 to 17 were enrolled in school. About 91 percent of children living in camps were enrolled, with female enrollment slightly higher than that for males (93 percent compared with 88 percent). Syrian refugee children ages 6 to 17 living outside of camps had lower enrollment rates: 83 percent, with no difference between females and males.

Financial constraints and a lack of interest—mainly that they do not see the prospect of education in their current circumstances—are top reasons for Syrian refugee children not attending school. Family obligations, financial challenges, child marriages, and child labor are other reasons.

To assess the factors determining school enrollment among Syrian refugee children, a linear probability model is estimated here. The results, presented in figure 2.7, show that the probability of refugee children's enrollment increases with the level of education of the head of household. Thus the educational attainment of household heads has a strong impact on children's school enrollment. Living in one of the camps is another factor that increases a child's chance of being enrolled in school. By contrast, being a male child, living in a rural area outside of the camps, being part of a household having a male head, and being part of a household having a widowed or divorced head are factors affecting school enrollment negatively. Consumption levels, receipt of remittances or

FIGURE 2.5

Level of education among Syrian refugees by sex and age cohort, 2021
(percent)

a. Inside camps

b. Outside of camps

■ None ■ Primary ■ Secondary ■ University

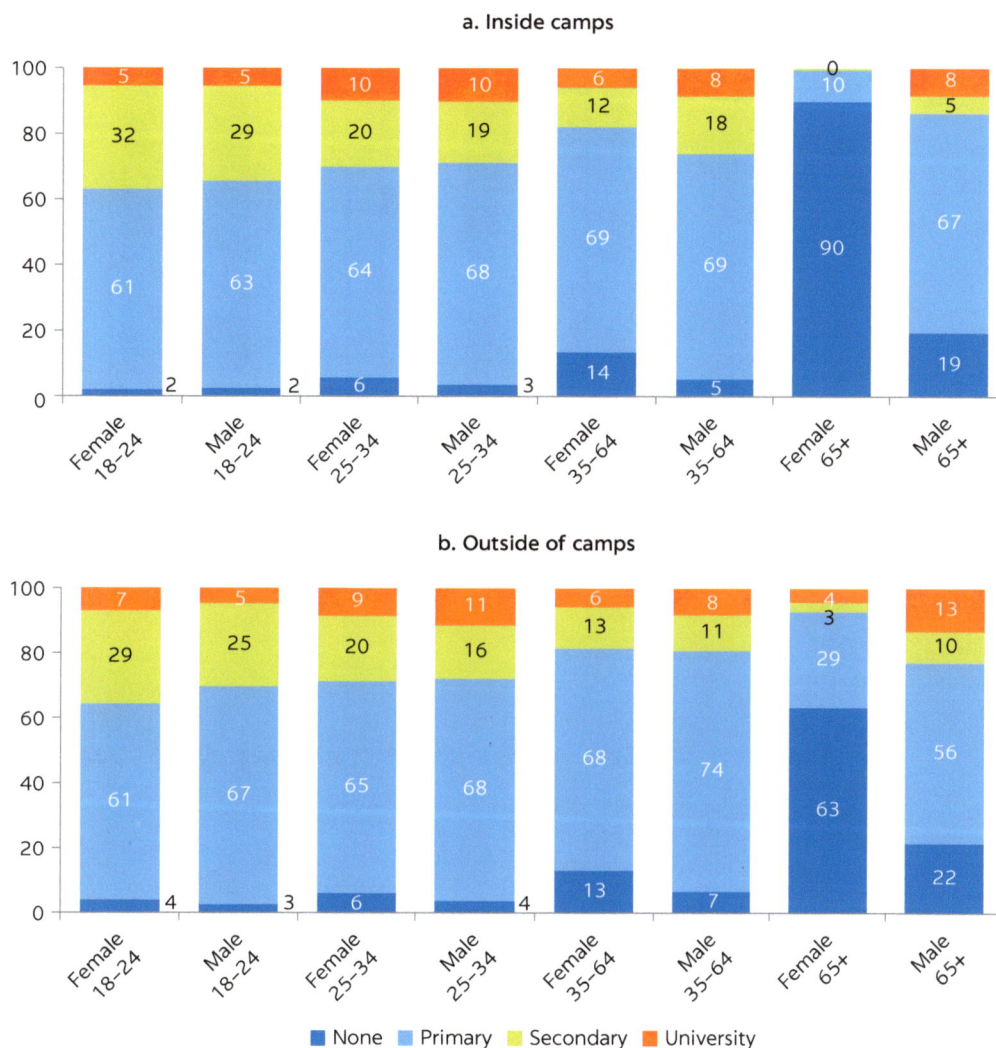

Source: Original figure for this publication using data from UNHCR 2021.

assistance, and the duration of stay in Jordan are found not to be statistically significant factors with respect to school enrollment.

In regard to health, a higher percentage of Syrian refugees with chronic illnesses live outside the camps than in them. According to the 2021 Vulnerability Assessment Framework survey, about 18 percent of Syrian refugees living outside of camps had serious medical or chronic conditions, compared with 11 percent of those living in camps. The camps provide no specialty health care services, and chronically ill refugees who live in the camps are often referred to seek treatment outside. Chronic illness was highest in 2021 among people age 65 years and older, 80 percent of whom reported illness. About a quarter of working-age refugees reported serious medical conditions. Diabetes was the most common serious medical condition reported by refugees with serious medical conditions (17 percent), followed by heart disease (13 percent) and respiratory illnesses (12 percent).

FIGURE 2.6

School enrollment of Syrian refugee children by location, 2021

(percent of children ages 6 to 17)

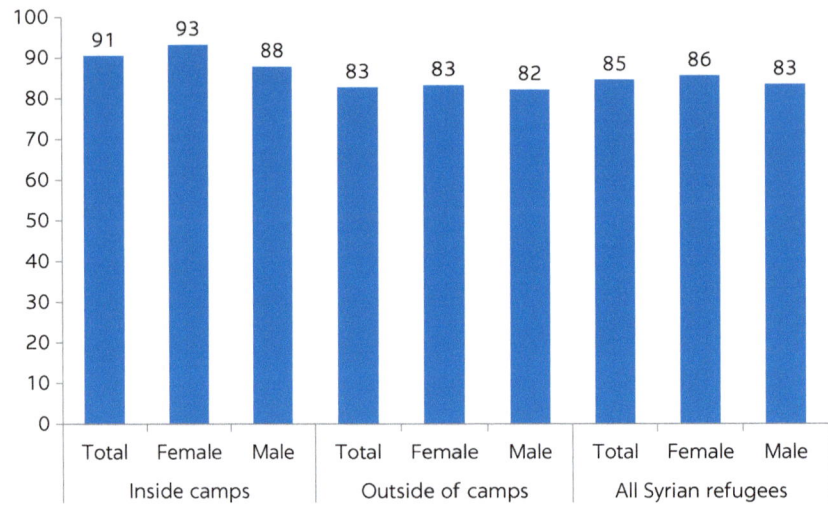

Source: Original figure for this publication using data from UNHCR 2021.

FIGURE 2.7

Determinants of Syrian refugee children's school enrollment, 2021

(percent)

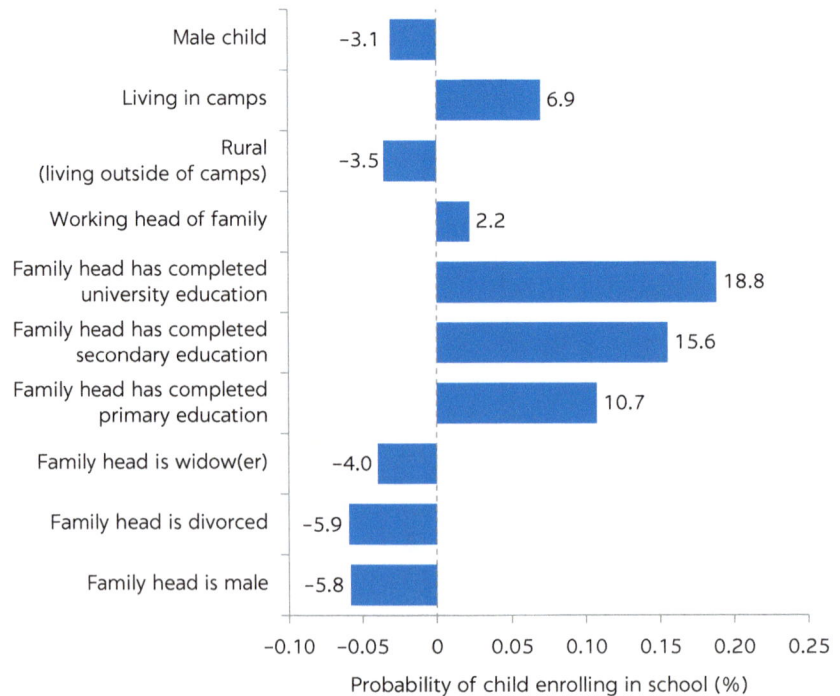

Source: Original figure for this publication using data from UNHCR 2021.

Note: Figure shows statistically significant variables only.

Housing and asset ownership

Syrian refugees in Jordan living in and outside of refugee camps differ in terms of the types, conditions, and cost of their housing. According to the 2021 Vulnerability Assessment Framework survey, most refugee households living outside the camps (90 percent) stayed in finished apartments with two or more rooms; 10 percent lived in substandard or informal settlements. Within the two camps for which information is available, housing consists of shelters. In Za'atari camp, these comprise fixed and mobile prefabricated units made of fiberglass and corrugated iron; in Azraq, all shelters are fixed and built from zinc and steel, making them hot during the summer and cold during winter.

Refugees in camps generally live in poorer conditions than those living outside of camps in host communities (figure 2.8). The former are more likely to be at risk of overcrowding and to live in a shelter with a substandard roof and unsafe latrine. About 57 percent of refugee households in camps as of the 2021 Vulnerability Assessment Framework survey lived in overcrowded conditions, compared with 14 percent of those outside. About 64 percent and 51 percent of refugees living in and outside of camps, respectively, lived in shelters with substandard roof conditions, experiencing problems like leakage during rain, dampness, and visible cracks. About 15 percent of households in camps did not have safe latrines, compared with 10 percent outside. The camp shelter challenge is more pronounced in Za'atari, mainly because most units in Za'atari have exceeded their life span of six to eight years. More than 70 percent of respondents to the survey who were living in the Za'atari camp said they had substandard walls, floors, and ceilings.

FIGURE 2.8

Housing conditions in and outside of Syrian refugee camps, 2021

(percent)

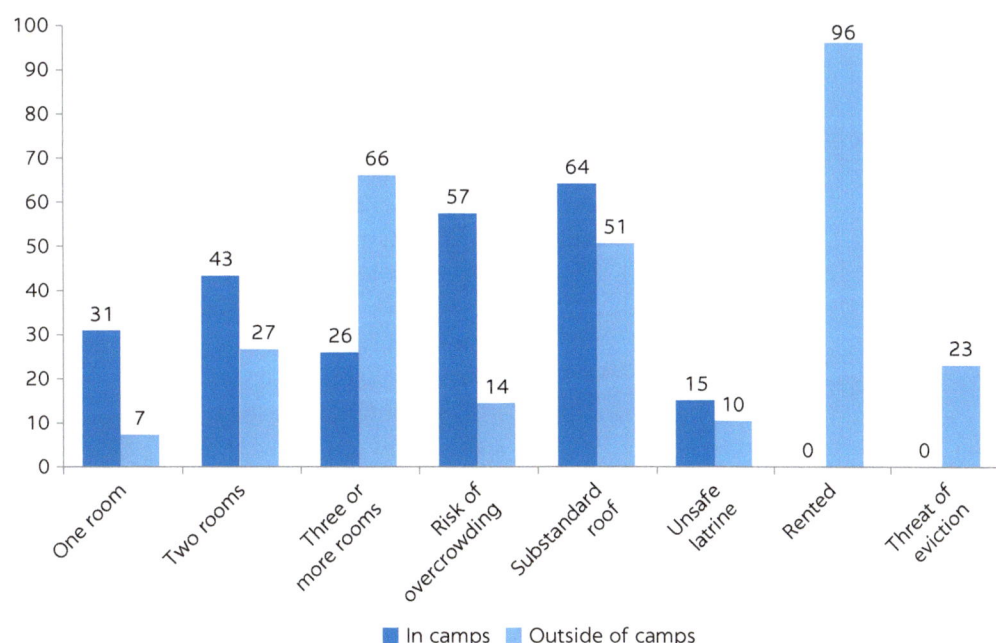

Source: Original figure for this publication using data from UNHCR 2021.

Most refugee households outside of camps (about 96 percent) rented their dwellings, according to data from the 2021 Vulnerability Assessment Framework survey; the rest lived with family members or had shelter as a result of their work. Of those who rented, almost a quarter reported a threat of eviction because of their inability to pay their rent (on average, JD 123 per month). Rent was mostly paid out of work salaries or Basic Needs assistance from UNHCR or, for almost a tenth of households, money borrowed specifically to pay it. As expected, Amman, which hosts the highest share of refugees, is also the most expensive governorate in terms of housing costs. Refugees living in camps do not face challenges of inability to afford rent and threat of evictions, as rent and utilities are provided in kind.

Over the years, Syrian refugees in Jordan have accumulated assets, with some differences among those living in and outside of camps (figure 2.9). Most Syrian refugees, irrespective of where they live, own common household items like mattresses, blankets, refrigerators, and cooking utensils. In other respects, refugees staying in camps show substantial differences from those living outside of camps in regard to assets owned. Bicycles, for instance, are a common means of transportation in camps, owned by 54 percent of camp households as of 2021, but are rarely owned by households living outside of camps. Households in camps are much more likely to own gas stoves and gas heaters, whereas households living outside of camps own electric appliances such as water heaters and electric ovens. Households living outside of camps are also more likely to own beds and sofas.

Assistance and access to services

All households in Syrian refugee camps in Jordan receive assistance, irrespective of their socioeconomic status; outside of camps, by contrast, assistance is targeted to the most vulnerable. Assistance is provided in different forms and in quantities that have varied over time. Key components are cash assistance (increasingly provided in the form of electronic wallets), which households can use to meet their basic needs, and food assistance, which is offered in the form of food vouchers that can be used only to buy food in supermarkets that have contracts for this purpose with the World Food Programme.

Cash for cooking gas is regularly provided to camp populations throughout the year. Water is supplied free of charge but is rationed to 25–50 liters per person daily. Electricity is provided for a limited number of hours a day, also free of charge. As of the 2021 Vulnerability Assessment Framework Survey, there were 57 schools for children and 17 kindergartens in the two refugee camps for which data were available. All children living in the camps have access to free education and free health care, though medical services remain limited and no specialty services are offered. As noted earlier in the chapter, chronically ill patients or those with complications are typically referred to off-camp hospitals for medical treatment.

UNHCR provides cash assistance to selected households living outside the camps in host communities to cover the costs of rent, water, and utilities. The World Food Programme also provides food assistance to vulnerable refugees, in the form of cash directly deposited into beneficiaries' bank accounts rather than food vouchers as for those living in camps.[10] All registered Syrian refugees living outside of camps can access Jordan's public services; for care at public health

FIGURE 2.9

Syrian refugee households owning assets by asset type, 2021
(percent)

Asset	Outside of camps	In camps
Floor mattress	93	97
Refrigerator	89	81
Kitchen utilities	88	93
Blankets	87	92
Electric fan	85	78
Smartphone	84	89
Washing machine	82	85
Television	76	88
Cabinets	69	51
Electric lamps	53	76
Gas or electric oven	52	34
Water heater	49	2
Gas heater	47	82
Beds	45	24
Sofa set	34	3
Gas stove	31	60
Water filter	24	40
Basic telephone	24	14
Table and chairs	21	7
Kerosene heater	12	1
Water pump	11	0
Computer or tablet	6	16
Freezer	5	7
Air conditioner	3	15
Bicycle	1	54
Car	1	0
Diesel boiler	0	8

■ In camps   ■ Outside of camps

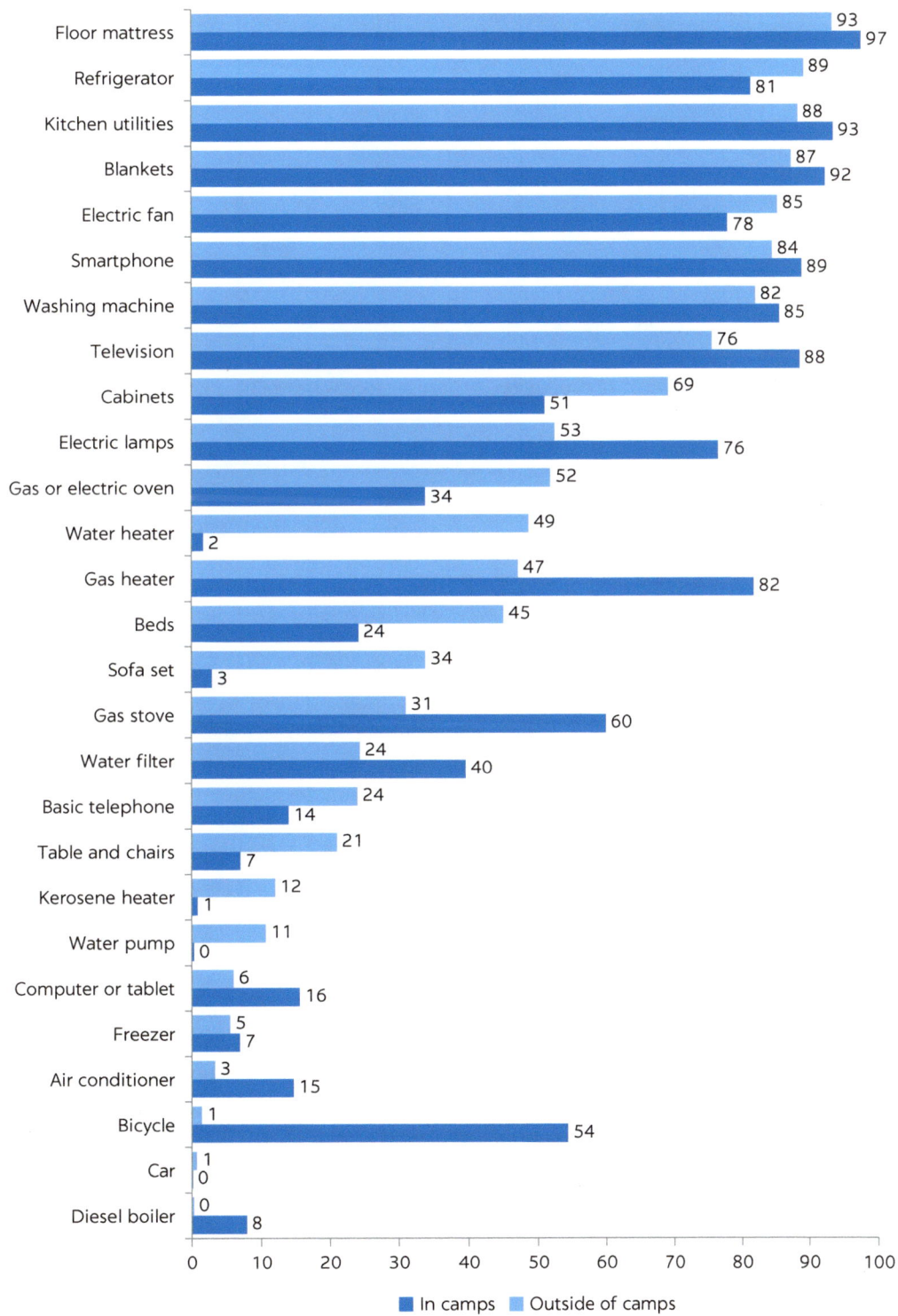

Source: Original figure for this publication using data from UNHCR 2021.

FIGURE 2.10

Access to services among Syrian refugee households, 2021
(percent)

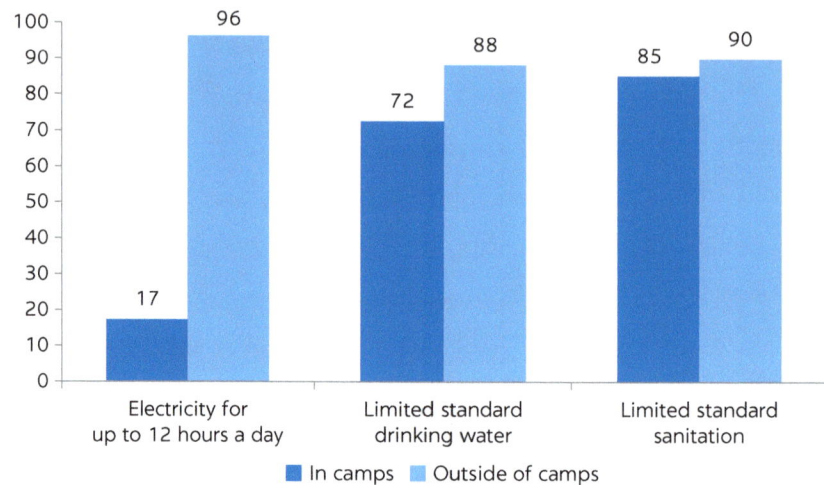

Source: Original figure for this publication using data from UNHCR 2021.

centers and public hospitals, they pay the non-insured Jordanian rate. They can also send their children to Jordanian public schools free of charge.

Households outside of camps report better access to infrastructure services than camp residents. Figure 2.10 compares the level of access to infrastructure services for those living in camps and outside of them. As the figure shows, as of 2021, 96 percent of out-of-camp households had access to electricity for more than half the day, compared with only 17 percent of those in the camps. About 88 percent of households living in host communities had access to standard drinking water, compared with 72 percent in camps. Almost half (46 percent) of respondents living in camps indicated a lack of satisfaction with the services provided there.

Employment

Whether they live in refugee camps or outside of them, only small percentages of working-age Syrian refugees have active work permits. Only 6.3 percent of working-age respondents living outside of camps and 12.4 percent of those living in camps had active work permits at the time of the 2021 Vulnerability Assessment Framework survey. Among those who did not have active work permits, 10 percent outside the camps and 22 percent in the camps said they had previously had them, and among those that had previously had work permits, only 40 percent outside the camps and 15 percent in them planned to renew them. Several factors contributed to their intention not to renew work permits (figure 2.11). Cost (43 percent), sector restrictions (18 percent), and unemployment (14 percent)— there is no point in obtaining a work permit unless employment has been secured—were the main reasons among out-of-camp Syrian refugees, whereas cost (85 percent) was the major reason for in-camp residents.

Syrian refugees living in camps had a labor force participation rate in 2021 of 46 percent, 11 percentage points higher than the rate for refugees living outside of the camps. A major factor contributing to this difference was the higher

FIGURE 2.11
Syrian refugees' reasons for not renewing work permits, 2021
(percent)

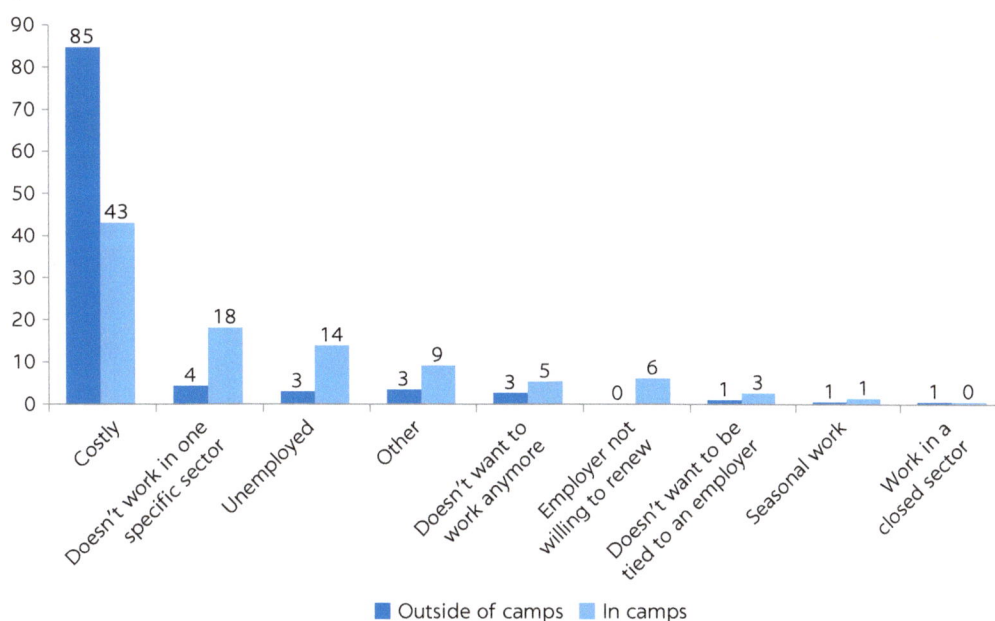

Outside of camps ■ In camps

Source: Original figure for this publication using data from UNHCR 2021.

proportion of women in the labor force within the camps, 21 percent, compared with only 6 percent outside the camps (figure 2.12). The higher participation of women who live in camps reflects the gender balance of refugee workers in incentive-based volunteer programs, in which aid agencies strive to allocate opportunities equally to men and women and which are offered only to those staying in camps. Working-age Syrian refugees who live in camps had an employment rate in 2021 of 22 percent, comparable to that for refugees living outside the camps (26 percent). Yet women in camps are twice as likely to be employed than those living outside; for men the reverse holds true. Whereas 49 percent of working-age men living outside camps in 2021 were employed, within camps, a considerably smaller share was: 37 percent.

Refugees living outside of camps have more job opportunities than those living inside them; workers living outside camps work longer hours and are also more likely to be exposed to hazardous conditions. As of the 2021 Vulnerability Assessment Framework survey, most employed refugees living in camps worked either as incentive-based volunteers (47 percent) or in one of three occupations: on farms around the camps (20 percent) or in construction (7 percent) and manufacturing (4 percent). Those living outside the camps had more varied occupation types, including construction (29 percent), accommodation (15 percent), manufacturing (12 percent), agriculture (10 percent), and wholesale (12 percent) (figure 2.13). Working hours for those living outside of camps averaged 42 hours per week, compared with 35 hours for those living in camps. Among employed out-of-camp refugees, 80 percent indicated they had been exposed to work hazards and 59 percent reported abuse, compared with 64 percent and 31 percent, respectively, of those living in camps. Child labor exists but is limited. In 2021, a little more than 1 percent of children between the ages of 5 and 14 living outside of camps worked, as opposed to 0.4 percent of those living in camps.

FIGURE 2.12

Distribution of working-age Syrian refugees by employment status, 2021

(percent)

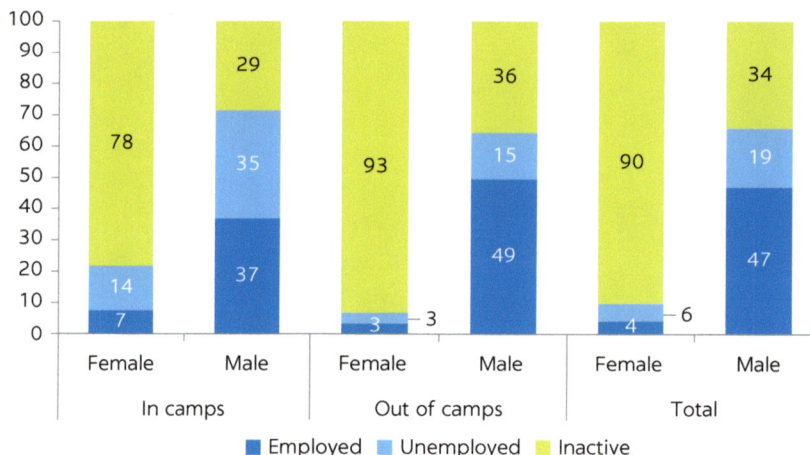

Source: Original figure for this publication using data from UNHCR 2021.
Note: Numbers in individual bars may not sum to 100 because of rounding. Working-age refugees are considered to be those ages 15 to 64.

FIGURE 2.13

Sector of employment among employed Syrian refugees, 2021

(percent)

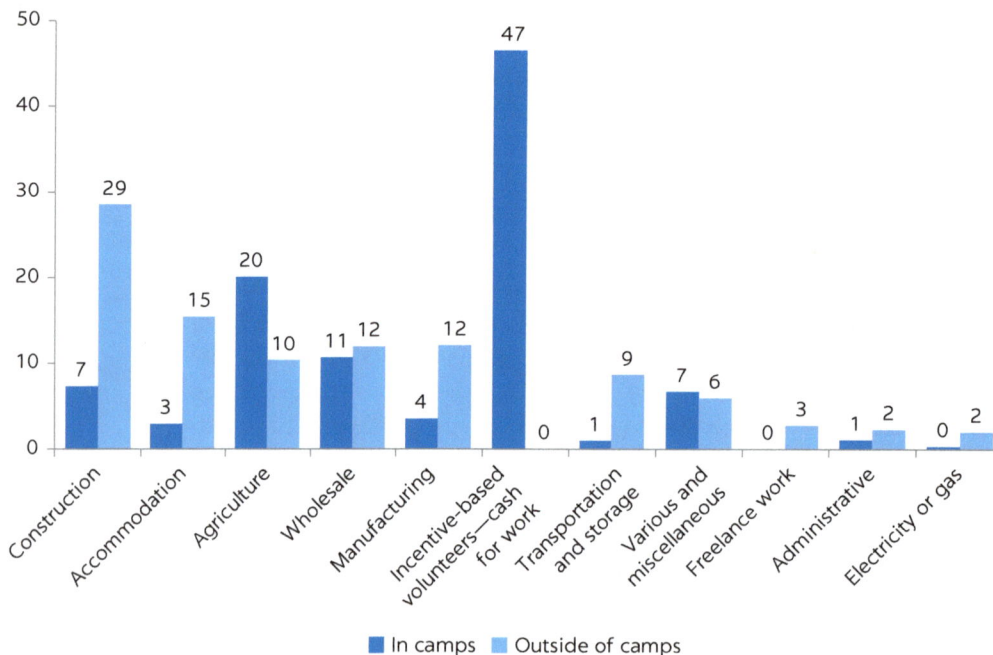

Source: Original figure for this publication using data from UNHCR 2021.

Sources of income

Syrian refugee households living outside of camps show a greater dependency on wage income than those living in camps, and those living in camps depend more on assistance than do those living outside (figure 2.14). Refugee households living outside of camps reported higher monthly wage incomes in 2021 than did those living within the camps (JD 110 versus JD 76). Despite this difference in earned incomes, households living in camps have higher total monthly incomes, on average, than those living outside, because of the greater amount they receive in the form of assistance. Those living in camps received total monthly assistance (from UNHCR, the United Nations Children's Fund, the World Food Programme, and other aid organizations) of JD 250 per month in 2021, compared with JD 111 for those living outside of camps.

Mental health and living inside or outside the camps

Jordanian government policies and procedures influence Syrian refugees' decisions to live inside or outside of refugee camps, as do individual considerations. The human wish for agency is one factor likely to play a big role. Syrian refugees living in Jordan's refugee camps are assured of free housing and sufficient financial assistance to sustain themselves. As noted earlier in the chapter, they also have access to free basic health care and education for their children; water and electricity are also free, but quantities are rationed.

Those living outside of camps undertake larger financial risks. These refugees face higher expenses, as they provide their own housing and pay for their own utilities, with less likelihood of receiving financial assistance from humanitarian agencies. As mentioned previously, households living outside of camps do have access to free education services and health services for which they typically pay.

FIGURE 2.14

Composition of household incomes among Syrian refugees, 2021
(Jordanian dinars)

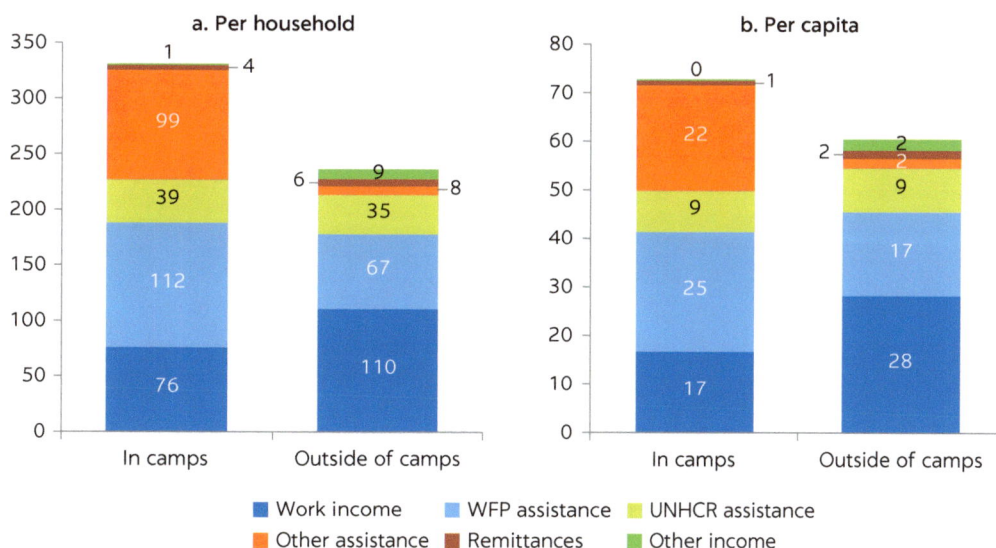

Source: Original figure for this publication using data from UNHCR 2021.
Note: UNHCR = United Nations High Commissioner for Refugees; WFP = World Food Programme.

Their water and electricity are not rationed, but they do have to pay for it. Those living outside the camps work more hours and earn more, but as the last subsection revealed, after assistance is included, they end up with less total income each month than households living in camps.

The largest difference, however, for those living inside or outside of refugee camps may be agency. Those living outside are free to go where they like. This freedom comes at a price, however, as life outside the camps is more stressful, at least financially. Figure 2.15 shows that refugee households living in camps systemically report less reliance on adverse coping strategies than those outside of them, illustrating the higher levels of stress the latter group faces.

Refugee mental health seems to reflect this difference in levels of financial and other stresses. The 2021 Vulnerability Assessment Framework survey asked refugees how often they felt depressed. As figure 2.16 shows, 43 percent of Syrian refugees living outside of camps reported experiencing depression on a weekly or daily basis (as did 51 percent of non-Syrian refugees outside the camps, not shown in the figure). By contrast, 35 percent of refugees living in camps reported weekly or daily depression. Also, those living outside of camps (whether refugees or Jordanians) experienced more intense levels of depression than those living in camps.

A reasonable hypothesis, then, would be that the secure accommodation and basic services, as well as the other assistance provided, help Syrian refugees living in camps better avoid symptoms of depression than those living outside of camps.[11]

FIGURE 2.15

Levels of coping strategies adopted by Syrian refugee households, 2021

(percent)

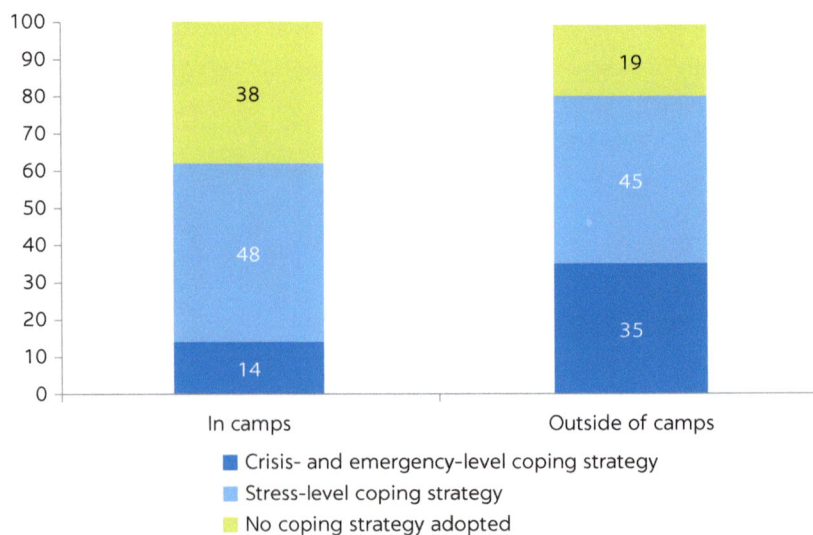

Source: Original figure for this publication using data from UNHCR 2021.
Note: Results are calculated using the reduced Coping Strategies Index, an indicator used to compare the hardships households face because of a shortage of food. The index measures the frequency and severity of the food consumption behaviors in which a household has had to engage in the seven days prior to the survey on account of a shortage of food. Numbers in individual bars may not sum to 100 because of rounding.

FIGURE 2.16

Syrian refugees' mental health by location, 2021

(percent)

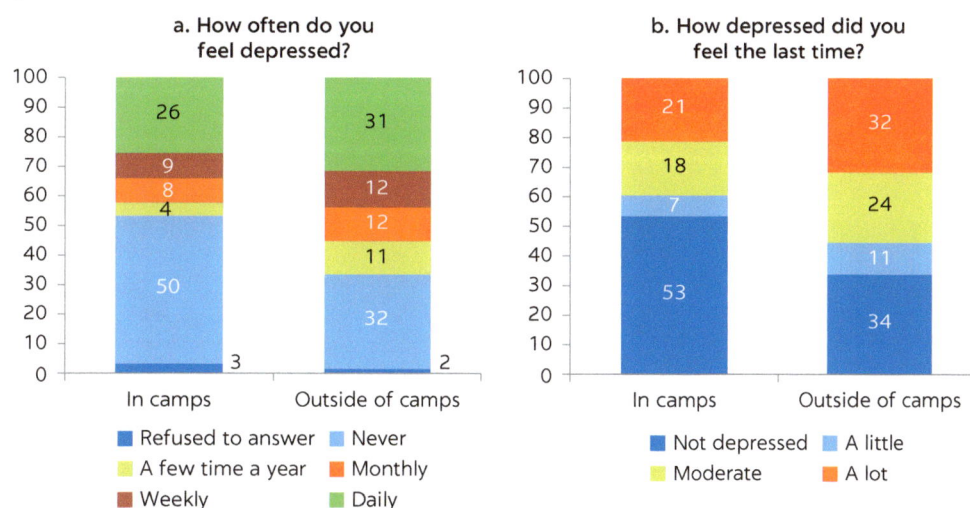

Source: Original figure for this publication using data from UNHCR 2021.
Note: Numbers in individual bars may not sum to 100 because of rounding.

The decision to live in or outside a camp

Policy variables—particularly those associated with when refugees arrived in Jordan—appear partly to drive the likelihood that a Syrian refugee household will live in one of Jordan's refugee camps, but household decisions are also an important determinant. As previously observed, households living outside of camps tend to be smaller than those living in camps and to have fewer dependents. Refugees living outside of camps are also more likely to be employed and more likely to be chronically ill. This section takes a more systematic approach to exploring the extent to which households living in camps and outside of them differ from one another. It conducts logistic regressions with the dependent variable taking the value 1 if a refugee lives in a camp and 0 otherwise. A combination of policy variables and household characteristics are selected as independent variables. Two regressions are specified. Model 1 includes only demographic characteristics, the household head's level of education, and whether the household head has a chronic illness. Model 2 includes, in addition, the household head's employment and occupation type and whether the household receives remittances. Table 2.4 shows the results.

There seems indeed to be self-selection in regard to refugees' decisions regarding their living situation, as the likelihood that a household will live outside of a refugee camp increases with the head's age and having a chronic illness and inversely with the head's years in Jordan, the household's dependency ratio, and household size. However, refugees living in camps have comparable household types, and their heads have comparable levels of education, to those living outside of camps.

TABLE 2.4 Logistic regressions explaining Syrian refugees' decision to live outside of camps

	SOCIODEMOGRAPHIC VARIABLES ONLY	INCLUDING ECONOMIC ACTIVITIES
Age of household head	−0.0570**	−0.0488*
Age of household head squared	0.000552**	0.000600**
Household head's number of years in Jordan	−2.100***	−2.082***
Household head's number of years in Jordan squared	0.153***	0.153***
Dependency ratio	−0.201***	−0.234***
Household size	0.171*	0.116
Household size squared	−0.275***	−0.220***
Household head is female	−0.304**	−0.762***
Household head is married	1.17e−05	0.140
Household head has primary education	0.0350	0.0952
Household head has secondary education	−0.327	−0.103
Household head has university education	−0.154	0.531*
Household head has chronic illness	0.615***	0.777***
Household head is employed in accommodation		2.563***
Household head is employed in administrative work		−2.660***
Household head is employed in agriculture		0.310
Household head is employed in construction		2.327***
Household head is employed in utilities		2.045***
Household head is employed in manufacturing		2.309***
Household head is employed in transportation and storage		3.633***
Household head is employed in miscellaneous work		0.739***
Household head is employed in wholesale		0.273
Household receives remittances		−0.375
Constant	10.49***	9.708***
Pseudo R-squared (McFadden)	0.0768	0.235
Pseudo R-squared (Tjur)	0.0725	0.2379
Metric of similarities (1 − Tjur R-squared) (percent)	93	76
Number of observations	8,176	8,176

Source: Original table for this publication using data from UNHCR 2021.
Note: Regressions are conducted at the household level. Models include weight and clustered error.
*$p < .1$ ** $p < .05$ *** $p < .01$

CHANGES OVER TIME

The displacement of Syrians in Jordan has become protracted. With most Syrian refugees arriving by 2013 or shortly after and few returning, most have been living in Jordan for 10 years or more. Because the first arrivals did not have the option to stay in a refugee camp, those living outside of camps have a slightly longer average duration of stay than those living in camps (figure 2.17).

FIGURE 2.17
Syrian refugees in Jordan by duration of displacement, 2023
(percent)

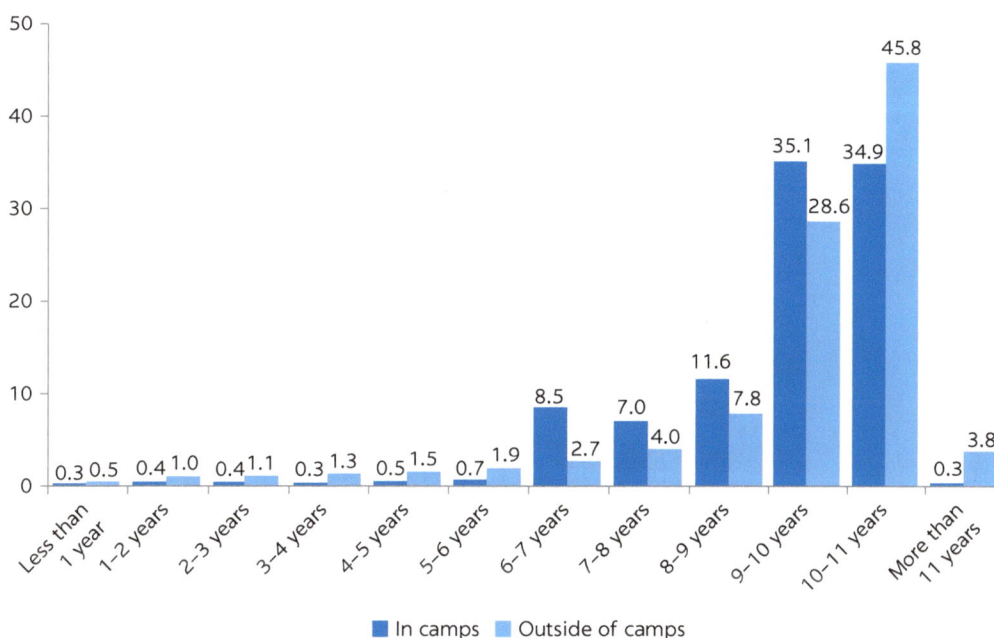

Source: Original figure for this publication using data from UNHCR 2021.

In 2015–16 the World Bank conducted surveys among Syrian refugees in the Kurdistan region of Iraq, in Jordan, and in Lebanon: the Survey of Syrian Refugee and Host Communities. This survey aimed to assess the socioeconomic and living conditions of a representative sample of the Syrian refugee and host community populations (Krishnan et al. 2016). For Jordan, data from this survey can be compared with results from the 2021 Vulnerability Assessment Framework survey. Though comparisons need to be made with care, as the two surveys had different sampling frames and asked questions differently and the Survey of Syrian Refugee and Host Communities collected data only for Jordanians in host communities, an analysis of both surveys does yield insights into how Syrian refugees in Jordan have fared over time.

Household composition

In terms of demographics, the Syrian refugee population in Jordan remained largely unchanged between the times of the two surveys (figure 2.18). The share of children under age 15 held constant at 48–49 percent, as did the proportion of people of working age at about 50 percent. Nonetheless, the dependency ratio increased slightly, because the number of refugees between ages 15 and 35 declined a little between 2015–16 and 2021.

The distribution of household sizes also remained largely unchanged. Noteworthy is the fact that Syrians in 2021 married later than Syrians in 2015–16, even though Syrians still tended to marry younger than Jordanians (figure 2.19).

FIGURE 2.18

Population pyramids for Syrian refugees, 2015–16 and 2021

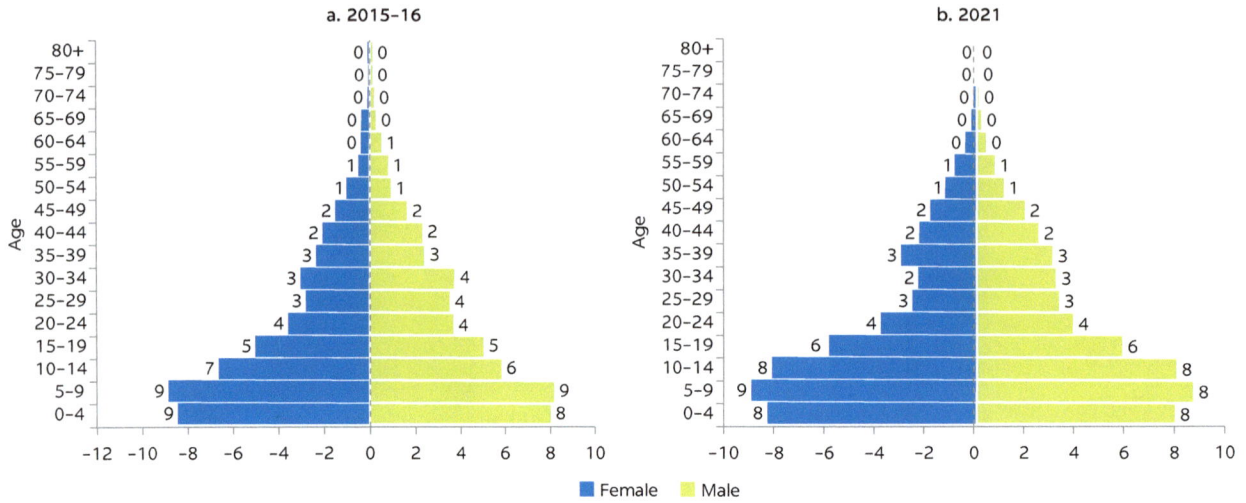

Source: Original figure for this publication using data from UNHCR 2021 and World Bank 2016.

FIGURE 2.19

Household demographics for Syrian refugees, 2015–16 and 2021

(percent)

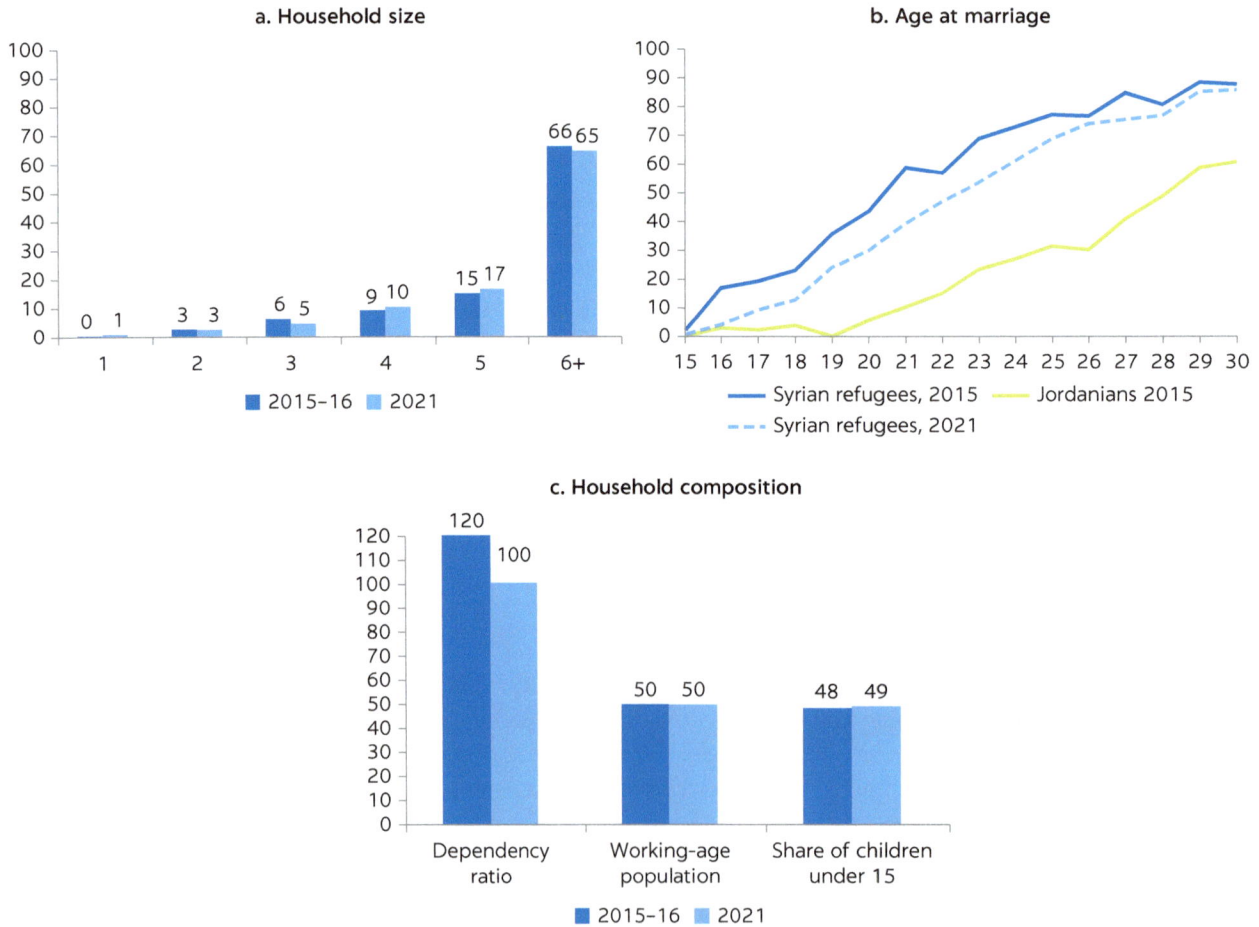

Source: Original figure for this publication using data from UNHCR 2021 and World Bank 2016.

FIGURE 2.20

School enrollment among Jordanians and Syrian refugees, 2015–16 and 2021

(percent)

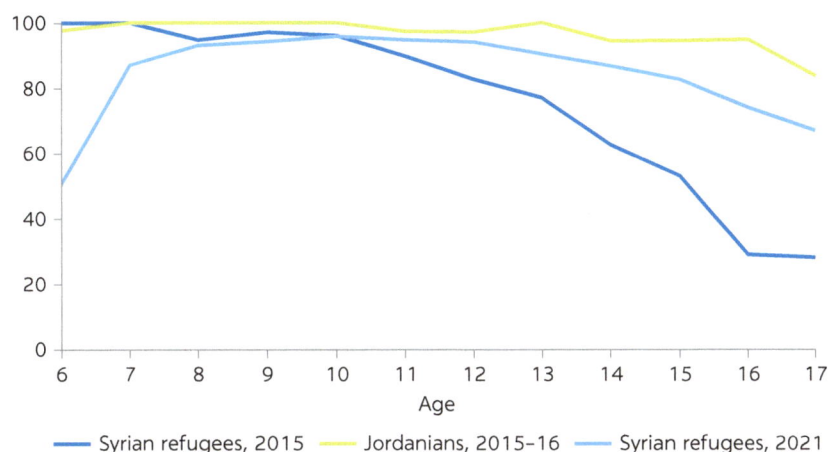

Source: Original figure for this publication using data from UNHCR 2021 and World Bank 2016.

Education

In 2015–16 Syrian refugee children had considerably lower school enrollment rates than Jordanian children. For the latter group, enrollment was almost universal between the ages of 6 and 16, but among Syrian children, enrollment dropped rapidly with age.

Figure 2.20 shows evidence of increases in the school enrollment of Syrian children over time, with the 2021 level coming closer to the Jordanian level in 2015–16. At the early stage of the conflict and refugee arrival, conflict and displacement widely disrupted Syrian children's education. The Jordanian government responded by hiring additional teachers, adding a second shift, and providing free basic and secondary schooling in camps and host communities (Jordan Ministry of Planning and International Cooperation 2016). School enrollment among Syrian refugee children increased from 78 percent in 2015–16 to 85 percent in 2021. Much of the enrollment gap between refugee and Jordanian children has been closed, though enrollment among the former group remains lower, more so for younger children. A recent study shows no evidence that the greater exposure to Syrian refugees has affected the educational attainment of Jordanians, as it has not changed the teacher-to-student ratio or classroom size (Assaad, Ginn, and Saleh 2023).

Employment

The employment rate among Syrian refugees ages 15 to 34 increased significantly between the two surveys. As figure 2.21 shows, the employment rate among Syrians ages 15 to 34 increased from 40–50 percent in 2015–16 to 60–80 percent in 2021. This increase brought refugees' employment rate in 2021 up to a level similar to that among Jordanians in 2015–16, with more pronounced increases among those living outside of camps.

FIGURE 2.21

Employment levels among Jordanians and Syrian refugees by age group, 2015–16 and 2021

(percent)

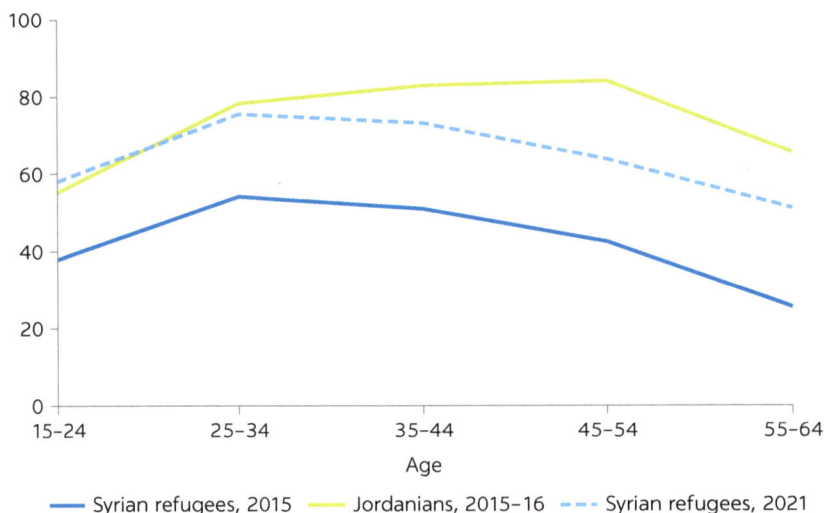

Source: Original figure for this publication using data from UNHCR 2021 and World Bank 2016.

FIGURE 2.22

Asset ownership among Syrian refugees, 2015–16 and 2021

(percent)

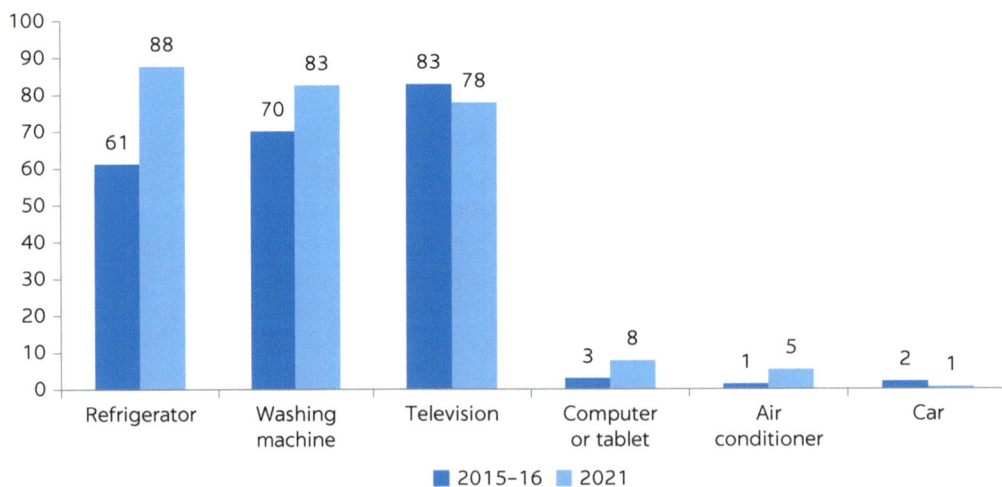

Source: Original figure for this publication using data from UNHCR 2021 and World Bank 2016.

Assets

With respect to asset ownership, some increases can be observed among Syrian refugees between 2015–16 and 2021. For example, the share of refugee households that owned a refrigerator or washing machine increased between the two surveys, as did ownership of computers or tablets and air conditioners, even though ownership of televisions decreased slightly (figure 2.22).

CONCLUSION

Using data primarily from the 2021 Vulnerability Assessment Framework survey, this chapter has reviewed the socioeconomic characteristics of Syrian refugees living in Jordan, making a distinction between refugees living in one of two camps, Azraq and Za'atari (on which the survey provides data) and refugees residing elsewhere in Jordan. Syrian refugees living in host communities benefit from closer connections with Jordanian society: refugees obtain their own housing; they have access to public facilities for health and education and are active in the labor market, albeit with restrictions.

Most Syrian refugees in Jordan live outside the refugee camps. Although time of arrival, as well as government policy toward refugees, plays a role in whether Syrians live in or outside of the camps, evidence suggests that refugee households make this decision themselves, which leads to self-selection in regard to certain characteristics. Camp populations, for instance, have greater numbers of younger people who live in larger households with higher dependency ratios; such self-selection is self-explanatory, as the camps offer greater economic security. Those residing outside of camps incur expenses camp dwellers do not, for housing and utilities, in particular, and they receive less in assistance. As a consequence, those living outside of camps are more likely to be gainfully employed, giving them greater agency overall, but they are more economically stressed and more likely to feel depressed.

One positive note: as the displacement of Syrians in Jordan has become increasingly protracted, the living conditions of Syrian refugees have improved a bit. Employment levels in 2021 were higher than those in 2015–16, and asset ownership among refugees increased between the two times. More refugees were being educated in 2021 than in 2015–16, and the share of girls who married at a very young age decreased during that time.

NOTES

1. Syrians accounted for less than 10 percent of the non-Jordanians, with Omanis (115,000) and Egyptians (112,000) the largest groups among the non-Jordanian population.
2. The Jordan Compact offered both concessional financing and beyond-aid incentives, like trade concessions that relaxed rules of origin for Jordanian exports to Europe, to support inclusive growth for Jordanians and Syrian refugees alike. Reforms under the compact aimed at increasing the number of work permits for Syrian refugees, as well as at improving Jordanians' ability to register businesses and the business environment in Jordan in general, thus facilitating better economic opportunities for all.
3. Not all Syrian refugees necessarily register with UNHCR, but UNHCR updates its records of registered Syrians on a yearly basis, as agreed upon with the government of Jordan.
4. These transit camps were created to enable Jordanian authorities to make safety checks before allowing refugees to enter Jordan and be directed to other refugee camps or settled through the *kafil* system (Doraï 2018).
5. UNHCR, "Jordan" (web page, accessed January 2024; https://www.unhcr.org/countries/jordan).
6. Even before the compact, the Jordanian government had been working to provide universal education to Syrian refugee children, mainly by expanding the use of double-shift schools, with Jordanian children attending the first shift in the morning and Syrian children mostly attending the second shift in the afternoon.
7. The profile of refugees living in and out of camps that is presented here is largely derived using data from the 2021 Vulnerability Assessment Survey, implemented by UNHCR,

which covered refugees living in host communities as well as refugees living in Azraq and Za'atari camps (but not refugees living in other camps in Jordan). Chapter 3 provides more information on the implementation and sampling (as well as other aspects) of the 2021 survey. In select instances, the chapter uses the 2022 Labor Force Survey, implemented by the Jordan Department of Statistics, and the Survey of Syrian Refugee and Host Communities 2015–2016, conducted by the World Bank.

8. The dependency ratio is the number of persons younger than age 15 or older than age 64 divided by the number of persons of working age (between 15 and 64 years old).

9. Throughout the chapter, "working age" is deemed to be 18 to 64 years, unless otherwise noted.

10. Chapter 4 delves more deeply into refugees' access to cash assistance.

11. Results from the 2023 Quality of Life Survey, an online survey discussed in chapter 3, also report better mental health for refugees living in camps than for those living outside.

REFERENCES

Achilli, Luigi. 2015. "Syrian Refugees in Jordan: A Reality Check." Policy Brief, Migration Policy Centre, Robert Schuman Centre for Advanced Studies, European University Institute, San Domenico di Fiesole, Italy. https://doi.org/10.2870/821248 2015/02.

Assaad, Ragui, Thomas Ginn, and Mohamed Saleh. 2023. "Refugees and the Education of Host Populations: Evidence from the Syrian Inflow to Jordan." *Journal of Development Economics* 164 (February): 103131. https://doi.org/10.1016/j.jdeveco.2023.103131.

Doraï, Kamel. 2018. "Conflict and Migration in the Middle-East: Syrian Refugees in Jordan and Lebanon." In *Critical Perspectives on Migration in the Twenty-First Century*, edited by Mariana Karakoulaki, Laura Southgate, and Jakob Steiner, 113–26. Bristol, UK: E-International Relations Publishing. https://www.e-ir.info/2018/09/04/conflict-and -migration-in-the-middle-east-syrian-refugees-in-jordan-and-lebanon/.

Jordan Department of Statistics. 2004. "General Results of Census 2004." Statistical Tables on Population and Housing. Department of Statistics, Hashemite Kingdom of Jordan, Amman. https://dosweb.dos.gov.jo/censuses/population_housing/census2004/census2004_tables/.

Jordan Department of Statistics. 2015. "General Results of Census 2015." Statistical Tables on Population and Housing. Department of Statistics, Hashemite Kingdom of Jordan, Amman. https://dosweb.dos.gov.jo/censuses/population_housing/census2015/census2015_tables/.

Jordan Department of Statistics. 2022. "Labor Force Survey 2022" (data set). Department of Statistics, Hashemite Kingdom of Jordan, Amman.

Jordan Ministry of Planning and International Cooperation. 2016. *Jordan Response Plan for the Syria Crisis, 2016–2018*. Amman: Ministry of Planning and International Cooperation, Hashemite Kingdom of Jordan. https://reliefweb.int/report/jordan/jordan-response-plan -syria-crisis-2016-2018.

Kelberer, Vicky, and Denis Sullivan. 2017. "Challenges and Successes of Jordan's Work Permit Program for Syrian Refugees after One Year." *SyriaSource* (blog), March 27, 2017. https:// www.atlanticcouncil.org/blogs/syriasource/challenges-and-successes-of-jordan-s-work -permit-program-for-syrian-refugees-after-one-year/.

Krishnan, Nandini, Juan Munoz, Flavio Russo Riva, Dhiraj Sharma, and Tara Vishwanath 2016. "Survey Design and Sampling: A Methodology Note for the 2015–16 Surveys of Syrian Refugees and Host Communities in Jordan, Lebanon, and Kurdistan, Iraq." United Nations High Commissioner for Refugees, Geneva. https://microdata.unhcr.org/index.php /catalog/406/download/1551/Mimeo.

NRC (Norwegian Refugee Council) and IHRC (International Human Rights Clinic). 2016. *Securing Status: Syrian Refugees and the Documentation of Legal Status, Identity, and Family Relationships in Jordan*. Oslo: NRC. https://www.nrc.no/resources/reports/securing-status -syrian-refugees-and-the-documentation-of-legal-status-identity-and-family-relation ships-in-jordan/.

UNHCR (United Nations High Commissioner for Refugees). 2021. "Vulnerability Assessment Framework Population Survey for Refugees in Host Communities: Jordan, 2021" (data set). UNHCR, Geneva.

UNHCR (United Nations High Commissioner for Refugees). 2023. "Total Registered Syrian Refugees" (accessed December 2023). https://data.unhcr.org/en/situations/syria /location/36.

World Bank. 2016. "Survey of Syrian Refugee and Host Communities, 2015–2016" (data set). World Bank, Washington, DC.

World Bank. 2022. *Syria Economic Monitor—Spring 2022: Lost Generation of Syrians.* Washington, DC: World Bank. https://openknowledge.worldbank.org/entities/publication /82c50366-fb28-5ae9-8fda-d5ab9bff51f0.

Yahya, Maha, Jean Kassir, and Khalil el-Hariri. 2018. *Unheard Voices: What Syrian Refugees Need to Return Home.* Beirut: Carnegie Endowment for International Peace Middle East Center. https://carnegieendowment.org/files/Yahya_UnheardVoices_INT_final.pdf.

3 Measuring Poverty among Syrian Refugees

CHINEDU OBI AND JOHANNES HOOGEVEEN

MAIN MESSAGES

The measurement of poverty among refugees remains in its infancy, and few existing studies calculate poverty using detailed consumption modules. This chapter estimates monetary poverty for Syrian refugees living inside camps and among host communities in Jordan. It provides the first available estimates of monetary poverty for refugees in both locations.

The results present a conundrum. Refugees living in camps have a lower likelihood of monetary poverty, yet refugees' revealed preference is to live in host communities. As measurement issues are unlikely to explain this result, the chapter uses a multidimensional measure of poverty to investigate whether the inclusion of additional aspects of deprivation can explain the puzzle. When the poverty measure used captures education and access to services in addition to monetary poverty, the welfare gap between refugees living in and outside of camps decreases, but refugees in camps nonetheless remain no less better off.

The chapter then explores whether freedom might be an overlooked dimension of welfare that seems obviously critical for populations who, like refugees, face restrictions in their movements. Unlike refugees living among the host population in Jordan, those living in camps are relatively freedom deprived, as they face restrictions in their movements and employment opportunities. It seems plausible that like anyone, refugees value their autonomy, experience dignity from their ability to earn their own keep, and appreciate possibilities for economic advancement in their own lives and those of their children. Once freedom is taken into account, the choice of a majority of refugees to live outside of camps is no longer a puzzle.

INTRODUCTION

Measures of monetary poverty have long been important indicators of social progress and a means to compare welfare over time and across different populations. Perhaps the most publicized monetary poverty measures are those the World Bank produces using the international poverty line. They demonstrate that global poverty has declined since the 1990s but that poverty levels vary from country to country. Countries generate and publish their own poverty numbers, using national poverty lines, allowing within-country comparisons between population groups, across districts, or between poor and nonpoor people.

Given the importance assigned to knowing levels of poverty, it is somewhat surprising that for one of the most vulnerable populations in the world, refugees, measures of poverty are rare. When poverty estimates for refugees are available, they typically have been derived using imputation methods (for example, Beltramo et al. 2020; Dang and Verme 2023), rather than through direct measurement, or have been calculated using abbreviated consumption modules (JDC, World Bank Group, and UNHCR 2020; Verme et al. 2016), which are known to bias consumption estimates downward and poverty rates upward (Beegle et al. 2010). Exceptions include Nguyen, Savadogo, and Tanaka (2021) and World Bank (2019), which present poverty estimates for refugees in Chad and Uganda, respectively, derived from detailed consumption modules comparable to those used in national household surveys.

This chapter presents monetary poverty estimates for Syrian refugees in Jordan derived from direct measurement of refugee households' consumption. It discusses challenges in measuring monetary poverty among refugees, which relies on determining the market value of refugees' consumption, especially for those living in refugee camps, which provide much of consumption as in-kind humanitarian assistance.[1] It estimates monetary poverty among Syrian refugees using a cost-of-basic-needs approach, which the World Bank recommends and the government of Jordan and the Global Compact on Refugees have adopted.[2] These estimates of monetary poverty are derived for refugees residing in and outside of camps—a first—allowing comparisons of welfare between the two groups.[3]

Comparing poverty among refugees living in and outside of camps generates some counterintuitive results. For instance, refugees staying in camps are found to have lower levels of monetary poverty than refugees living in host communities. Why, then, would refugees who have the option to live in camps voluntarily opt to stay outside them and, in doing so, accept a lower level of welfare than they might have otherwise? Plausibly, the market value of consumption does not capture all aspects of welfare. Verme (2023) suggests going beyond monetary-welfare metrics when assessing the welfare of refugees and internally displaced persons by considering their access to jobs, services, and basic infrastructure. Obi (2021) does so, comparing subjective quality-of-life indicators for Syrian refugees living in camps with those for refugees living outside of camps, and finds that the latter group has a higher self-reported quality of life than the former. To explore the puzzle of why some Syrian refugees in Jordan voluntarily expose themselves to circumstances in which they are more likely to end up as monetarily poor, this chapter considers indicators of nonmonetary poverty—in particular, the Multidimensional Poverty Measure—to conclude that when additional aspects of poverty are accounted for, refugees living in host communities are on balance worse off than those living in camps.[4]

The chapter then explores whether the literature on welfare of refugees has overlooked freedom as a dimension of well-being, particularly when comparisons are made between Syrian refugees living in and outside of refugee camps. After all, people living in host communities have greater liberty to move around as they please, greater agency, and more economic opportunities. Equating welfare to the consumption of tangible goods and access to infrastructure and services ignores, among other things, the value individuals may attach to the ability to move about freely.[5]

The next section of the chapter offers a brief overview on measuring refugee poverty, with a focus on Jordan. The third section presents, in some detail, the approach used to measure poverty among Syrian refugees living in and outside of Jordan's refugee camps, to allow an adequate discussion of the issues that arise when measuring poverty among refugees. Readers less interested in such details can skip this section and focus on the results, which the chapter's fourth section presents, including estimates of monetary poverty for refugees living in and outside of camps, along with a brief poverty profile. The fifth section presents estimates of nonmonetary poverty, in particular, the Multidimensional Poverty Measure, and proposes a Freedom Index. The sixth section discusses measuring refugees' welfare, and a final section offers conclusions.

MEASURING POVERTY AMONG REFUGEES IN JORDAN: A BRIEF HISTORY

Measuring refugee poverty is receiving increasing attention but is still at an early stage (Pape and Verme 2023). The Indicator Framework accompanying the Global Compact on Refugees illustrates the issue's infancy, presenting for only eight countries the proportion of refugee and host community populations living below the host countries' national poverty lines (UNHCR 2022).

Measuring monetary poverty requires substantial resources, and only a limited number of completed surveys have the necessary elements to enable measurement of refugees' poverty levels.[6] Estimating refugee poverty rates requires survey data that are representative of refugee populations. Surveys must include enough information to enable researchers to compute a comprehensive estimate of consumption or income (including consumption or income from refugees' own production), correctly address differences in prices across space and time, and construct a correctly weighted distribution of consumption or income per person.

Jordan has, for some time now, been at the forefront of measuring poverty among refugees. Verme et al. (2016) present the first refugee poverty estimates the United Nations High Commissioner for Refugees (UNHCR) or World Bank has ever undertaken. They estimate poverty for Syrian refugees living outside of Jordan's refugee camps using the UNHCR's proGres registration database and data obtained through home visits to refugees. Though their estimates come with methodological limitations, the extensive analysis they offer demonstrates the value of analyzing poverty among refugees.

In 2017–18, undoubtedly to better inform its decisions regarding the large number of refugees residing in the country, the government of Jordan fielded a Household Income and Expenditure Survey to collect detailed consumption data from Jordanians as well as from non-Jordanians residing in the country. Data from the survey have been used to calculate an estimate of the national poverty rate (15.7 percent), but no estimates of poverty among any subpopulations in Jordan have to date been published.[7]

Amid these efforts at measuring refugee poverty, UNHCR's Jordan office implemented its own surveys to assess refugee well-being. These Vulnerability Assessment Framework surveys initially focused on protection issues and encompassed refugee demographics, shelter, water and sanitation, health, food security, livelihoods, financing, and coping mechanisms, but not household consumption. That changed in 2021.

To strengthen poverty measurement among refugees, the World Bank–UNHCR Joint Data Center on Forced Displacement, the World Bank, and UNHCR Jordan collaborated to reimagine the 2021 Vulnerability Assessment Framework survey—the fifth in the series—with the aim of estimating refugee poverty in a way that meets the requirements of the Global Compact on Refugees. The collaboration's first objective was to estimate poverty among Syrian refugees in way that replicated Jordanian authorities' poverty measurement and overcame limitations of Verme's earlier poverty estimates.[8] To this end, the team responsible for the reimagining introduced a consumption module into the Vulnerability Assessment Framework survey that mirrored the Household Income and Expenditure Survey consumption module.

ESTIMATING MONETARY POVERTY AMONG REFUGEES

The estimation of poverty starts with accurately measuring household consumption. Measures of this type are typically obtained from detailed consumption surveys. Implementing such surveys takes a substantial amount of time, however, not least because consumption modules can be very detailed. The consumption module in Jordan's Household Income and Expenditure Survey, for instance, collects information on more than 500 items.

To avoid making the Vulnerability Assessment Framework survey unwieldy and difficult to implement, the team sought to balance collecting sufficiently detailed consumption data to approximate the Household Income and Expenditure Survey estimate against gathering data so detailed that the survey became unmanageable. After all, in addition to collecting consumption information, the survey also included questions related to water, sanitation, and hygiene; shelter; food security; coping strategies; finances; documentation; health; education; and livelihoods. Moreover, as the 2021 survey was fielded during the pandemic, a module on COVID knowledge, attitudes, and practices was added.

Survey data were collected face to face over 16 weeks between July and October 2021 for refugees living outside of camps and between October and December 2021 for those living in camps. The remainder of this section discusses key aspects of the survey.[9]

Sampling

The sample for the 2021 Vulnerability Assessment Framework survey was drawn from proGres, UNHCR's main registration database,[10] which includes all data collected from Syrian refugees in Jordan during their initial registration as well as during (annual) updates. Upon arrival in Jordan, refugees belonging to the same family are registered jointly as a single "case": a processing unit headed by a principal applicant and including the applicant's dependents. At registration, personal information for every case is collected, as well as other information relevant for the case.[11] Upon registration, UNHCR issues an asylum-seeker certificate, valid for 12 months, that must be renewed annually. Each time a refugee renews the certificate, registration information is verified, validated, and updated as appropriate. Regularly updating as to who is registered as a refugee makes proGres an excellent source for the survey's sample.

Using proGres, the team developed a stratified sampling strategy both for refugees living in camps and for those living outside of them. For out-of-camp refugees, sampling procedures accounted for refugees' nationality and governorate of residence. The strata employed included Iraqi, Syrian, and other nationalities from all 12 governorates of Jordan. Refugee households within each governorate were first classified according to the three nationality groups, after which the probability-proportional-to-size method was used to determine the number of cases to interview.

For refugees living in camps, sampling was limited to the two largest refugee camps, Azraq and Za'atari, which host only Syrian refugees. Overall, 10,765 surveys were completed, of which 8,557 involved refugees living outside of camps and 2,208 those living inside camps.

Sampling respondents from proGres is a strength as well as a limitation of the Vulnerability Assessment Framework survey. Most Syrian refugees in Jordan have probably been registered at some point in time (Verme et al. 2016), but it is less evident how many renew their registrations annually. Only those who expect benefits from having an up-to-date asylum-seeker certificate can be reliably expected to do so. As a consequence, and because the sample was drawn from active refugees, it might be biased in favor of Syrian refugees receiving assistance.

Defining households

As noted in the last subsection, the proGres database makes reference to cases: usually a nuclear family whose members registered jointly upon arrival in Jordan. The database defines "case" differently from "household" as used in consumption surveys, which use a combination of criteria such as "time spent in the household, pooling of resources, and communal eating habits" (Oseni et al. 2021, p. 16). In practice, most cases and households are identical, but they are not always. For instance, refugees may opt for living arrangements in which they share their house, but not their meals, with others. Hence, even though the case is the unit of sampling in proGres, for the purpose of computing poverty among Syrian refugees in Jordan, those who both live and eat together must be identified.

To make this feasible, the Vulnerability Assessment Framework survey identifies who shares what with whom. Those who share a house but do not share food are treated as individual households, each of which responds separately to the consumption module. By contrast, only one consumption module is completed when two cases (families) live together and also share meals. Of the 10,765 cases surveyed, 8,093 were sharing a dwelling, comprising 8,051 households.

Consumption module

The Vulnerability Assessment Framework survey's consumption module collects information on both food and nonfood items. Food consumption data are gathered based on a seven-day recall period. The food portion of the consumption module is divided into two parts. The first part comprises three leading questions that assess whether any household member, within the seven-day recall period, consumed a food item, purchased a food item, or received a food item as humanitarian aid or in-kind assistance. The second part asks those who answered yes to any of the leading questions in the first part to identify how much of each item was consumed, purchased, or received as humanitarian aid.

The nonfood consumption module, by contrast, has different recall periods depending on the subcategory being surveyed. Transportation, communication, and personal care items have a one-month recall period, clothing and footwear an annual recall period, and housing and utilities an open recall period ranging from per day to annual. The in-camp and out-of-camp samples have identical recall periods.[12]

The Household Income and Expenditure Survey consumption module collects information on 553 items, which, as noted, the team considered too burdensome to include unabbreviated in the Vulnerability Assessment Framework survey. As the latter's interest is primarily in identifying the poorest households correctly (for decisions related to assistance, it is less important to estimate the consumption of wealthy households correctly), the team used the results of the 2017–18 Household Income and Expenditure Survey to rank all items consumed by the poorest 20 percent of non-Jordanians at subcategory levels, then selected from each subcategory the top items in terms of quantity consumed and number of households consuming them. Through various iterations, the team created an abbreviated consumption module that accounted for approximately 80 percent of the total consumption of the poorest non-Jordanians.

To further reduce the burden on interviewees, the team constructed two consumption modules: a short one with 62 consumption items and a long one with 96 items (table 3.1). To arrive at unit prices needed to value consumption and determine caloric intake, the long form (but not the short one) asks

TABLE 3.1 **Number of items in the consumption modules of 2021 Vulnerability Assessment Framework (VAF) survey and 2017–18 Household Income and Expenditure Survey**

	VULNERABILITY ASSESSMENT FRAMEWORK SURVEY		
CATEGORY AND SUBCATEGORY	VAF SHORT	VAF LONG	HIES
Nonfood			
Cleaning materials	1	2	37
Clothing and footwear	1	3	67
Education	1	4	19
Health	2	3	15
Housing, water, electricity, and gas	7	8	48
Personal care	5	11	36
Tobacco	1	1	14
Transport and communication	2	4	37
Other	1	2	54
Durables (camps only)	4	4	41
Subtotal	25	42	368
Food			
Beverages, spices, and sweets	8	10	46
Fruits and vegetables	11	16	63
Grains and products	5	6	20
Meals in restaurants	1	6	10
Proteins and fats	12	16	46
Subtotal	37	54	185
Total	62	96	553

Source: Original table for this publication using data from Jordan Department of Statistics 2018 and UNHCR 2021.
Note: HIES = Household Income and Expenditure Survey, 2017–18.

respondents who purchased particular items how much they paid for them and the quantity they purchased. To assist respondents in recalling quantities of food purchased or consumed, the survey provides a photograph displaying different types of food packaging and their corresponding equivalents in kilograms. In the 2021 Vulnerability Assessment Framework survey, 75 percent of the interviewees in each governorate completed the short form of the consumption module, and the remaining 25 percent completed the long one.

Figure 3.1 presents results from the 2021 survey for the long and short form. In line with what the literature reports (Beegle et al. 2010), the long form records higher levels of consumption than the short form. The differences are generally small, however, typically less than JD 0.5; only for households living in camps in the top decile are the differences larger.

Valuing in-kind assistance

Refugees living in Jordan's refugee camps for Syrians receive certain assistance like shelter, water, and electricity in kind. Thus, survey respondents living in camps are unable to value their use of water or electricity. Also, the Vulnerability Assessment Framework survey does not ask these respondents for the rental value of the shelter they occupy. Yet to estimate monetary poverty in a way that allows the welfare of refugees living in and outside of camps to be compared, it is critical to obtain estimates for the consumption of these goods.

To arrive at a valuation for water for refugees living in camps, the survey uses the average per capita cost for those living outside of camps. For electricity, under the assumption that each household living in one of the camps uses equal amounts of electricity, camps' total electricity expenses are divided by the number of households in the camps.[13]

Rent is estimated using the fact that some camp refugees rent out the shelter that is put at their disposal. To capture the value of this rent for the 2021 survey, the team conducted interviews with camp administrators to inquire about the rental rates and found that the rent ranged from JD 75 to JD 150 per month depending on the shelter's condition. This information was used to approximate

FIGURE 3.1

Syrian refugees' reported per person monthly nominal consumption according to long and short forms by consumption decile and location, 2021

(Jordanian dinars)

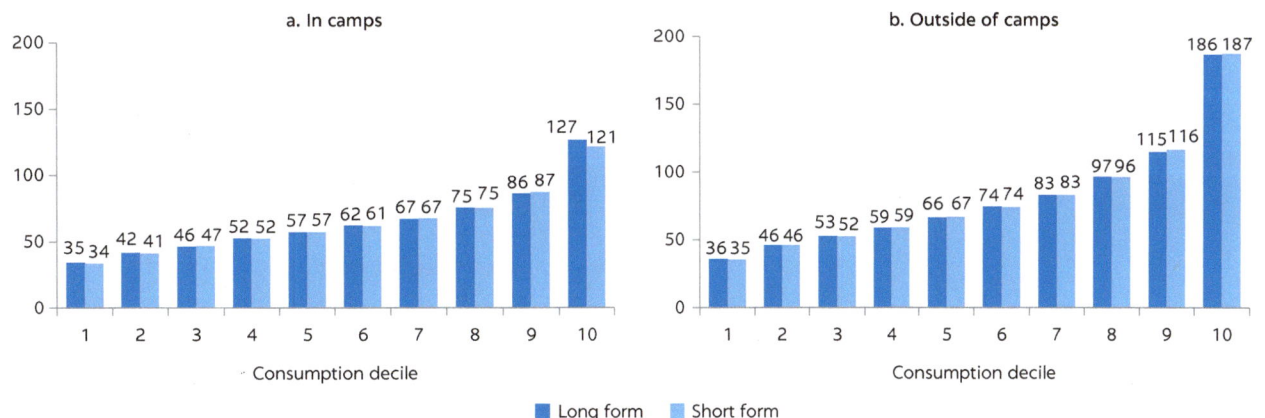

Source: Original figure for this publication using data from UNHCR 2021.
Note: For Syrian refugees living in camps, consumption does not include imputed rent and utilities.

a monthly rental value. Starting from a minimum rental value of JD 75, each camp shelter was assigned an assessed value based on the condition of the dwelling as captured in the Vulnerability Assessment Framework survey, such as whether it had a makeshift extension or a concrete floor and the condition of the roof, walls, doors, electrical connections, lights, and ventilation, among other things.

Consumption aggregates

The team constructed a consumption aggregate for poverty measurement, starting with a nominal aggregate and then spatially deflating it before adjusting it to account for the different lengths of the two forms of the consumption module. The resulting consumption aggregate is used to measure refugee poverty.

Comparisons of welfare need to be based on real (as opposed to nominal) differences, implying that price adjustments may be necessary as prices differ over time and across space. The 2021 Vulnerability Assessment Framework survey required no adjustments for temporal changes, as the individual surveys were completed within a short period of time (three months) and Jordan's annual inflation in 2021 was low (1.3 percent). It did require spatial deflation, however, as prices varied inside and outside of camps, between the north and south of the country, and between rural and urban areas. A Paasche index was used to account for regional price variations.[14]

Next, the team adjusted the consumption aggregate for the fact that the short form of the module reports lower levels of consumption than the long form. The long form was deemed as correctly estimating consumption, so the team applied to short-form consumption a correction factor that is sensitive to distributional differences:

$$CF_{ith} = \frac{\alpha_{ith}}{\beta_{ith}}, \tag{3.1}$$

in which α_{ith} is the mean of the spatially deflated consumption aggregate at each percentile in the long form and β_{ith} is the mean of spatially deflated consumption aggregate at each percentile in the short form. A t-test analysis confirms that after the correction has been applied, the consumption aggregates for the short and long forms of the consumption module are not statistically different.

Table 3.2 shows real monthly total (adjusted) per capita consumption for those living in and outside of the camps for the 2021 survey. Refugees in camps were found to consume JD 92 per person per month, higher than the JD 83 consumed by those outside the camps. Imputed rent constituted 19 percent of total consumption in camps, less than the share of rent outside, at 29 percent. Food consumption among those living in camps was JD 31 per person per month, constituting 34 percent of total consumption. For those living outside of camps, food consumption was JD 24 per capita per month, constituting 29 percent of total consumption. Refugees living in camps spent more on food than those living outside, but higher food costs were not the reason, as the data showed no major difference in the cost of food in and outside the camps or in the share of consumption of different food classes. About 40 percent of food consumption in both locations came from cereals and sugar.

TABLE 3.2 **Monthly consumption per capita per month for Syrian refugees in Jordan, 2021**

	OUTSIDE OF CAMPS		IN CAMPS	
	JORDANIAN DINARS	PERCENT	JORDANIAN DINARS	PERCENT
Per capita consumption	83.0		91.8	
Transportation and communication	6.6	7.9	6.2	6.7
Personal care	4.1	4.9	4.7	5.2
Tobacco	3.4	4.1	8.2	9.0
Health	8.4	10.1	6.8	7.4
Education	1.1	1.3	0.5	0.6
Clothing	2.0	2.4	5.1	5.5
Cleaning	2.1	2.5	2.3	2.5
Utilities	7.6	9.1	8.7	9.5
Rent	24.0	28.9	17.8	19.4
Food	23.9	28.8	31.4	34.2
Cereals		31.5		32.9
Fruits and vegetables		20.1		18.1
Legumes		2.2		1.2
Meat and fish		14.2		13.5
Dairy		17.0		17.1
Oil and fat		6.4		8.0
Sugar		8.5		9.1

Source: Original table for this publication using data from UNHCR 2021.

Determining cost-of-basic-needs poverty line

The poverty line is the benchmark against which individuals' consumption is assessed. Those consuming less than the poverty line are considered poor; those who consume more are nonpoor. The poverty line consists of two components: a food poverty line and an allowance to account for basic nonfood needs.

Food poverty line

In the cost-of-basic-needs approach employed here, the food poverty line reflects the cost of consuming a reference basket of basic needs, that is, the food corresponding to a predetermined minimum caloric intake. In the case of Jordan, the food poverty line corresponds to the cost of consuming 2,300 kilocalories (kcal), the number of calories used to determine Jordan's national poverty line.

Establishing the basic needs basket requires a reference population—in this instance, those in the second to seventh consumption deciles, on the conjecture that their consumption pattern reflects that of poor households. Composite items and prepared meals are not considered because they are too heterogenous to enable prices and caloric values to be meaningfully derived, leaving a list of 34 food items from which the basic needs food basket is constructed. For the reference population, the average quantity of each food item consumed is determined, along with the total kcal consumed. As this total is less than the recommended daily calorie intake of 2,300 kcal per capita, the average quantity of each food item is then scaled upward such that total kcal sum to 2,300 kcal. This yields the food basket that, once priced using the unit prices of each food item, defines the food poverty line. The food poverty line is then calculated after pooling observations for refugees living in and outside of camps. For the 2021 Vulnerability Assessment Framework survey, it was estimated at JD 200 per person per year or JD 16.7 per person per month.

Nonfood poverty line

To fully reflect basic needs, the poverty line includes an allowance for nonfood essentials required to sustain the minimum standard of living. This nonfood component of the poverty line is calculated using the "upper Ravallion" method, by calculating the spending on nonfood consumption by households whose food consumption equals the food poverty line. For the 2021 Vulnerability Assessment Framework survey, the nonfood allowance was estimated at JD 64 per person per month.

Setting the refugee poverty line

The overall poverty line, then, is the sum of the food poverty line and the nonfood allowance: JD 80.7 (rounded to JD 81) per month for the 2021 Vulnerability Assessment Framework survey (table 3.3). Refugees are therefore defined as poor if the total value of their monthly per capita consumption is less than JD 81.

Monetary poverty

Using real adjusted per capita consumption and the poverty line, it is now possible to calculate poverty among Syrian refugees in Jordan. Table 3.4 presents poverty incidence, depth, and severity for those living in and outside of camps, based on data from the 2021 Vulnerability Assessment Framework survey. About 62 percent of the Syrian refugees living outside of camps in 2021 were poor, compared with 45 percent of those living in camps. The combined poverty rate for Syrian refugees in both living situations was 58 percent.

TABLE 3.3 **Composition of the poverty line for Syrian refugees in Jordan, 2021**
(Jordanian dinars)

Food component	16.7
Nonfood component	64.0
Poverty line	80.7

Source: Original table for this publication using data from UNHCR 2021.

TABLE 3.4 **Estimates of poverty among Syrian refugees in Jordan, 2021**
(percent of population)

RESIDENCE	HEADCOUNT RATIO	POVERTY GAP DEPTH	POVERTY SEVERITY
In camps	45	9	3
Outside of camps	62	19	7
All Syrian refugees in Jordan	58	17	6

Source: Original table for this publication using data from UNHCR 2021.
Note: The statistics in the table are based on a poverty line of JD 81 per month.

Refugees living outside of camps had a greater poverty depth (a measure of how much it would take to bring their consumption up to the poverty line) than those living in camps (19 percent versus 9 percent).[15] So not only were refugees living outside camps more likely to be poor, they were also further removed from the poverty line (that is, the intensity of their poverty was greater) than refugees living in camps.

Poverty severity, a measure that squares the poverty gap and thus gives greater weight to those further removed from the poverty line, also shows that poverty was more extreme among out-of-camp refugees than among those living in camps. Severe poverty, based on the 2021 survey, was 7 percent for those living outside of camps and 3 percent for those living in camps.

The finding that as recently as 2021, the rate of monetary poverty for Syrian refugees living in host communities in Jordan was higher than that for those living in camps is noteworthy and in fact, surprising. All Syrian refugees in Jordan have the option of living in a refugee camp. That many choose to live outside of the camps, where they have a higher likelihood of living in poverty and the depth and severity of poverty are greater, is counterintuitive, at least at first sight.

Sensitivity analyses

To assess the robustness of the finding that Syrian refugees who live outside of camps are poorer, the team conducted sensitivity analyses in which the construction of the consumption aggregate for those living in camps was varied, as was the construction of the poverty line. After all, when constructing the consumption aggregate, the team had to make a number of nonstandard assumptions to deal with in-kind consumption by refugees living in camps. These assumptions affect the amount consumed, and because one common poverty line is used for both refugees living in camps and those living outside, the assumptions could have an impact on the comparison of poverty rates for the two groups.

Four specific scenarios were constructed for the analysis. Scenario 1 calculates the food and nonfood components of the poverty line separately for refugees living in camps and those living outside them, using a consumption aggregate that does not consider the value of in-kind assistance (rent, electricity, and water) provided in camps. This scenario accepts the difficulty of estimating in-kind consumption for refugees living in camps and treats refugees living in and outside of camps as if they are two different populations with their own poverty lines.

Scenario 2 calculates the food component of the poverty line jointly for the camp and out-of-camp populations. After all, even though nonfood consumption is calculated differently for refugees living in and outside of camps, the Vulnerability Assessment Framework survey uses identical food modules for the two groups.

Scenario 3 deducts the values of rent and utilities from the consumption aggregates of both the in-camp and out-of-camp populations, then assesses the food and absolute poverty lines jointly.

Scenario 4—the preferred scenario—has already been presented. It calculates the poverty line jointly for the in-camp and out-of-camp populations, using consumption aggregates that account for the values of rent and utilities in the camps, based on expenditures, as outlined in the subsection "Valuing In-Kind Assistance."

The results of the analysis show that the various assumptions in the scenarios affected the measured incidence of poverty in camps in 2021 (they tended to lower it) but did not change the striking pattern of refugees living outside of camps being poorer than those living in camps (table 3.5). This finding is robust.

Considering the cumulative density function of consumption for refugees living in and outside of camps (under the preferred scenario) reinforces this conclusion. Consumption for the out-of-camp population stochastically dominates that for the in-camp population until per capita consumption reaches JD 130. The percentages on the vertical axis in figure 3.2 can be interpreted as the poverty incidence for a given poverty line, because they measure the share of the population consuming less than the corresponding point on the vertical axis. The figure therefore shows that as long as the poverty line is less than JD 130—where the graph lines for the in-camp and out-of-camp populations cross in the figure—irrespective of the value chosen for the line, those living outside of camps had higher poverty levels in 2021 than those living in camps.[16]

TABLE 3.5 **Sensitivity of the poverty line**

	SCENARIO 1		SCENARIO 2		SCENARIO 3		SCENARIO 4 (PREFERRED SCENARIO)	
	OUTSIDE OF CAMPS	IN CAMPS	OUTSIDE OF CAMPS	IN CAMPS	OUTSIDE OF CAMPS	IN CAMPS	OUTSIDE OF CAMPS	IN CAMPS
Food component (Jordanian dinars)	16.7	14.9	16.7	16.7	16.7	16.7	16.7	16.7
Nonfood component (Jordanian dinars)	64.4	31.5	64.9	32.7	32.1	32.1	64.0	64.0
Poverty line (Jordanian dinars)	81.1	46.4	81.6	49.4	48.8	48.8	80.7	80.7
Poverty incidence (percent)	61.9	22.6	62.4	26.1	55.3	25.1	61.8	44.9

Source: Original table for this publication using data from UNHCR 2021.

FIGURE 3.2

Cumulative density function of consumption for Syrian refugees living in and outside of camps, 2021

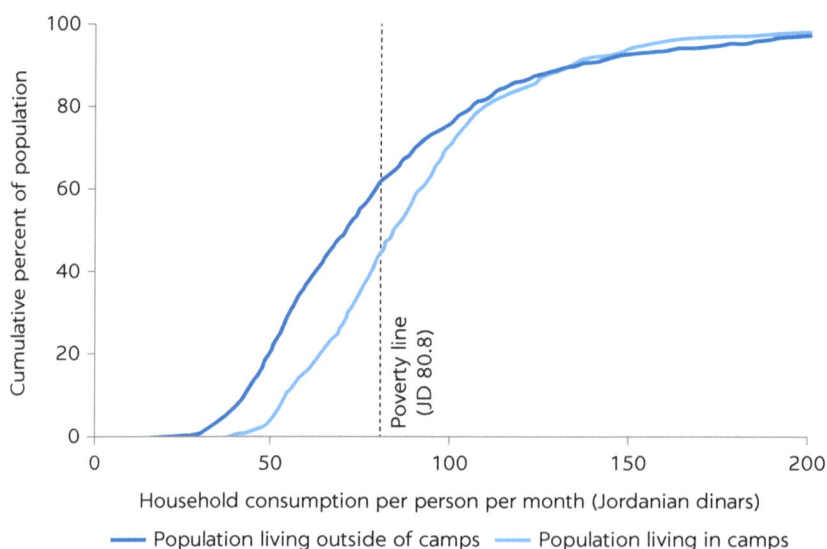

Source: Original figure for this publication using data from UNHCR 2021.

POVERTY PROFILE

This section presents a brief poverty profile of Syrian refugees living in Jordan. This profile has three purposes. It provides a first indication of the socioeconomic characteristics of the poor among the Syrian refugee population. It also offers some useful indications of the important variables that a welfare model tailored to a refugee population should consider, and it highlights the dimensions of poverty to which policy should accord priority.

Location

The incidence of poverty among Syrian refugees in Jordan in 2021 showed disparities across locations (see figure 3.3), with refugees living in the relatively rural governorates of Ma'an and Jerash having the highest poverty rates. Among the camps, Za'atari camp had a lower incidence of poverty (40 percent) than Azraq camp (53 percent). This difference aligns with the observation that the area around Za'atari offers economic opportunities, whereas Azraq is more isolated.

Refugees residing in Jordanian cities, Amman and Aqaba in particular, had the lowest incidence of poverty in 2021: less than 55 percent. Although Amman had one of the lowest poverty rates, it nonetheless housed the highest share of the poor, with about 34 percent of all poor Syrians in Jordan living there. So although the rate of poverty was lower among the Syrian population in Amman, because of the high concentration of refugees in the capital, poverty was actually more prevalent there.

Socioeconomic characteristics

Household demographics are strongly correlated with poverty among Syrian refugees whether they live in or outside the camps. Figure 3.4 shows that according to data from the 2021 Vulnerability Assessment Framework survey, the incidence of poverty increased with household size and was highest among

FIGURE 3.3

Poverty rates among Syrian refugees by location, 2021

(percent)

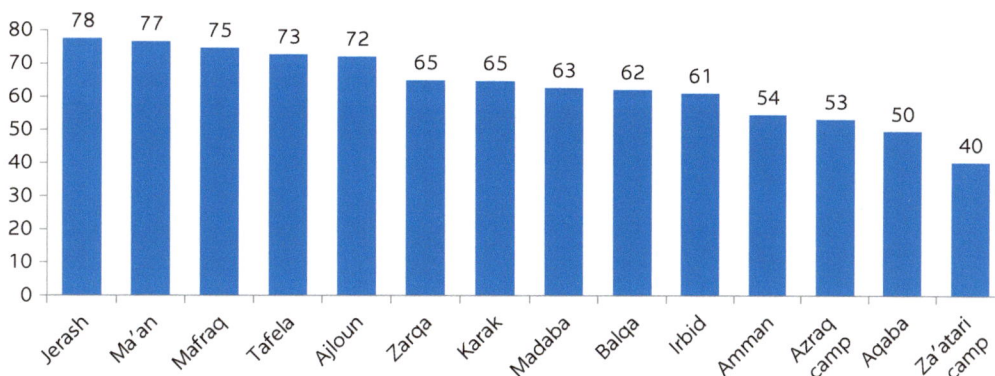

Source: Original figure for this publication using data from UNHCR 2021.

FIGURE 3.4

Poverty rates and household size among Syrian refugees by location, 2021

(percent)

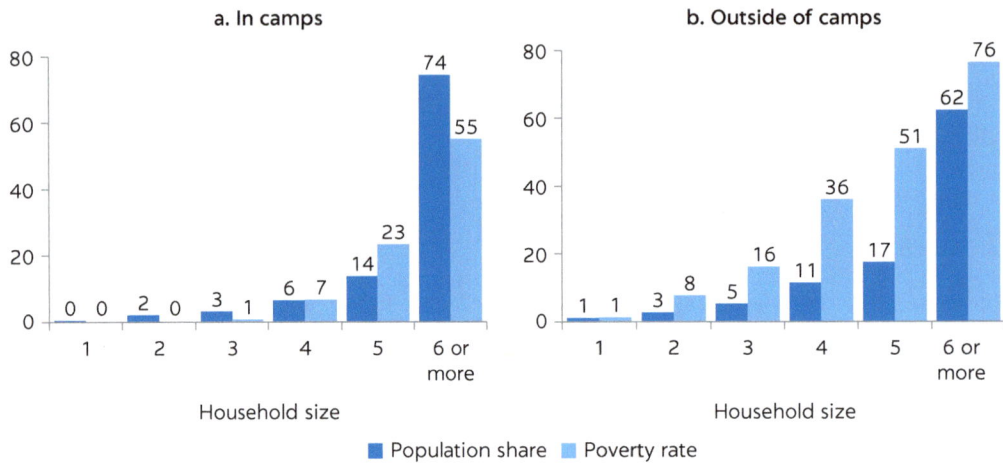

a. In camps

b. Outside of camps

Household size

Household size

■ Population share ■ Poverty rate

Source: Original figure for this publication using data from UNHCR 2021.

FIGURE 3.5

Poverty and family composition among Syrian refugees by location, 2021

(percent)

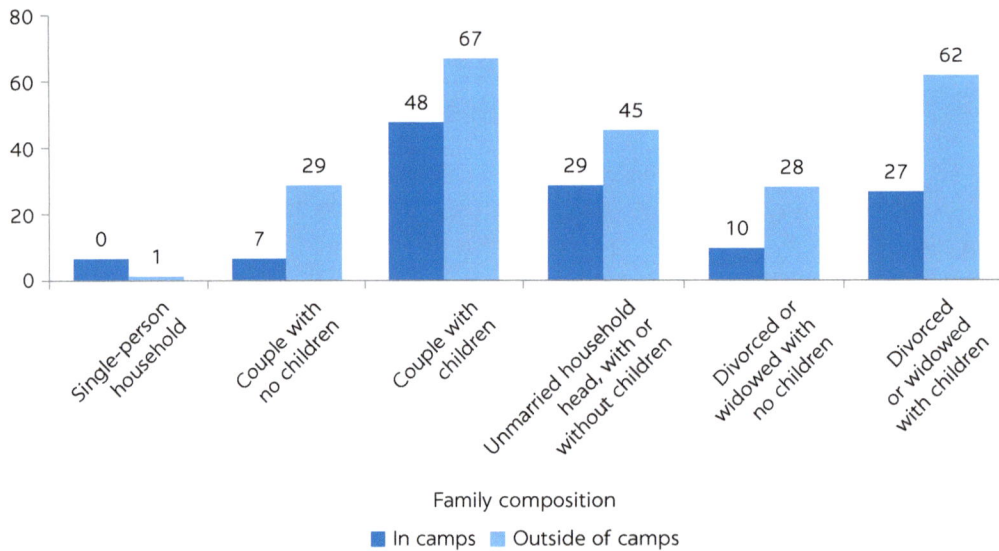

Family composition

■ In camps ■ Outside of camps

Source: Original figure for this publication using data from UNHCR 2021.

households with six or more persons. Despite the likelihood that poverty will increase with household size, the majority of Syrian refugee households were on the larger side, more so among those living in the camps than among those living outside of them.

A positive correlation between family composition and poverty mirrors that between household size and poverty, as figure 3.5 illustrates. The figure shows that according to the 2021 survey data, households with children were more likely to be poor than those without. The correlation between poverty and household size was stronger for those refugees living outside of camps than for those living in them.

The age of the head of a refugee household correlated with poverty among refugees living outside of camps but not among those living in camps. As figure 3.6 shows, in both locations, households in the 2021 Vulnerability Assessment Framework survey that had elderly household heads (older than 65 years) had lower poverty rates than those whose head was of working age (25 to 64 years).

For Syrian refugees living in camps, the household head's level of education does not play a systematic role in explaining poverty. This lack of a correlation (which would be expected to exist and be negative) is somewhat surprising. The importance of assistance and relative unimportance of labor income in camps may explain it. Outside of camps, by contrast, where refugees rely more on labor income to make ends meet, poverty rates are higher among households whose heads have lower levels of education, confirming the typical pattern often observed in poverty assessment, as figure 3.7 illustrates. According to data from the 2021 Vulnerability Assessment Framework survey, households whose heads had no or only primary education had a poverty rate of 63–65 percent, compared with 52 percent for those whose heads had secondary education and 43 percent for those whose heads had university education.

Employment

Being employed reduces the likelihood of being poor for both those living in and those living outside of Jordan's refugee camps for Syrians. In the 2021 Vulnerability Assessment Framework survey, households in refugee camps whose heads were employed showed a poverty rate of 42 percent, against 46 percent among those whose heads were not. Among those living outside of camps, households with heads who worked had a poverty rate of 58 percent, against 65 percent for those with unemployed heads. The sector in which a household head is employed also matters. Whether they lived in or outside of

FIGURE 3.6

Poverty rate and age of household head among Syrian refugees by location, 2021

(percent)

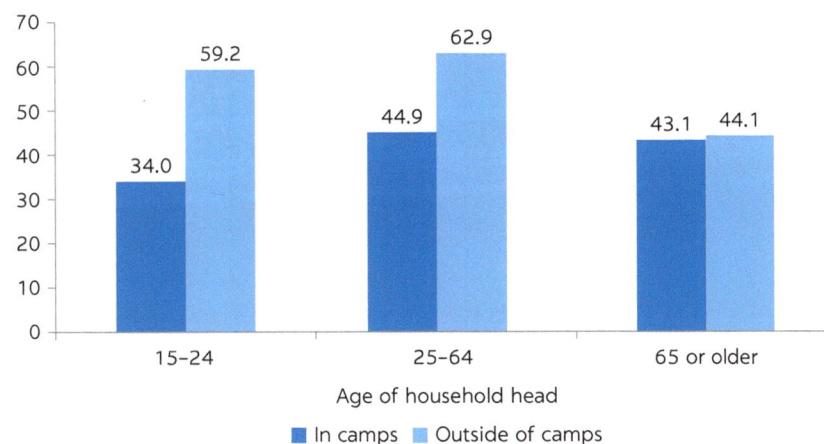

Source: Original figure for this publication using data from UNHCR 2021.

Poverty rate and household heads' level of education among Syrian refugees by location, 2021
(percent)

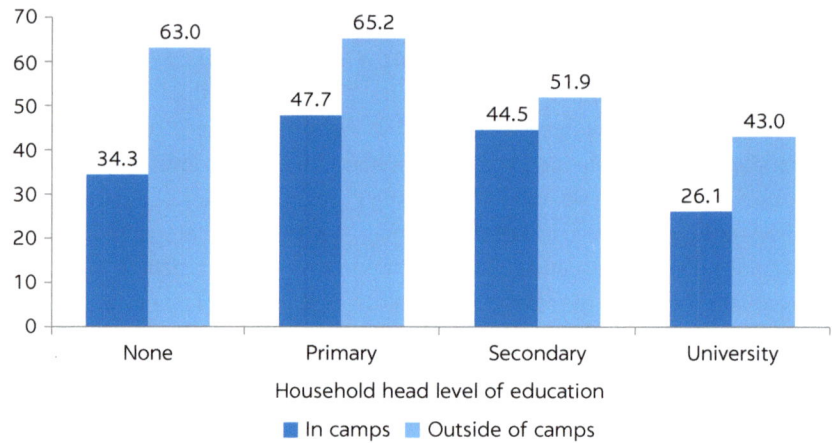

Source: Original figure for this publication using data from UNHCR 2021.

FIGURE 3.8

Poverty rate and occupation type among Syrian refugees by location, 2021
(percent)

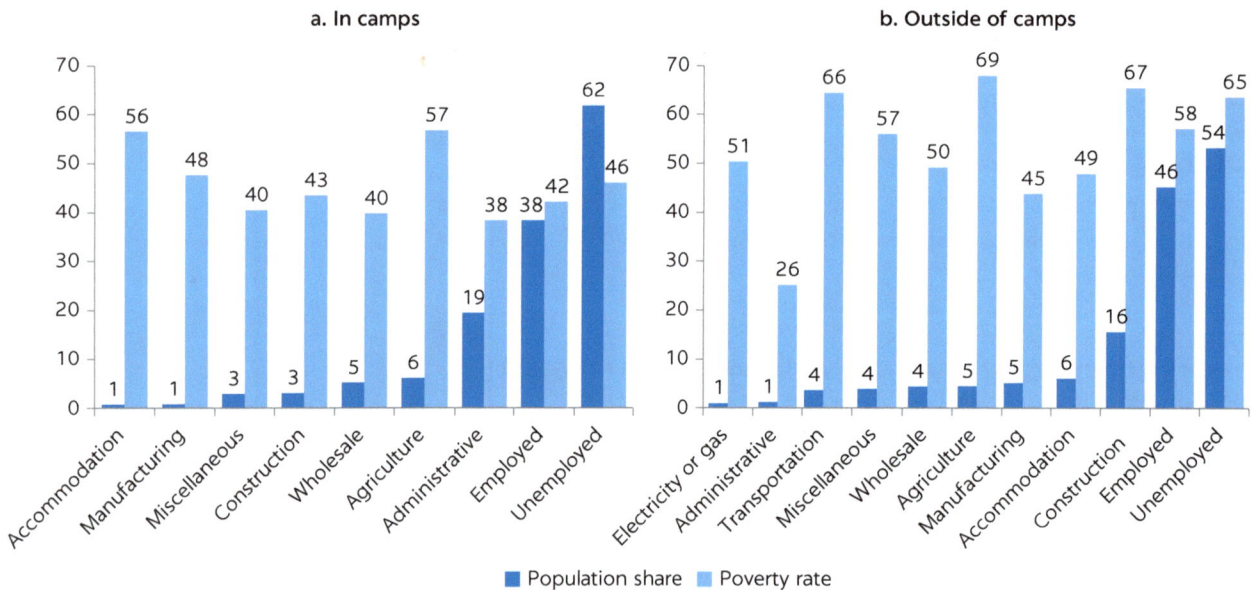

Source: Original figure for this publication using data from UNHCR 2021.

camps, refugee households whose head managed to be employed as administrative staff (often in the formal sector) were least likely to be poor in the 2021 survey. By contrast, having a head working as manual labor in the agricultural sector or in construction was associated with higher levels of poverty. Remarkably, figure 3.8 shows that refugee households with heads working in agriculture, whether they lived in or outside of camps, had a higher prevalence of poverty than households with unemployed heads.

Length of stay

The length of Syrian refugees' stay in Jordan is also an important correlate of poverty among them. As the duration of stay increases, the likelihood of being poor declines. In the 2021 Vulnerability Assessment Framework survey, households outside of camps that had lived in Jordan for 10 years or more were 13 percentage points less likely to be poor than those that had lived in Jordan for 5 years or less, and the difference was even higher among households in camps, about 34 percentage points. One reason for the decline in poverty over time is the positive correlation between employment and duration of stay (figure 3.9). Another is that refugees build up assets over time, and ownership of household assets (beds, tables, sofa sets, ovens, gas stoves, water heaters, and air conditioners) is correlated with lower rates of poverty, presumably because many assets also have an impact on household members' productivity.

FIGURE 3.9

Poverty rate and employment among Syrian refugees by length of stay and location, 2021

(percent)

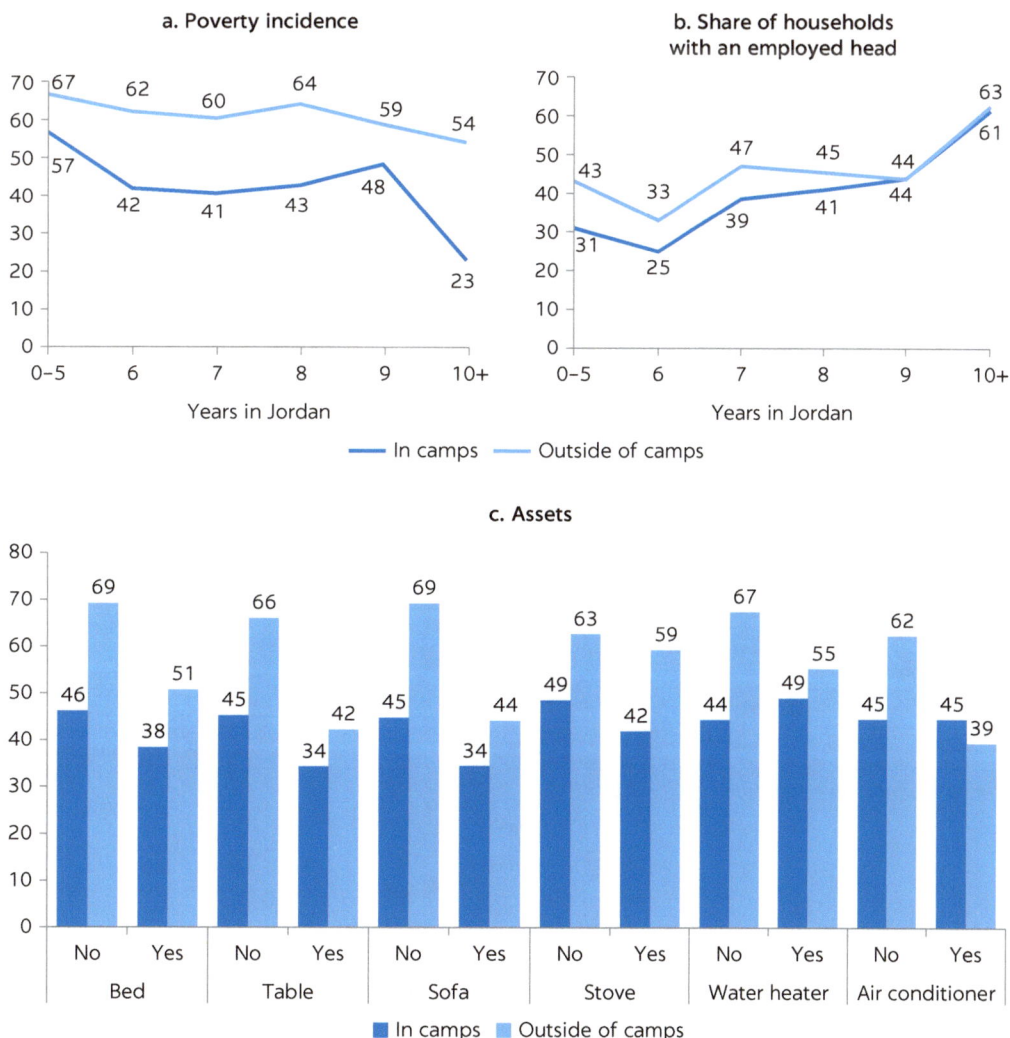

Source: Original figure for this publication using data from UNHCR 2021.

Poverty regression

Previous subsections have noted that household size, family composition, and household heads' education and sector of employment are correlated with poverty among Syrian refugees in Jordan. Poverty is also associated with unemployment, owning fewer assets, and a shorter stay in Jordan. Many of these factors measure the same thing: larger families are more likely to have young children, and people with low levels of education tend to be employed to perform manual labor in agriculture or construction.

To identify the association between each individual variable and poverty, this subsection presents three regressions with poverty as the dependent variable (1 = household is poor, 0 = household is nonpoor) and observable characteristics as right-hand-side variables. Using data from the 2021 Vulnerability Assessment Framework survey, the first regression considers together both refugees living in camps and those living outside of camps, the second is restricted to the camp population only, and the third confines itself to refugees living outside of camps.

The regressions show that household demographics, including gender, household size, and age of the head, as well as the head's education level and employment and household asset ownership, explained poverty among Syrian refugees in Jordan, according to 2021 survey data, with statistical significance (table 3.6). Refugees living outside of camps were more likely to be poor; those staying in Amman were less likely to be poor. Length of stay was statistically significant only in the regression for those staying outside camps, as was level of education, presumably because its impact operates through the labor market, in which people are sorted into sectors according to their education characteristics.

TABLE 3.6 **Correlates of being poor among Syrian refugees, 2021**

VARIABLES	ALL SYRIANS IN JORDAN	IN CAMPS	OUTSIDE OF CAMPS
Residence (base: outside of camps)	2.108***		
Age of household head	0.0689***	0.0229	0.0791***
Age of household head squared	−0.000754***	−8.26e−05	−0.000895***
Household head's years in Jordan	−0.0349	−0.450	−0.0554*
Household head's years in Jordan squared	0.000432	0.0370*	0.000883
Dependency ratio	0.221***	0.355***	0.208***
Household size	0.779***	1.305***	0.773***
Household size squared	−0.292***	−0.927***	−0.254***
Sex of household head (base: male)	−0.247***	0.0388	−0.274***
Marital status of household head (base: single)			
Married	−0.112	0.382	−0.168
Divorced or widowed	−0.353*	−0.265	−0.349
Education level of household head (base: no education)			
Primary education	0.286	0.748**	0.183
Secondary education	0.122	0.730**	−0.0566
University education	−0.272	0.000683	−0.348
Vulnerability			
Household head has chronic illness	−0.104	−0.0707	−0.103
Household receives remittance	−1.269***	−0.217	−1.679***
Multiple sharing family	−0.536***	−0.191	−0.651***

continued

TABLE 3.6., *continued.,*

VARIABLES	ALL SYRIANS IN JORDAN	IN CAMPS	OUTSIDE OF CAMPS
Occupation type of household head (base: unemployed)			
Accommodation	−0.509**	0.768	−0.583**
Administrative	−0.298	−0.108	−0.768
Agriculture	0.0492	0.548	−0.137
Construction	−0.0511	−0.666*	−0.0445
Electricity or gas	−0.0826		−0.0275
Manufacturing	−0.456**	−0.0491	−0.498**
Transportation	0.209		0.228
Miscellaneous work	−0.111	−0.311	−0.0789
Wholesale	−0.447***	−0.470	−0.466**
Shelter			
Number of rooms	−0.308***	−0.0547	−0.353***
Household has bed	−0.199**	−0.311	−0.169*
Household has table	−0.496***	−0.504*	−0.480***
Household has sofa	−0.271**	−0.347	−0.245
Household has oven	−0.292***	−0.650**	−0.255**
Household has stove	−0.322**	−0.708***	−0.273*
Household has water heater	−0.251*	0.227	−0.258*
Household has air conditioner	−0.508***	−0.296*	−0.768***
Household has electric heater	−0.452**	2.023***	−0.493**
Household has access to sanitation	0.254*	0.526**	0.116
Household has access to electricity	0.150	0.318*	0.00670
Household has access to water	0.341*	0.000211	0.535*
Location (base: Ajloun)			
Balqa	−0.310		−0.309
Karak	0.291		0.289
Amman	−0.341*		−0.344*
Aqaba	0.0557		0.226
Azraq camp	0.683***		
Irbid	−0.226		−0.178
Jerash	0.280*		0.307*
Ma'an	0.540***		0.517***
Madaba	−0.334**		−0.349**
Mafraq	0.0912		0.120
Tafela	−0.0129		−0.0431
Zarqa	0.195		0.209
Za'atari camp		−1.075***	
Constant	−4.598***	−2.994*	−2.301***
Number of observations	8,176	2,200	5,968
Pseudo-*R*-squared	0.246	0.209	0.256

Source: Original table for this publication using data from UNHCR 2021.
Note: Blank cells in the table indicate variables that could not be included in the regressions or were dropped from them.
*p < .1 **p < .05 ***p < 0.01

According to data from the 2021 Vulnerability Survey, poverty among Syrian refugees in Jordan increased with household size, but once other variables like dependency ratio are controlled for, the relationship is weaker than figure 3.6 suggests: the nadir is reached at a household size of 1.3, after which the likelihood of poverty declined as households grew larger. Poverty also increased with the age of the head of household, up until the head reached 45 years of age, at which point the likelihood of poverty declined with age of the household head.

BEYOND MONETARY POVERTY

Poverty is a complex concept, and a measure of poverty that focuses on the monetary aspects of consumption may not capture all its facets well (Verme 2023). That Syrian refugees in Jordan living outside of camps voluntarily seek out living arrangements that lower their material welfare and increase their risk of monetary poverty provides a stark illustration of this point. Syrian refugees' revealed preference for not living in a camp (83 percent opt not to do so) suggests that monetary poverty does not capture all dimensions of welfare adequately—at least not for refugees. This section explores whether other dimensions of refugee welfare might have been overlooked.

Multidimensional poverty

Considering poverty as a phenomenon with multiple dimensions can broaden poverty assessment. The World Bank employs an official Multidimensional Poverty Measure that comprises five indicators in addition to monetary poverty to capture two additional dimensions of welfare: education (two indicators) and access to basic infrastructure (three indicators) (see table 3.7). The Multidimensional Poverty Measure thus broadens the concept of poverty beyond simply monetary poverty.[17]

Each of the measure's indicators has a deprivation threshold, a binary variable, that takes the value 1 when an individual or household is deprived and 0 otherwise. The overall measure then aggregates information across these indicators, giving equal weight (one-third) to each dimension: monetary poverty,

TABLE 3.7 Composition of Multidimensional Poverty Measure for Syrian refugees and deprivation levels, 2021

DIMENSION	INDICATOR	DEFINITION	WEIGHT (FRACTION)	IN CAMPS (PERCENT)	OUTSIDE OF CAMPS (PERCENT)
Monetary	Monetary	Poor at refugee poverty line	1/3	44.9	61.8
Education	Educational attainment	No adult in household (age of grade 9 or above) has completed primary education	1/6	30.1	24.1
	Educational enrollment	At least one school-age child up to the age of grade 8 is not enrolled in school	1/6	6.1	20.0
Basic infrastructure	Electricity	Household has no access to electricity for half of time	1/9	83.1	3.5
	Sanitation	Household lacks access to limited standard sanitation	1/9	15.3	11.2
	Drinking water	Household lacks access to limited standard drinking water	1/9	27.5	13.1

Source: Original table for this publication using data from UNHCR 2021.

education, and basic infrastructure, and within each dimension, equal weight to each indicator. The measure considers households multidimensionally poor if they are deprived according to indicators whose weight adds up to one-third or more. Because the monetary dimension is measured using only one indicator, the measure attaches to monetary poverty a weight of one-third, which means that individuals or households who are monetarily poor are automatically considered poor under the broader multidimensional poverty measure. The final two columns of table 3.7 show the shares of Syrian refugees living in and outside of camps who were deprived, according to each indicator, in the 2021 Vulnerability Assessment Framework survey.

The first row of table 3.7 replicates the monetary poverty incidence statistics that were presented earlier in the chapter, with poverty rates being higher among those living outside of camps than among those living in camps. The education indicator shows mixed results: refugee households living in camps were more likely, according to Vulnerability Assessment Framework survey data from 2021, to have no educated adult, but their children, by contrast, were more likely to be enrolled in school. The share of refugees living in camps who were deprived of access to services was much higher than that for those living outside of camps. Deprivation levels regarding access to electricity, water, and sanitation were, respectively, about 80, 14, and 4 percentage points higher for those in camps than for refugees outside camps. This is not surprising at all. Outside the camps there is often constant power from public grids, while the camps use solar power, which provides insufficient electricity.

Bringing it all together, the Multidimensional Poverty Measure's composite index shows that 67 percent of Syrian refugees living outside of camps in the 2021 survey were multidimensionally poor versus 57 percent of those living in camps, as figure 3.10 depicts. Among the measure's three dimensions, also shown in the figure, only on the infrastructure dimension did the measure find refugees in camps to be worse off than refugees living outside the camps. Hence the puzzle of poverty's being more common among refugees living outside of camps remains unresolved, even though when additional dimensions of welfare beyond monetary poverty are considered, the difference between the two groups becomes less pronounced.

FIGURE 3.10

Multidimensional poverty among Syrian refugees by location, 2021
(percent)

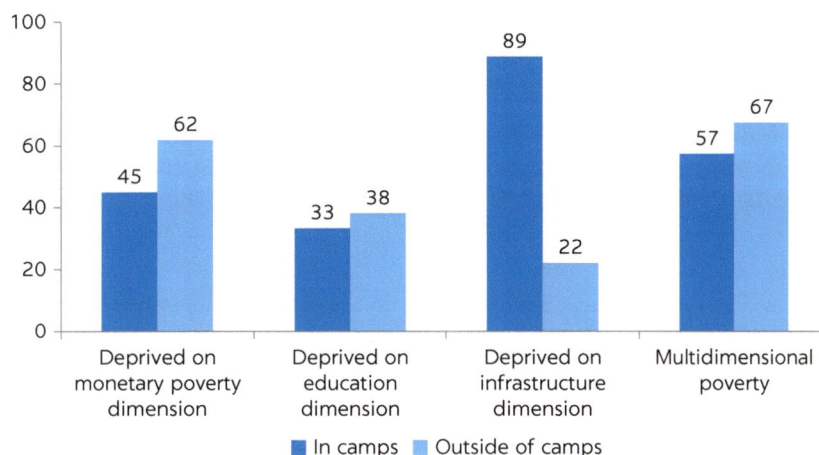

Source: Original figure for this publication using data from UNHCR 2021.

Freedom

So far the chapter has considered refugee poverty through the lens of monetary poverty and access to education and infrastructural services. This approach has yielded at least one surprising result in revealing that by choosing to live outside of refugee camps, Syrian refugees in Jordan seem to opt for a higher probability of poverty. Yet it can be argued that welfare is about more than low income or access to electricity or education; it's about freedom as well.

Nobel Prize–winning economist Amartya Sen, a strong proponent of this view, argues that economic development is about expanding freedoms. According to Sen (1999), poverty should not be just about the amount of income an individual makes; rather, Sen argues, individual well-being stems from the ability to be and do what the individual values. Sen calls this freedom to pursue meaningful lives "capabilities" and says capabilities comprise the resources, opportunities, and constraints—including financial resources, education, legal status, access to health care, and social networks—that influence whether and how individuals can realize their aspirations. Both individual factors, such as skills and health, and structural factors, such as policies, discrimination, and conflict, influence capabilities, Sen notes.

The capabilities framework can be expanded to capture individuals' desires or aspirations as well, an approach that is more common in the international migration literature but is equally relevant in explaining refugees' decisions and well-being (Carling and Schewel 2018). The capabilities-aspirations framework recognizes that individuals' aspirations shape which capabilities they make it a priority to develop and how they strive to actualize their capabilities in the face of constraints (de Haas 2021).

When deciding whether to live in a refugee camp or outside of the camps, Syrian refugees in Jordan weigh their aspirations against their capabilities. Individuals have agency and can make choices about their lives, even within constrained circumstances, but each individual's unique situation, along with the individual's priorities and resources, influences the individual's choices. For example, a young, skilled male refugee might choose to live outside of the camps to pursue work opportunities, even if it means less assistance and greater chances of poverty, because his capabilities (skills) and aspirations (economic independence) align better with his freedom-seeking behavior. On the other hand, an elderly couple without jobs might make security and the basic needs provided in camps a higher priority than the greater freedom offered outside the camps.

The interplay between aspirations and capabilities can have a profound impact on refugees' well-being. Fulfilling aspirations, such as achieving economic independence, gaining an education, or reuniting with family members, can bring a sense of accomplishment, life satisfaction, and emotional well-being. However, limited capabilities due to policies, discrimination, or lack of resources can restrict agency and trap refugees in unfavorable situations.

Recognizing the interplay between aspirations and capabilities can inform policies that put a priority on refugee inclusion, expanding refugees' capabilities, addressing structural inequalities, and offering diverse support options to empower refugees to pursue their desired lives, whether within camps or outside them. By understanding the complex dynamics of the aspirations-capabilities framework, policy makers can better support refugees in navigating their circumstances and achieving their aspirations.

Analytically, the framework pushes for broader ways of measuring refugee poverty that go beyond monetary well-being and include other areas, such as agency and life satisfaction. It aims for greater recognition that refugees have aspirations beyond financial stability, including the desire for autonomy and the ability to live a meaningful life.

The Multidimensional Poverty Measure captures one dimension of the capabilities-aspirations framework: education. As noted previously, in regard to the 2021 Vulnerability Assessment Framework survey data, the measure has ambiguous results in regard to education, as it finds that refugees living outside of camps were better educated (had more capabilities), but their children were less likely to attend school (had lower aspirations).

Individuals can conceptualize freedom in many different ways, however. Subjective life satisfaction, physical and mental health, and freedom to live life without discrimination or fear of insecurity all represent dimensions of capability, and including them in the analysis of refugee welfare can deliver a better understanding of constraints refugees face in reaching their desired lives (Stiglitz, Sen, and Fitoussi 2009).

The 2021 Vulnerability Assessment Framework survey did not comprise such dimensions, but the World Bank's Quality of Life Survey, an internet survey fielded in 2022, did. This survey captured 2,266 observations for Jordanians and 517 for Syrian refugees living in and outside of camps. Table 3.8 shows how this survey can be used to capture various dimensions of freedom.[18]

TABLE 3.8 Syrian refugees' scores on Freedom Index components, 2022

DIMENSION	DEFINITION	WEIGHT (FRACTION)	IN CAMPS (PERCENT)	OUTSIDE OF CAMPS (PERCENT)
Life satisfaction	All things considered, how satisfied are you with your life these days? (scale: 1 [very dissatisfied] to 10 [very satisfied]; a score of 5 or above signifies higher life satisfaction.)	1/3	23	25
Optimism for self	I am optimistic about my future. (yes or no)	1/9	33	32
Optimism for children	I am optimistic about my children's future. (yes or no)	1/9	30	29
Not being discriminated against	1. You are treated with less courtesy or respect than other people. 2. You receive poorer service than other people at restaurants or stores. 3. People act as if they think you are not smart. 4. People act as if they are afraid of you. 5. You are threatened or harassed. (options: almost every day, at least once a week, a few times a month, a few times a year, less than once a year, never. Not feeling discrimination is defined as not experiencing discrimination within a month.)	1/9	47	56
Mental health	How often over the past two weeks have you (1) felt cheerful and in good spirits, (2) felt calm and relaxed, (3) felt active and vigorous, (4) woke up feeling fresh and rested, and (5) felt that daily life has been filled with things that interest you. (options: all the time, most of the time, more than half the time, less than half the time, some of the time, at no time.) Index score of 0 to 100 is obtained, and a score of 50 and above is taken to signify good mental health; World Health Organization's Wellbeing Index WHO-5.	1/9	15	11

continued

TABLE 3.8., *continued.,*

DIMENSION	DEFINITION	WEIGHT (FRACTION)	IN CAMPS (PERCENT)	OUTSIDE OF CAMPS (PERCENT)
Freedom to make life decisions	To what extent do you agree or disagree with the following statement: I feel free to decide how to live my life. (options: strongly agree, agree, neither agree nor disagree, disagree, strongly disagree; freedom to make life decisions is defined as agreeing or strongly agreeing.)	1/9	34	37
Sense of security	How safe do you feel on the street after dark? (scale: 1 [not at all safe] to 10 [very safe]; a score of 5 and above is taken to signify a sense of security.)	1/9	66	68
Absence of freedom	Binary variable (takes value of 1 if household's Freedom Index score is less than one-third, 0 if its index score is one-third or greater).	Binary	56	53

Source: Original table for this publication using data from World Bank 2022.

To measure freedom, the survey creates a composite Freedom Index, mirroring the approach used in the Multidimensional Poverty Measure. It considers seven dimensions: *life satisfaction,* a composite indicator of welfare that measures more than an individual's command over material goods; *optimism for self and children,* a measure of future opportunities; *not being discriminated against; mental health; freedom to make life decisions;* and *sense of security.* Table 3.8 shows the weights assigned to these variables. The index gives life satisfaction (an umbrella concept) a weight of one-third and weights the other six dimensions equally at one-ninth each. The weighted average of these variables, calculated for each household, is labeled the Freedom Index and used to determine the degree of absence of freedom a household perceives. Following the approach taken for the Multidimensional Poverty Measure, the index creates a binary variable, absence of freedom, that takes a value of 1 if a household's Freedom Index score is less than one-third, indicating that the household lacks freedom, or 0 if its index score is one-third or greater, indicating that it experiences freedom. Note that although all components of the index are defined in a positive way (the presence of freedom), the absence of freedom variable measures a negative.

The last two columns of table 3.8 present scores on the Freedom Index's indicators for refugees living in camps and those living outside of camps, based on data from the 2022 Quality of Life Survey, and show only small differences between the two groups. In terms of overall life satisfaction, refugees living outside of camps did slightly better, and they were also less likely to feel discriminated against (the only indicator on which the two groups' scores showed a large difference), felt more empowered to make decisions, and had a greater sense of security. Refugees living in camps, by contrast, were more likely to be optimistic about their own future and that of their children and less likely to have mental health issues. On balance, refugees living outside of camps were more likely to experience freedom, at least according to the Freedom Index.

DISCUSSION

Freedom is an important aspect of personal self-determination, particularly for refugees who have been forced to flee their country of origin on account of a well-founded fear of persecution. For them, the freedom to leave is a prerequisite to securing protection against (anticipated) persecution. Freedom is, however, about more than the freedom of movement alone: it is about having opportunities to build a life for oneself and one's children, to be safe, and not to be discriminated against.

For Syrian refugees in Jordan, freedom is a dimension on which they are deprived. Even if the lack of monetary means to attain an acceptable standard of living experienced by many refugees is set aside, they are restricted in the work they are allowed to do, and many experience discrimination. Those living in camps are even more freedom deprived, as they experience restrictions in their movement.

Refugees experience a deprivation of freedom of a different order than that typically experienced by citizens, who, even though they may also experience freedom deprivations because they are discriminated against and insecure, do not face the kind of legal restrictions that refugees do. As freedom is an important aspect of welfare (so important that many societies' preferred way of punishing criminals is to deprive them of freedom), existing measures of poverty such as monetary poverty and multidimensional poverty indexes fail to capture this aspect. As a consequence, any comparisons of welfare between host country citizens and refugees that limit themselves to monetary poverty or multidimensional poverty likely underreport the deprivations refugees experience.

With the data at hand, it is not possible to calculate, for Syrian refugees in Jordan, a Multidimensional Poverty Measure that is enhanced to include freedom, as the 2001 Vulnerability Assessment Framework survey did not include dimensions of freedom, but table 3.9 illustrates what such an expanded Multidimensional Poverty Measure could look like.

It is beyond this chapter and this volume to detail how a freedom dimension for refugee welfare surveys should be defined and measured. An extensive literature discusses how to do so, but measurement of freedom typically relies on subjective data, which complicates the matter. The use of subjective data to measure welfare objectively is a challenging field (see Ravallion 2012). Personality, for instance, is likely to affect an individual's responses to a question about optimism regarding the future. Frame of reference also matters. A Syrian refugee living outside of refugee camps may be satisfied with life when comparing

TABLE 3.9 **Components of an extended Multidimensional Poverty Measure for refugees**

DIMENSION	INDICATOR	DEFINITION	WEIGHT (FRACTION)	IN CAMPS (PERCENT)	OUTSIDE OF CAMPS(PERCENT)
Economic means	Monetary poverty	Poor at refugee poverty line	1/4	44.9	61.8
Education	Educational attainment	No adult in household (age of grade 9 or above) has completed primary education	1/8	30.1	24.1
	Educational enrollment	At least one school-age child up to the age of grade 8 is not enrolled in school	1/8	6.1	20.0
Basic infrastructure	Electricity	Household has no access to electricity for half of time	1/12	83.1	3.5
	Sanitation	Household lacks access to limited standard sanitation	1/12	15.3	11.2
	Drinking water	Household lacks access to limited standard drinking water	1/12	27.5	13.1
Freedom	Absence of freedom composite	Experiences less than a threshold of freedom	1/4	55.5	53.2

Sources: Original table for this publication using data from UNHCR 2021 and World Bank 2022.

herself with those living in camps, but very unsatisfied when comparing her life outside the camps to her life before displacement. Which reference frame does she use? Furthermore, frames of reference can be manipulated, which can lead to different answers on a survey even when objective circumstances have not changed. For example, Kristensen and Westergaard-Nielsen (2007) find that 20 percent of respondents on a survey in Europe gave a different answer on job satisfaction when asked twice within the same interview.

Such complications to measurement leave unchanged the importance of capturing freedom as a dimension of welfare for refugees and create a strong case for including it in future refugee welfare surveys.

CONCLUSION

The measurement of poverty among refugees is still in its infancy, and few studies have undertaken it. This chapter started out by producing monetary poverty estimates for Syrian refugees in Jordan living in refugee camps and in host communities. The chapter demonstrated that estimating monetary poverty is an involved exercise, requiring detailed consumption modules and careful data processing. Even with those elements present and available, producing comparable poverty estimates for Syrian refugees living in camps and those living outside of camps proved to present challenges, because many in-camp refugees receive in-kind assistance (such as housing provided to refugees staying in camps) to which it is hard to attach a market value. Certain ad hoc decisions had to be made to determine a poverty line for registered Syrian refugees. Sensitivity analyses confirmed that the observed pattern for monetary poverty was independent of these decisions, leading to the noteworthy result that Syrian refugees living in host communities are more likely to be monetarily poor than those living in camps.

Not only is the incidence of poverty higher among refugees living outside of camps, but the depth and severity of monetary poverty are greater. This presents a conundrum: Why do people who have the option to live in a camp and experience a lower likelihood of deprivation decide against doing so?

As measurement issues do not appear to drive this result, the chapter explored whether monetary poverty adequately measures refugee poverty or other dimensions of deprivation should be considered. To this end, it calculated, for participants in UNHCR's 2021 Vulnerability Assessment Framework survey, the World Bank's Multidimensional Poverty Measure, which captures, in addition to monetary poverty, deprivations with respect to education and access to services. Using this measure reduces the poverty gap between refugees living in and outside of camps, but it does not eliminate it. Those living in host communities remain (multidimensionally) poorer.

The chapter then considered another dimension of well-being: freedom. It presented data representing different aspects of freedom and showed that Syrian refugees living outside of camps tend to score better on this dimension. It argued that to measure refugees' welfare, the Multidimensional Poverty Measure might have to be enlarged with a freedom dimension.

The chapter's results have several implications related to the measurement of poverty among refugees:

- Including an (abbreviated) consumption module in the Vulnerability Assessment Framework survey proved feasible and worthwhile; countries with sizable refugee populations should preferably include a refugee stratum in national surveys to allow for direct comparisons between host and refugee populations.

- Measuring poverty among those who receive many benefits in kind, such as refugees living in camp or camplike situations, will require additional methodological work to assess how receiving benefits in kind affects measures of monetary poverty.
- Monetary poverty alone, and even multidimensional poverty indexes, may not satisfactorily capture refugees' welfare. An extended multidimensional poverty index that includes a freedom dimension seems more appropriate, and future surveys may want to consider capturing this dimension of refugee welfare. Additional research is needed to determine how best to do so.

The most important finding of this chapter, however, is the high degree of deprivation among Syrian refugees: as recently as 2021, 62 percent of Syrian refugees living in host communities in Jordan, and 45 percent of Syrian refugees living in Jordan's refugee camps, were monetarily poor.

ANNEX 3A. ADDITIONAL TABLE

TABLE 3A.1 Composition of food poverty basket

ITEM	DAILY KILOCALORIES CONSUMED PER CAPITA (ADJUSTED)	MEDIAN UNIT PRICE	PRICE PER KILOCALORIE	COST	SHARE OF COST	SHARE OF KILOCALORIES
Apples	2.12	1.000	1.887	0.1215	0.7%	0.1%
Bananas	3.01	1.000	1.070	0.0979	0.6%	0.1%
Beans	28.05	0.001	0.000	0.0004	0.0%	1.2%
Biscuits	11.33	0.002	0.001	0.0002	0.0%	0.5%
Bread	944.09	0.400	0.154	4.4207	26.5%	41.0%
Cheese	9.33	3.000	0.854	0.2425	1.5%	0.4%
Chicken	34.57	2.000	1.572	1.6528	9.9%	1.5%
Chips	15.85	0.004	0.001	0.0004	0.0%	0.7%
Chocolate	46.42	0.200	0.040	0.0560	0.3%	2.0%
Cucumbers	9.46	0.500	2.924	0.8416	5.0%	0.4%
Dates	4.87	0.002	0.001	0.0001	0.0%	0.2%
Eggs	24.12	0.092	1.637	1.2012	7.2%	1.0%
Fish	1.90	0.625	0.328	0.0190	0.1%	0.1%
Frozen fish	1.49	2.750	1.460	0.0659	0.4%	0.1%
Garlic	4.77	0.008	0.005	0.0008	0.0%	0.2%
Grapes	3.55	0.650	1.940	0.2094	1.3%	0.2%
Greens	3.06	1.400	5.192	0.4836	2.9%	0.1%
Hummus	3.11	1.000	0.692	0.0654	0.4%	0.1%
Ice cream	88.49	0.100	0.039	0.1051	0.6%	3.8%
Infant milk	13.70	0.011	0.002	0.0009	0.0%	0.6%
Juice	3.64	0.800	1.667	0.1847	1.1%	0.2%
Labneh	3.48	0.004	0.006	0.0006	0.0%	0.2%
Lemons	2.57	1.000	2.857	0.2232	1.3%	0.1%

continued

TABLE 3A.1., *continued.,*

ITEM	DAILY KILOCALORIES CONSUMED PER CAPITA (ADJUSTED)	MEDIAN UNIT PRICE	PRICE PER KILOCALORIE	COST	SHARE OF COST	SHARE OF KILOCALORIES
Macaroni	53.77	0.001	0.000	0.0005	0.0%	2.3%
Mandarins	0.73	0.700	1.333	0.0298	0.2%	0.0%
Margarine	15.05	0.004	0.000	0.0002	0.0%	0.7%
Meat	10.19	5.000	2.632	0.8156	4.9%	0.4%
Milk	0.58	0.900	1.299	0.0230	0.1%	0.0%
Nuts	0.60	4.000	0.708	0.0130	0.1%	0.0%
Oil	243.59	0.002	0.000	0.0016	0.0%	10.6%
Onions	17.29	0.500	1.276	0.6706	4.0%	0.8%
Oranges	1.15	0.625	1.330	0.0466	0.3%	0.1%
Other spices	10.45	0.007	0.002	0.0006	0.0%	0.5%
Peaches	1.07	0.667	1.626	0.0528	0.3%	0.0%
Potatoes	45.11	0.500	0.762	1.0458	6.3%	2.0%
Powdered milk	32.09	0.005	0.001	0.0010	0.0%	1.4%
Rice	252.66	1.000	0.288	2.2115	13.2%	11.0%
Salt and pepper	15.17	0.002	0.001	0.0002	0.0%	0.7%
Soda	1.16	0.600	1.395	0.0491	0.3%	0.1%
Sugar	262.15	0.001	0.000	0.0013	0.0%	11.4%
Tahini	3.49	0.004	0.001	0.0001	0.0%	0.2%
Tomatoes	30.06	0.350	1.620	1.4816	8.9%	1.3%
Tomato purée	2.70	0.002	0.005	0.0004	0.0%	0.1%
Watermelon	9.24	0.313	0.944	0.2655	1.6%	0.4%
Yogurt	28.72	0.001	0.002	0.0019	0.0%	1.2%
Total	2,300			16.7	100%	100%

Source: Original table for this publication using data from UNHCR 2021.

NOTES

1. Sohnesen and Schmieding (2021) underline that monetary income may not be a tenable welfare indicator for displaced populations who are entirely dependent on humanitarian assistance, as even monetary consumption may be distorted for these populations, because they do not participate in typical markets for the food and nonfood items they need. For refugees in Jordan specifically, however, such estimates are feasible, not the least because much assistance is provided in cash and the value of in-kind assistance can be reasonably proxied.
2. Those interested in measuring monetary poverty are referred to Haughton and Khandker (2009).
3. Verme et al. (2016) limit themselves to poverty measurements for refugees living outside of camps and use an arbitrary poverty line.
4. For more information about the Multidimensional Poverty Measure, see World Bank, "Brief: Multidimensional Poverty Measure" (web page, accessed January 2024; https://www.worldbank.org/en/topic/poverty/brief/multidimensional-poverty-measure).
5. This omission is all the more remarkable given that the main way societies punish criminals and others is to take away their freedom by putting them in prison. Yet as few people are in prison or live in refugee camps, the absence of freedom as a welfare metric is easily overlooked.

6. UNHCR (2023) presents poverty estimates for eight countries: Brazil, Chad, Chile, Colombia, Costa Rica, Ethiopia, Kenya, and Uganda.

7. JDC, World Bank Group, and UNHCR (2020) provides other poverty estimates for Syrian refugees in Jordan, based on microsimulations.

8. Verme and colleagues had to contend with limited consumption information. They had at their disposal data conducted during home visits to refugees that asked three questions on welfare: one question on income, structured in 7 items, and two questions on expenditure, the first structured in 6 items and the second in 10. As Verme and colleagues readily acknowledge and as Beegle et al. (2010) and Christiaensen, Ligon, and Sohnesen (2022) show, the length of the items' recall period and the small number of items involved limit the precision of the resulting poverty estimates. Unable to calculate caloric values from the consumption information at their disposal, Verme and colleagues adopted an arbitrary poverty line of JD 50 per capita per month, the amount UNHCR used at the time for its cash assistance.

9. Obi (2023) provides additional details.

10. UNHCR, "Guidance on Registration and Identity Management: Planning and Preparing Registration and Identity Management Systems; 3.6 Registration Tools" (web page, accessed January 2024; https://www.unhcr.org/registration-guidance/chapter3/registration-tools/).

11. The data set collected includes all relevant personal data, such as name, date of birth, place of birth, gender, date of flight, arrival date in Jordan, registration date, ethnicity, religion, specific needs, and vulnerabilities. It also includes a very short summary of the refugee claim; the whereabouts of close relatives, whether in the refugee's country of origin, the country of asylum, or other countries; educational details; professional skills; occupation in countries of origin and asylum, if any; addresses in country of origin and country of asylum, including key movements within the country of origin; and reasons for flight. If refugees have relatives who are registered refugees in Jordan, the cases are linked.

12. The surveys for those living in camps and those living outside of camps use nearly identical consumption modules, with a few notable exceptions, such as the omission of rent from the in-camp surveys and ownership of durable goods from the out-of-camp surveys.

13. This is a strong assumption. An alternative approach would be to estimate the cost based on the availability of various household electrical appliances. The Vulnerability Assessment Framework survey gathers information on appliances, but it does not ask about usage levels, making this method impractical.

14. Spatial deflators were derived using food consumption only, because for nonfood items, the survey did not collect information on quantities purchased (which is necessary for calculating spatial deflators). The deflators were then applied to total consumption (both food and nonfood).

15. Poverty depth is generally expressed as a percentage. For example, a poverty depth, or poverty gap, of 19 percent means that the monetary equivalent of 19 percent of the poverty line is needed to bring household consumption up to the poverty line.

16. Syrian refugees have a higher incidence of poverty than Jordanians. Jordanians had a poverty rate of 16 percent in 2018, whereas the poverty rate of Syrians at the refugee poverty line was 58 percent. (It is important to note that Household Income and Expenditure Survey poverty—the measure used for Jordanians here—is based on the national poverty line, which differs from the refugee poverty line; poverty as calculated using the Vulnerability Assessment Framework survey is therefore not strictly comparable to that calculated using the Household Income and Expenditure Survey.) The Household Income and Expenditure Survey uses a more detailed consumption module that results, all other things being equal, in higher recorded levels of consumption and lower levels of poverty. It also uses a higher poverty line. At first this may be seem surprising, because the two surveys use the same methodology. Both anchor their poverty lines at 2,300 kcal and not on the number of items used to record consumption. Food poverty lines are, however, weakly relative: when people get wealthier, they consume more expensive kcal. Moreover, the Household Income and Expenditure Survey will have higher values for the nonfood component, which is calculated as a top-up based on the nonfood consumption of refugees whose total consumption lies at approximately the poverty line, because of the combined effect of the more detailed consumption module and weak relativity.

17. Other prominent global multidimensional measures exist, particularly the Multidimensional Poverty Index developed by the United Nations Development Programme and Oxford University. The Multidimensional Poverty Measure differs from these other multidimensional measures in one important aspect: it includes monetary poverty.

18. Results obtained through the Quality of Life Survey are not representative of the populations surveyed—for instance, young men are overrepresented among the respondents—because respondents were approached through Facebook advertisements and then opted to take (or not take) the internet survey. Thus, the results have to be interpreted with care, with a focus on general patterns and on differences between different subpopulations, such as those between refugees and Jordanians or between refugees living in camps and those living outside of camps.

REFERENCES

Beegle, Kathleen, Joachim De Weerdt, Jed Friedman, and John Gibson. 2010. "Methods of Household Consumption Measurement through Surveys: Experimental Results from Tanzania." World Bank Working Paper 5501, World Bank, Washington, DC.

Beltramo, Theresa, Hai-Anh H. Dang, Ibrahima Sarr, and Paolo Verme. 2020. "Estimating Poverty among Refugee Populations: A Cross-Survey Imputation Exercise for Chad." Policy Research Working Paper 9222, World Bank, Washington, DC.

Carling, Jørgen, and Kerilyn Schewel. 2018. "Revisiting Aspiration and Ability in International Migration." *Journal of Ethnic and Migration Studies* 44 (6): 945–63. https://doi.org/10.1080/1369183X.2017.1384146.

Christiaensen, Luc, Ethan Ligon, and Thomas Pave Sohnesen. 2022. "Consumption Subaggregates Should Not Be Used to Measure Poverty." *World Bank Economic Review* 36 (2): 413–32. https://doi.org/10.1093/wber/lhab021.

Dang, Hai-Anh H., and Paolo Verme. 2023. "Estimating Poverty for Refugees in Data-Scarce Contexts: An Application of Cross-Survey Imputation." *Journal of Population Economics* 36 (2): 653–79. https://doi.org/10.1007/s00148-022-00909-x.

de Haas, Hein. 2021. "A Theory of Migration: The Aspirations-Capabilities Framework." *Comparative Migration Studies* 9: art. 8. https://doi.org/10.1186/s40878-020-00210-4.

Haughton, Jonathan, and Shahidur R. Khandker. 2009. *Handbook on Poverty and Inequality.* Washington, DC: World Bank.

JDC (Joint Data Center on Forced Displacement), World Bank Group, and UNHCR (United Nations High Commissioner for Refugees). 2020. *Compounding Misfortunes: Changes in Poverty since the Onset of COVID-19 on Syrian Refugees and Host Communities in Jordan, the Kurdistan Region of Iraq and Lebanon.* Washington, DC: World Bank. http://hdl.handle.net/10986/34951.

Jordan Department of Statistics. 2018. "Household Income and Expenditure Survey, 2017–18." Department of Statistics, Hashemite Kingdom of Jordan, Amman.

Kristensen, Nicolai, and Niels Westergaard-Nielsen. 2007. "Reliability of Job Satisfaction Measures." *Journal of Happiness Studies* 8: 273–92. https://doi.org/10.1007/s10902-006-9027.

Nguyen, Nga Thi Viet, Aboudrahyme Savadogo, and Tomomi Tanaka. 2021. *Refugees in Chad: The Road Forward.* Washington, DC: World Bank.

Obi, Chinedu Temple. 2021. "The Impact of Living Arrangements (In-Camp versus Out-of-Camp) on the Quality of Life: A Case Study of Syrian Refugees in Jordan." Policy Research Working Paper 9533, World Bank, Washington, DC. http://hdl.handle.net/10986/35106.

Obi, Chinedu Temple. 2023. "Poverty Measurement for Refugees in Jordan: VAF Welfare Study—A Technical Note." United Nations High Commissioner for Refugees, Geneva, and World Bank, Washington, DC. https://data.unhcr.org/fr/documents/download/99518.

Oseni, Gbemisola, Amparo Palacios-Lopez, Harriet Kasidi Mugera, and Josefine Durazo. 2021. *Capturing What Matters: Essential Guidelines for Designing Household Surveys.* Washington, DC: World Bank.

Pape, Utz Johann, and Paolo Verme. 2023. "Measuring Poverty in Forced Displacement Contexts." Policy Research Working Paper 10302, World Bank, Washington, DC. https://documents1.worldbank.org/curated/en/099330002082336067/pdf/IDU0f21f2e9f0f7b704c420a5af038bbbbb4f592.pdf.

Ravallion, Martin. 2012. "Poor, or Just Feeling Poor? On Using Subjective Data in Measuring Poverty." Working Paper 5968, World Bank, Washington, DC.

Sen, Amartya. 1999. *Development as Freedom.* New York: Knopf.

Stiglitz, Joseph E., Amartya Sen, and Jean-Paul Fitoussi. 2009. "Report by the Commission on the Measurement of Economic Performance and Social Progress." Commission on the Measurement of Economic Performance and Social Progress, European Commission, Brussels. https://ec.europa.eu/eurostat/documents/8131721/8131772/Stiglitz-Sen-Fitoussi-Commission-report.pdf.

Sohnesen, Thomas Pave, and Felix Schmieding. 2021. *Measuring Monetary Poverty among Forcibly Displaced Populations in Camps and Their Hosts.* Copenhagen: Joint Data Center on Forced Displacement. https://unece.org/sites/default/files/2021-11/PPP_A.%202030%20Agenda_UNHCR_eng.pdf.

UNHCR (United Nations High Commissioner for Refugees). 2021. "Vulnerability Assessment Framework Population Survey for Refugees in Host Communities: Jordan, 2021" (data set). UNHCR, Geneva.

UNHCR (United Nations High Commissioner for Refugees). 2022. *Global Compact on Refugees—Indicator Framework 2022.* 2nd ed. New York: UNHCR. https://www.unhcr.org/media/global-compact-refugees-indicator-framework-2022-0.

UNHCR (United Nations High Commissioner for Refugees). 2023. *2023 Global Compact on Refugees Indicator Report.* New York: UNHCR. https://www.unhcr.org/media/2023-global-compact-refugees-indicator-report.

Verme, Paolo. 2023. "Poverty Measurement for Forcibly Displaced Populations: Challenges and Prospects of a New Field." In *Research Handbook on Measuring Poverty and Deprivation,* edited by Jacques Silber, 430–38. Cheltenham, UK: Elgar. https://doi.org/10.4337/9781800883451.

Verme, Paolo, Chiara Gigliarano, Christina Wieser, Kerren Hedlund, Marc Petzoldt, and Marco Santacroce. 2016. *The Welfare of Syrian Refugees: Evidence from Jordan and Lebanon.* Washington, DC: World Bank. doi: 10.1596/978-1-4648-0770-1.

World Bank. 2019. *Informing the Refugee Policy Response in Uganda: Results from the Uganda Refugee and Host Communities 2018 Household Survey.* Washington, DC: World Bank.

World Bank. 2022. "Quality of Life Survey" (data set). World Bank, Washington, DC.

World Bank. 2023. "Welfare in Forcibly Displaced Populations: From Measuring Outcomes to Building and Leveraging Harmonized Data to Improve Welfare among Forcibly Displaced Populations and Their Hosts; A Technical Brief Series." Issue Brief 3, Poverty and Equity Global Practice, World Bank, Washington, DC.

4 Humanitarian Assistance to Syrian Refugees

CHINEDU OBI AND JOHANNES HOOGEVEEN

MAIN MESSAGES

This chapter delves into the realm of assistance extended to Syrian refugees in Jordan, with a focus on cash programs offered by two of the largest humanitarian agencies: the World Food Programme (WFP) and the United Nations High Commissioner for Refugees (UNHCR). It assesses the methods aid organizations use to provide cash aid and the impact of that aid on poverty.

The chapter underscores two critical points. First, aid organizations can enhance the ways they deliver humanitarian assistance to Syrian refugees to make support systems more effective and efficient at reducing poverty. Second, even the most efficient programs of assistance will fail to eliminate poverty among refugees unless levels of assistance increase, refugees start to earn more income, or both.

An estimated $899 million annually would be needed to bring all Syrian refugees in Jordan to the minimum standard of living reflected by the refugee poverty line. Refugees currently earn more than half this amount, $539 million, and receive $206 million in assistance, leaving an annual shortfall of $154 million. At a targeting efficiency of 63 percent, the total shortfall in humanitarian financing in Jordan is estimated at $244 million per year.

Regrettably, in the current landscape, the probability of substantial increases in assistance remains low. This reality argues for a transformative change in the way humanitarian assistance is provided by aligning it much more strongly with the promotion of refugee self-reliance.

INTRODUCTION

For many Syrian refugees in Jordan and especially those living in refugee camps, assistance, whether provided in cash or in kind, is the main source of income.[1]

Multiple humanitarian agencies aid Syrian refugees. To coordinate their actions, the UNHCR's Refugee Assistance Information System (RAIS) acts as an interagency tool for tracking cash and in-kind assistance. Merging data from the UNHCR's 2021 Vulnerability Assessment Framework survey (UNHCR 2021b) with RAIS data makes it feasible in this chapter to evaluate the impact of assistance on refugees' welfare. This in turn allows the chapter to assess targeting efficiency through a series of scenario exercises, as well as by updating the proxy means test used to determine refugee eligibility for assistance.

The chapter thus provides insights into whether and how humanitarian agencies might be able to improve their current cash assistance programs for refugees. The chapter's analysis suggests that there is scope for such improvement. Yet the chapter's most critical finding is a general shortfall of humanitarian assistance and the inability of this assistance to eliminate poverty at current funding levels. Even with perfect targeting and no provision of assistance to refugees who do not actually need it, the chapter finds, poverty among refugees will remain high, unless assistance or refugee self-reliance increases.

Funding for refugee assistance, however, is unlikely to grow in a global context in which crises are multiplying, with increased competition for development assistance, including that for financing adaptation to and resilience against climate change. This leaves, then, a need to improve refugees' income-earning ability as an important objective.

The next section of the chapter discusses existing humanitarian cash programs for Syrian refugees. The second section considers the impact of existing assistance on poverty reduction and explores whether changing the way assistance is provided could improve its efficiency in targeting those most in need. The analysis in the third section goes a step further by exploring the impact on targeting efficiency of an updated proxy means test for refugees. The fourth section concludes the chapter.

HUMANITARIAN ASSISTANCE FOR REFUGEES IN JORDAN

The international community provides significant levels of humanitarian assistance to refugees in Jordan. RAIS enables humanitarian partners in this refugee assistance to share assistance records, cross-check aid recipient lists, and combine different types of data. RAIS is synchronized with proGres, UNHCR's refugee registration database, which is updated daily.

RAIS, like any database, has its specifics and its limitations. Monetary values of in-kind assistance go unrecorded, for instance, making it difficult to calculate the total value of such assistance. Not all humanitarian organizations report their assistance in RAIS, and those that do, don't always update their information regularly. Also, RAIS doesn't factor transaction costs and overheads into the assistance values it records. It does, however, make available the actual value of cash assistance refugees receive and the frequency with which they receive it.[2]

This section presents an overview of cash assistance provided to refugees in Jordan, as recorded in RAIS. It covers assistance given to all refugees registered with UNHCR in Jordan, not Syrian refugees alone. Because (as noted) RAIS lacks information on the value of in-kind assistance, the analysis is limited to cash assistance, data for which are provided at the case level.[3] It does not include assistance provided at the individual level or in-kind assistance.

Cash assistance

Table 4.1 presents the total cash assistance provided to refugees in Jordan between 2018 and 2021. WFP and UNHCR provided the vast majority (90 percent or more), with WFP providing slightly more than UNHCR.

TABLE 4.1 Cash assistance provided to refugees in Jordan, as recorded in RAIS, 2018–21

	2018		2019		2020		2021	
	ASSISTANCE (MILLION US DOLLARS)	SHARE (PERCENT)	ASSISTANCE (MILLION US DOLLARS)	SHARE (PERCENT)	ASSISTANCE (MILLION US DOLLARS)	SHARE (PERCENT)	ASSISTANCE (MILLION US DOLLARS)	SHARE (PERCENT)
WFP	118	50	163	59	164	60	170	54
UNHCR	98	42	102	37	85	31	129	41
Others	19	8	11	4	24	9	13	5
Total	235	100	276	100	273	100	312	100

Source: Original table for this publication using data from UNHCR 2023.
Note: RAIS = Refugee Assistance Information System.

More than 20 different organizations provided the remainder of the assistance, including the United Nations Children's Fund, Norwegian Refugee Council, International Organization for Migration, and International Committee of the Red Cross. The table shows a large increase in cash assistance during the COVID-19 years, from $235 million in 2018 to $273 million in 2020 and $312 million in 2021.

UNHCR and WFP provide cash assistance to refugees in Jordan through multiple programs summarized in table 4.2. The largest among these are UNHCR's monthly multipurpose cash assistance and WFP's monthly food assistance. Together these programs account for 80 percent of the cash assistance UNHCR and WFP provide to refugees in Jordan. The remaining 20 percent is distributed through an array of programs with narrower objectives. Of these, winter cash provided by UNHCR is the largest (14 percent), with the remaining 6 percent covering expenses for health, protection, education, and emergencies.[4]

WFP's monthly food assistance program offers cash transfers to refugees in Jordan—both those living in camps and those living in host communities—worth, in 2021, more than $170 million. Syrians accounted for about 95 percent of the 2021 recipients. The program provides all refugees living in camps (where the program is universal) with food assistance in the form of vouchers valued, in 2021, at $32 (JD 23) per person every month.[5] Refugees can use these vouchers in WFP-contracted supermarkets and bread shops located in the camps. Some, but not all, refugees living outside of camps receive WFP food assistance in the form of e-vouchers redeemable for cash at WFP-contracted automated teller machines or in WFP-contracted shops. These vouchers had a value, in 2021, of $32 (JD 23) per person per month for extremely vulnerable refugees and $21 (JD 15) for vulnerable refugees.[6]

UNHCR's Basic Needs program provides quarterly multipurpose cash assistance to refugees residing in camps and in host communities that was worth, in 2021, more than $69 million. All refugees registered as residing in camps receive this assistance, valued at $38 per month or more in 2021, depending on household composition (for example, the presence of women of reproductive age and the number of children under two years of age). Of the 2021 total, UNHCR provided $4 million to camp residents. This assistance is provided quarterly and is intended to help camp-residing households meet their most basic survival needs. (Camp residents also receive free shelter, utilities, medical care, education, and other basic services.)

TABLE 4.2 **Types of cash assistance provided by UNHCR and WFP in Jordan, all refugees, 2021**

ASSISTANCE TYPE, BY REFUGEE RESIDENCE	PROVIDER	TOTAL (DOLLARS)	SHARE OF TOTAL ASSISTANCE (PERCENT)	NUMBER OF RECIPIENT CASES
Outside of camps				
Food assistance	WFP	127,231,045	42.5	103,351
Multipurpose cash assistance	UNHCR	65,438,729	21.9	38,029
Winter cash assistance	UNHCR	31,091,490	10.4	73,332
In camps				
Food assistance	WFP	43,209,213	14.4	23,941
Multipurpose cash assistance	UNHCR	4,181,449	1.4	17,404
Winter cash assistance	UNHCR	10,525,674	3.5	7,113
Cash assistance for new arrivals/relocations	UNHCR	421,973	0.1	542
Cash assistance for newborn babies	UNHCR	126,030	0.0	4,201
Both				
Emergency cash assistance	UNHCR	14,210,636	4.7	42,457
Cash for health	UNHCR	1,401,201	0.5	3,489
Cash for education	UNHCR	857,645	0.3	465
Protection cash assistance	UNHCR	611,822	0.2	3,180
Total		299,306,908	100.0	317,504

Source: Original table for this publication using data from UNHCR 2023.
Note: UNHCR = United Nations High Commissioner for Refugees; WFP = World Food Programme.

UNHCR is unable to provide all refugees living outside of camps with multipurpose cash assistance. It applies a proxy means test to identify eligible refugees and complements it with categorical targeting, giving priority to refugee families who have little to no capacity for self-reliance because of age, disability, or serious medical conditions among family members or because of caregiving responsibilities for such family members. Assistance is provided monthly and is intended to help families meet their most basic survival needs, including rent, utilities, transportation, health, and other expenses. The amount received is comparable to the cash equivalent of the quarterly multipurpose cash assistance transfers and in-kind services that camp residents receive. In 2021, UNHCR provided approximately $65 million in multipurpose cash assistance transfers to refugee families living outside of camps, 90 percent of whom were Syrian refugees.

Figure 4.1 presents the amounts of multipurpose cash assistance refugees staying in host communities in Jordan received in 2021, based on a small postdistribution survey among eligible beneficiaries. The amount of assistance provided varied with household size, as the figure shows, much in line with the logic behind the assistance, which is to assist with (lumpy) housing costs and spending on utilities.

In addition to the regular Basic Needs multipurpose cash assistance, UNHCR provides seasonal cash assistance to help vulnerable households meet basic winter needs. In 2021,[7] the program transferred approximately $31 million in winter cash assistance targeted toward two groups residing outside of camps: poor or vulnerable families who were already beneficiaries of its Basic Needs multipurpose cash assistance, as well as families qualifying as poor under the targeting approach in use in that year but not receiving regular multipurpose cash assistance from UNHCR.

FIGURE 4.1

Amounts of UNHCR basic needs multipurpose cash assistance transfers to Syrian refugees living outside of camps, 2021
(dollars)

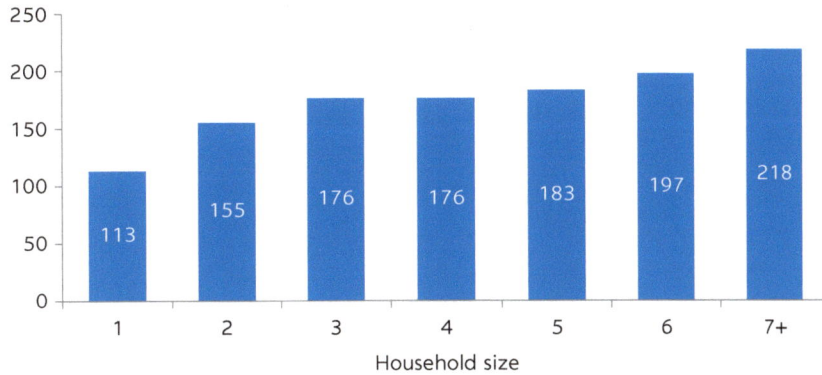

Source: Original figure for this publication using data from UNHCR 2022.

Coverage

As designed and delivered, cash assistance programs cover a smaller percentage of the total refugee population living in host communities than of the population residing in camps. As discussed in the last subsection, 100 percent of refugees living in camps receive transfers under both WFP's monthly food assistance program and UNHCR's quarterly multipurpose cash assistance program, in the amounts noted there. Refugees living in host communities, in contrast, do not receive blanket coverage and instead are provided with a different cash transfer value based on their specific needs. As of 2021, food assistance, for instance, reached 59 percent of refugees living outside camps, winter cash benefits reached approximately 25 percent, and assistance under UNHCR's largest program, multipurpose cash assistance, reached only 22 percent of refugees living outside of camps (figure 4.2). As a consequence, refugees living in host communities received less per capita, on average, than for those living in camps. In 2021, refugees residing in camps received on average an annual $447 in cash assistance; those living outside of camps received, on average, $418.

With multiple cash assistance programs operating in Jordan, households can feasibly receive more than one type of assistance. Indeed, the number of aid programs beneficiaries access varies considerably. Figure 4.3 presents a picture of unequally distributed assistance: 39 percent of registered cases living in host communities in Jordan received no assistance at all in 2021. In fact, assistance provided to refugees that year was bimodal: most received no assistance at all, but 34 percent received three or more types of assistance, suggesting that once a beneficiary manages to access one type of assistance, obtaining another type is easier. Within camps, all beneficiaries received at least two types of assistance, and a majority received as many as seven or more types of assistance.

Minimum expenditure basket or poverty line

Figure 4.1 shows that the amount of UNHCR's multipurpose cash assistance increases with household size; the same is true of WFP's food assistance. To guide how much assistance refugees should receive, UNHCR and WFP rely

FIGURE 4.2

Beneficiaries of largest cash programs among refugees in Jordan, 2023
(percent)

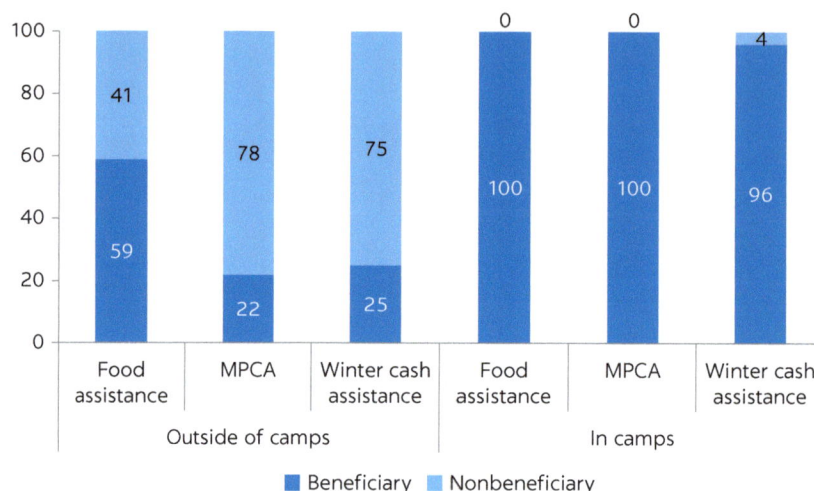

Source: Original figure for this publication using data from UNHCR 2023.
Note: MPCA = multipurpose cash assistance.

FIGURE 4.3

Number of different aid programs under which refugee cases received assistance by location, 2021

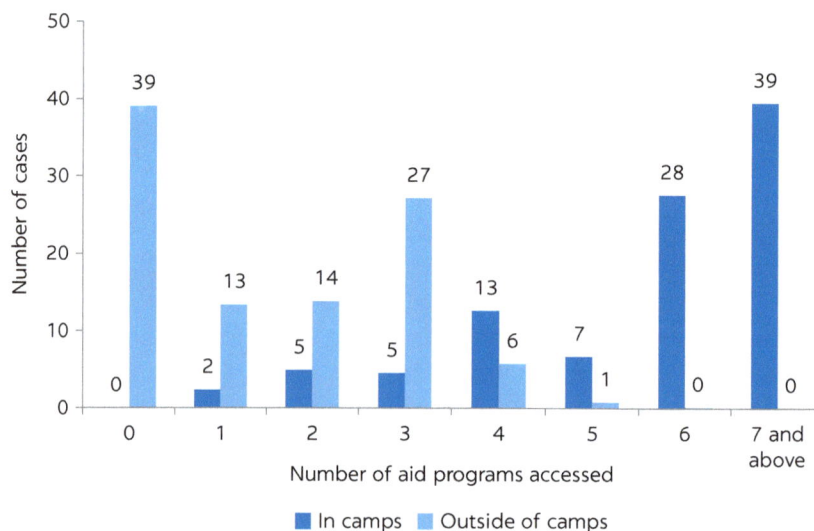

Source: Original figure for this publication using data from UNHCR 2023.
Note: Analysis includes assistance received from the United Nations High Commissioner for Refugees, the World Food Programme, and other providers.

on a minimum expenditure basket and a survival minimum expenditure basket. The first of these follows a cost-of-basic-needs approach and calculates, for instance, the minimum amount of food that needs to be consumed out of a group of commodities to provide 2,100 kilocalories (kcal) per capita (UNHCR 2019). The minimum expenditure basket, which is updated periodically, identifies eight different expenditure categories: basic needs; education; food security; health; livelihoods; protection; shelter; and water, sanitation, and hygiene. The survival minimum expenditure basket, a subset of the minimum expenditure basket, covers the latter's items under basic needs; food security; shelter; and water, sanitation, and hygiene.

Table 4.3 presents both expenditure baskets for 2021. In that year, the monthly cost of the minimum expenditure basket ranged from JD 177 for a household of one person to JD 779 for households of seven or more people. The cost of the survival minimum expenditure basket ranged from JD 97 for a one-person household to JD 329 for a household of seven or more people.

TABLE 4.3 **Minimum and survival minimum expenditure baskets, Jordan, 2021**
(Jordanian dinars)

SECTOR	ITEM	IN SMEB	FAMILY SIZE						
			1	2	3	4	5	6	7+
Basic needs	Basic household items	No	1.2	1.5	1.6	1.7	1.8	1.8	2.0
	Utilities	Yes	12.8	18.5	21.3	22.7	24.6	25.8	26.2
	Subtotal		14.1	19.9	22.9	24.4	26.4	27.6	28.2
Education	Access to education (transport)	No	n. a.	22.0	44.0	66.0	88.0	110.0	132.0
	Uniforms	No	n. a.	2.0	4.0	6.0	8.0	10.0	12.0
	Supplementary school supply	No	n. a.	6.0	12.0	18.0	24.0	30.0	36.0
	Daily allowance for child	No	n. a.	15.4	30.8	46.2	61.6	77.0	92.4
	Subtotal		0.0	45.4	90.8	136.2	181.6	227.0	272.4
Food security	Bulgur	Yes	5.1	10.2	15.3	20.3	25.4	30.5	35.6
	Cheese spread	Yes	1.2	2.5	3.7	4.9	6.1	7.3	8.6
	Eggs	Yes	0.6	1.2	1.8	2.4	3.1	3.7	4.3
	Green vegetables	Yes	0.3	0.5	0.8	1.1	1.4	1.6	1.9
	Lentils	Yes	1.3	2.6	3.9	5.2	6.5	7.8	9.1
	Pasta	Yes	1.8	3.6	5.4	7.2	9.0	10.7	12.5
	Poultry	Yes	1.8	3.7	5.5	7.3	9.2	11.0	12.8
	Rice	Yes	5.7	11.4	17.2	22.9	28.6	34.3	40.1
	Salt	Yes	0.1	0.1	0.2	0.2	0.3	0.3	0.4
	Sugar	Yes	0.7	1.4	2.0	2.7	3.4	4.0	4.7
	Vegetable oil	Yes	0.8	1.5	2.3	3.1	3.9	4.6	5.4
	Subtotal		19.3	38.7	58.0	77.3	96.7	116.0	135.4
Health	Primary	No	2.7	5.5	8.2	10.9	13.7	16.4	19.1
	Secondary	No	1.1	2.1	3.2	4.3	5.3	6.3	7.4
	Tertiary and catastrophic	No	1.5	3.0	4.6	6.1	7.6	9.1	10.6
	Deliveries	No	0.3	0.6	0.9	1.3	1.6	1.9	2.2
	Baby kit	No	0.0	0.1	0.1	0.2	0.2	0.3	0.3
	Subtotal		5.7	11.3	17.0	22.6	28.3	34.0	39.6

continued

TABLE 4.3., *continued.,*

SECTOR	ITEM	IN SMEB	FAMILY SIZE						
			1	**2**	**3**	**4**	**5**	**6**	**7+**
Livelihoods	Working tools and personal protective equipment	No	41.0	82.0	82.0	82.0	82.0	82.0	82.0
	Work permits	No	2.2	4.4	4.4	4.4	4.4	4.4	4.4
	Transportation	No	13.0	26.0	26.0	26.0	26.0	26.0	26.0
	Subtotal		56.2	112.4	112.4	112.4	112.4	112.4	112.4
Protection	Transport	No	10.0	16.0	16.0	16.0	16.0	16.0	16.0
	Communications	No	7.0	7.0	7.0	7.0	7.0	7.0	7.0
	Birth certificates	No	0.1	0.1	0.1	0.1	0.1	0.1	0.1
	Subtotal		17.1	23.1	23.1	23.1	23.1	23.1	23.1
Shelter	Rent	Yes	58.3	127.3	146.0	153.0	139.8	145.0	155.0
	Subtotal		58.3	127.3	146.0	153.0	139.8	145.0	155.0
Water, sanitation, and hygiene	Water (bottled)	Yes	1.2	1.4	1.5	1.7	2.0	2.0	2.6
	Water (network, tanker, dislodging, etc.)	Yes	4.4	4.8	4.9	5.2	5.7	5.7	7.5
	Hygiene items	Yes	1.4	1.6	1.7	1.8	1.9	2.1	2.5
	Subtotal		6.9	7.7	8.1	8.6	9.5	9.8	12.6
Total, minimum expenditure basket			177.5	385.9	478.2	557.8	617.8	694.8	778.7
Minimum expenditure basket per capita			177.5	192.9	159.4	139.4	123.6	115.8	111.2
Total, survival minimum expenditure basket			97.3	192.1	233.3	261.7	270.6	296.6	329.1
Survival minimum expenditure basket per capita			97.3	96.1	77.8	65.4	54.1	49.4	47.0

Source: Original table for this publication using data from UNHCR 2021a.

Note: n. a. = not applicable; SMEB = survival minimum expenditure basket.

Like the poverty line presented in chapter 3, the minimum expenditure basket offers a way of expressing the minimum expenditure a family needs to make to meet its basic needs. Yet even though the concepts behind the two measures are similar, the way they are determined differs. Poverty lines follow a revealed-preference approach and are based on observed household consumption. The minimum expenditure basket uses a multisectoral approach to define an illustrative basket of essential items that households generally consume in a particular country or other location, based on expert opinion about minimum required kcal and in consultation with members of the target population on their preferences and consumption norms. Similarly, the education expenses that poverty lines capture reflect what households actually spend on the education of their children. In contrast, the amount included for education expenses in the minimum expenditure basket is normative and reflects how much it would cost if all school-age children went to school.

In addition to these differences, data are collected differently as well for the minimum expenditure basket and chapter 3's poverty line: the latter relies exclusively on data from a detailed consumption module, whereas the minimum expenditure basket obtains its data from a combination of market and administrative prices.

Figure 4.4 presents the 2021 minimum expenditure basket and average household consumption for Jordan, as collected through the 2021 Vulnerability

FIGURE 4.4

Minimum expenditure basket categories and consumption for refugees in Jordan's host communities, 2021 Vulnerability Assessment Framework survey

(Jordanian dinars)

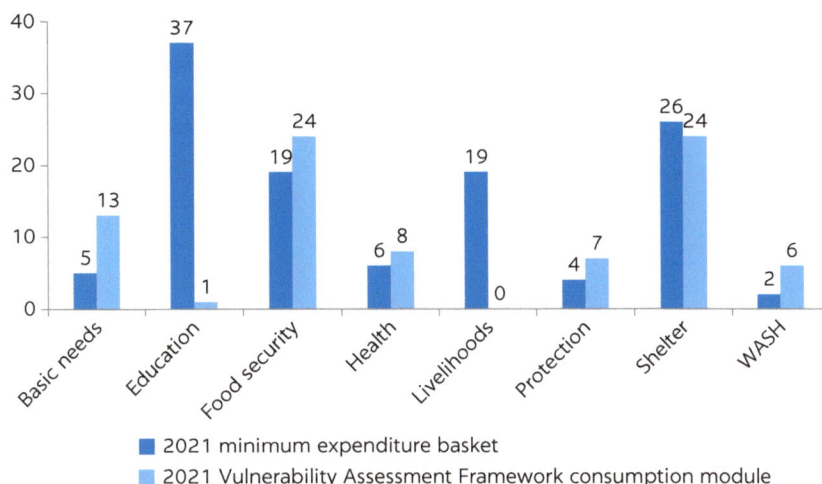

Source: Original figure for this publication using data from UNHCR 2021a and UNHCR 2021b.
Note: WASH = water, sanitation, and hygiene.

Assessment Framework survey's consumption module (see table 3.2). It shows substantial differences between the two. Whereas the minimum expenditure basket for that year allocated a significant amount to education (twice as much as it allotted to food), data collected through the survey recorded little household spending on education. A similar observation can be made in regard to livelihoods, which makes sense in a context of limited access to economic opportunities. By contrast, the survey records that households spent more on basic needs and food in 2021 than the minimum expenditure basket allocated to it. On average, the difference between the cost of the minimum expenditure basket and *average* per capita consumption in 2021 is considerable.[8] The average minimum expenditure basket per capita in 2021 cost JD 118, whereas average consumption as measured by the survey cost JD 83, and the average cost of the survival minimum expenditure basket per capita for 2021 was JD 53. The minimum expenditure basket thus had a cost higher than the poverty line (JD 81), whereas the survival minimum expenditure basket had a lower one.

Closer inspection of the minimum expenditure basket reveals ways it differs from observed consumption. For instance, although the minimum expenditure basket's food security category is based on 2,100 kcal, the food items included vary from those in the diet selected for the 2021 Vulnerability Assessment Framework survey's consumption module. According to that survey, for instance, refugees in Jordan obtain 41 percent of their kcal from consuming bread (World Bank 2023), yet bread does not feature at all in the commodities in the minimum expenditure basket's food security category (UNHCR 2019). Bread is a cheap source of energy in Jordan, and refugees make consuming bread a priority over a nutritionally diverse and balanced diet, which the minimum expenditure basket prescribes.

Spending on education increases linearly for households of two or more persons because the minimum expenditure basket assumes that households comprise one adult only and all remaining household members are school-age children. Hence, for households of seven persons, for example, the minimum expenditure basket assumes one adult and six children of school age (UNHCR 2021a).

One peculiarity of the minimum expenditure basket is that whereas it consistently increases the expenditure associated with household size for households of one to seven people, it stops doing so for households larger than that. As table 4.3 shows, the basket assigns a minimum amount for households of seven or more people of JD 779—as if having more than seven mouths to feed or more than six children to send to school or to a doctor does not involve any additional expense—even though 30 percent of refugee households living outside of camps include more than seven people (figure 4.5).

Household composition and economies of scale

The discussion thus far might prompt a conclusion that the poverty line is a better way to estimate refugee basic needs than is the minimum expenditure basket. But poverty lines do not take two aspects of expenditure into account that the minimum expenditure basket does: household composition and economies of scale.

It is commonly understood that children consume less food than adults, and that certain things, such as bathrooms, televisions, and living rooms, can be shared. So where assistance is concerned, it makes sense to take into consideration adult equivalence and economies of scale at the household level. The minimum expenditure basket does so, though not consistently (figure 4.6). For instance, the amounts allocated to utilities, protection, and shelter increase with household size, but as households grow larger, the size of the increase becomes smaller. Household economies of scale are particularly strong in regard to livelihoods and protection in the minimum expenditure basket, as the amounts assigned for them increase when household size increases from one to two, then remain constant at household sizes above two. The linear increase in the amounts allocated to health and food security suggests that adult equivalence is ignored

FIGURE 4.5

Distribution of refugee household size by location, Jordan, 2021

(percent)

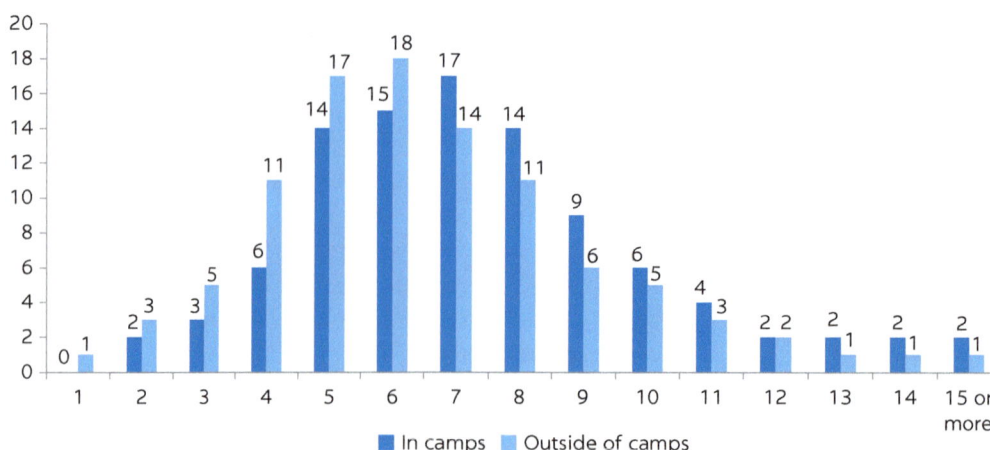

Source: Original figure for this publication using data from UNHCR 2021b.

FIGURE 4.6
Cost of components of minimum expenditure basket by household size, Jordan, 2021
(Jordanian dinars)

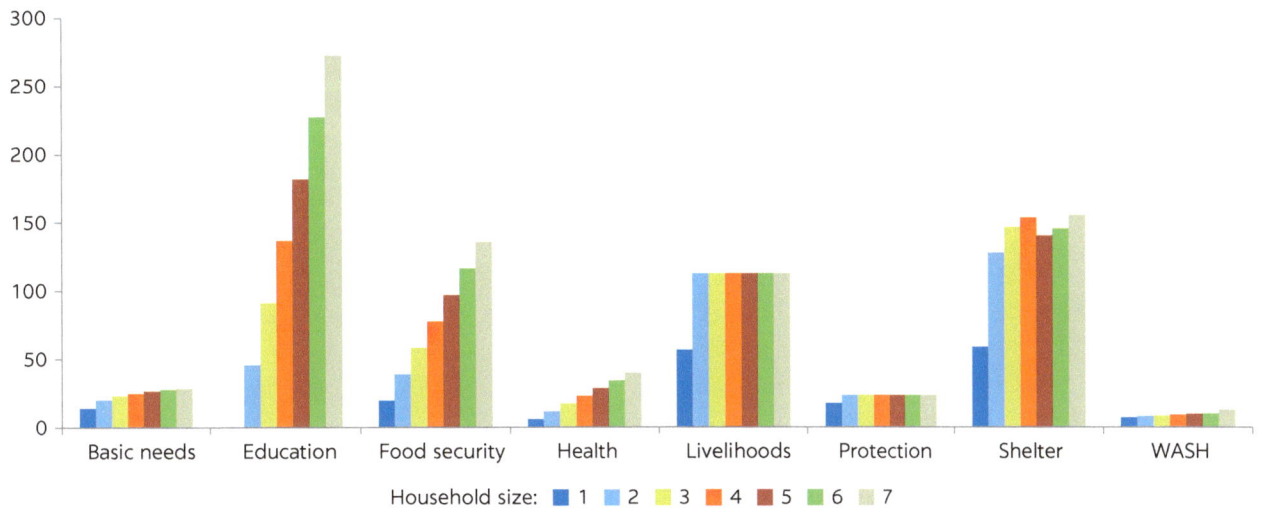

Source: Original figure for this publication using data from UNHCR 2021a.
Note: WASH = water, sanitation, and hygiene.

in regard to these two expenditure categories. For health, this seems defensible; for food security, less so.

Unlike the minimum expenditure basket, the poverty line derived in chapter 3 ignores adult equivalence and economies of scale; it is expressed in per capita terms, and the total minimum amount increases linearly with household size. For poverty profiling, this may be adequate, provided it is recognized that adult equivalence and economies of scale partly drive correlations between poverty and household size. But should a poverty line be used to inform what constitutes a reasonable amount for transfer? Figure 4.7 compares the transfer amount required, for 2021, when chapter 3's poverty line is used and the amounts needed to fund the survival minimum expenditure basket and minimum expenditure basket for different household sizes.

The amount needed to fund the survival minimum expenditure basket and minimum expenditure basket for 2021 exceeded or coincided with the poverty line for households having up to three family members, but as households grew larger, the amount needed to fund the minimum expenditure basket fell increasingly above the poverty line, whereas that required for the survival minimum expenditure basket fell increasingly below it. From here on in this section, the minimum expenditure basket is ignored as an indicator for the minimum amount of assistance refugees need, as it lies too far above the poverty line to function as a realistic minimum. But what about the poverty line? Should it be considered an upper bound for minimum expenditure, as it ignores economies of scale and adult equivalence? Could adult equivalence and household economies of scale be taken into account in the poverty line?

Deaton (2003) discusses a straightforward way to include household composition and economies of scale in poverty line calculations by expressing household composition and size in adult equivalents, using the formula $(AE = A + \alpha K)^h$, in which A is the number of adults in a household; K is the number of children; a is the "cost" of a child relative to that of an adult, which lies

FIGURE 4.7

Cost of minimum expenditure baskets, by household size, and composition of refugee households, Jordan, 2021

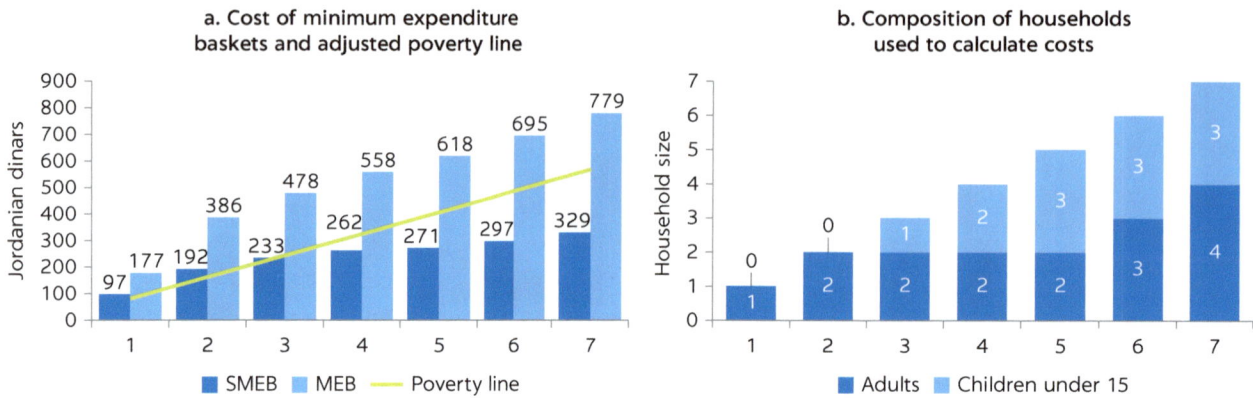

Source: Original figure for this publication using data from UNHCR 2021a and UNHCR 2021b.
Note: MEB = minimum expenditure basket; SMEB = survival minimum expenditure basket.

somewhere between 0 and 1; and h, which also lies between 0 and 1, controls the extent of economies of scale. When both a and h are 1—the most extreme case, with no discount for children or for size—the number of adult equivalents is simply the household size.

Although Deaton's approach has intuitive appeal, sensible values for a and h are not obvious. Adult-equivalence parameters vary from country to country, so national standards should dictate the values to be used. Unfortunately, few countries apply them in practice, and their application in a protracted refugee situation is even less well understood.

In conclusion, the poverty line lies between the cost of the minimum expenditure basket and that of the survival minimum expenditure basket for all but the smallest household sizes, and the minimum expenditure basket and survival minimum expenditure basket could be considered an upper and lower bound, respectively, for minimum expenditure needs, with the survival minimum expenditure basket truly being a survival minimum: thus, using it to determine amounts refugees need for survival would imply that all refugees are monetarily poor. All three measures have the advantage of operational simplicity, as all providers of assistance need to know to implement them is household size. Yet the survival minimum expenditure basket and the minimum expenditure basket have conceptual limitations that per capita poverty does not, as the latter is rooted in observed household consumption. Thus, humanitarian actors have important scope to revise the composition of the minimum expenditure basket based on the preferences revealed by observed household consumption and to explore further the potential for the poverty line to capture household composition and economies of scale. The latter might support increased use in humanitarian settings.

IMPACT OF ASSISTANCE ON POVERTY

This section explores how assistance reduces poverty among Syrian refugees in Jordan and whether it does so efficiently. To analyze the impact of cash assistance on poverty, the section calculates consumption excluding cash or in-kind assistance, referred to as "preassistance consumption." It then determines assistance's impact on poverty by comparing refugee poverty levels before and after assistance is included in consumption aggregates.[9] The calculation used for this comparison implicitly assumes that refugee households do not save from the cash assistance they receive. Given the degree of destitution among Syrian refugees, this assumption seems reasonable (recall from chapter 3 that even after receiving assistance, 58 percent of refugees are monetarily poor), at least in the aggregate. For individual cases, it may not hold, as it has been well documented that refugee families borrow money and incur debt, which, of course, has to be repaid as well. If one ignores savings, preassistance consumption can also serve as a proxy for income refugees earn.[10] The subsection "Estimating the Shortfall in Assistance" and chapter 6 use this interpretation of preassistance consumption.

Figure 4.8 and box 4.1 illustrate how removing assistance affects the distribution of consumption among Syrian refugees in Jordan. Preassistance consumption in 2021 was less than postassistance consumption, and the preassistance lines in the figure lie to the left of those for full consumption. All graphs in the figure show little dispersion, demonstrating that refugee households had relatively small differences in consumption, as Gini indexes, which measure inequality, underscore. For the full consumption aggregate, the Gini index for refugees living in host communities was 0.26; that for refugees living in camps was even lower: 0.20. These indexes show remarkably low levels of inequality. Preassistance Gini indexes, however, were higher: 0.38 and 0.36, respectively, for those living outside of and in camps. The drop in Gini indexes in postassistance consumption, suggests that assistance in 2021 favored poorer refugees.

FIGURE 4.8

Distribution of welfare among Syrian refugees with and without assistance by location, 2021

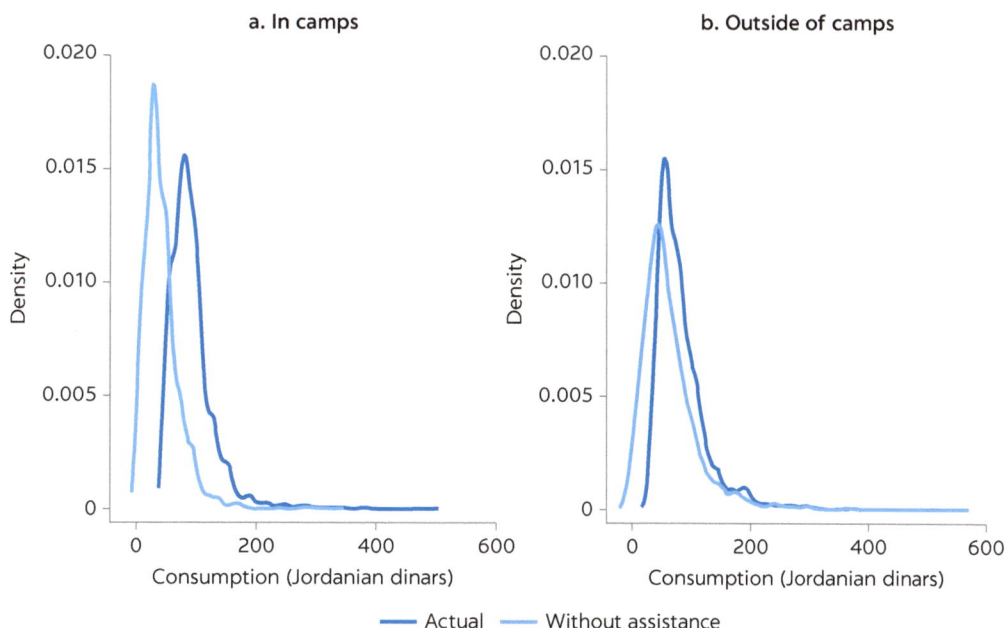

Source: Original figure for this publication using data from UNHCR 2021b.

Figure 4.9 shows the impact of assistance on poverty among Syrian refugees in Jordan according to 2021 data. The baseline scenario starts with a poverty incidence of 45 percent among those living in camps and 62 percent among those living outside of camps, as presented in chapter 3. Were cash assistance taken away, the poverty rate among those living in camps would increase to 77 percent; among refugees living in host communities, it would rise to 75 percent. If in-kind assistance, provided exclusively in camps, were also eliminated, the poverty rate among those living in camps would increase to 91 percent, while the rate for those living outside of camps would remain unchanged at 75 percent (since those living outside of camps receive no in-kind assistance).

Two observations are worth noting. First, assistance has an enormous impact on poverty, and second, without cash assistance, refugees living in host communities would be less likely to be poor than refugees living in camps. The second observation is unsurprising, since refugees residing in host communities exhibit higher preassistance consumption levels than refugees living in camps and have more exposure to job opportunities.

Distribution of assistance across wealth categories

Using the estimates of preassistance consumption and in-kind assistance presented in the previous subsection, as well as information on cash assistance, it is possible to measure how humanitarian assistance is distributed across Syrian refugees of different poverty status. To this end, this subsection sorts refugees into deciles based on their estimated level of consumption, with the first decile reflecting the poorest consumption levels and the tenth decile the least poor. Figure 4.10 presents the results.

The two panels in the figure offer several different messages. First, the in-kind assistance available only to households residing in camps has a value comparable to that of the cash assistance they receive. Next, the cash assistance

FIGURE 4.9

Headcount poverty among Syrian refugees before and after assistance by location, 2021

(percent)

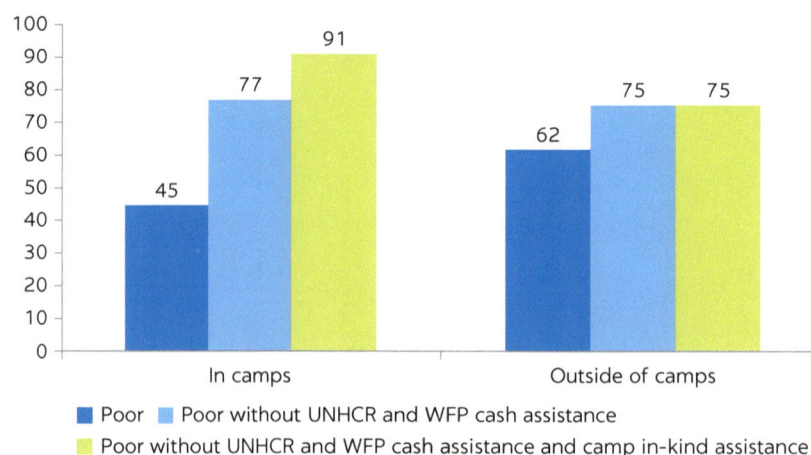

Source: Original figure for this publication using data from UNHCR 2021b.
Note: UNHCR = United Nations High Commissioner for Refugees; WFP = World Food Programme.

Reductions in funding and increases in poverty among Syrian refugees

The approach this section presents can be used to assess the impact on poverty of changing levels of assistance provided to Syrian refugees in Jordan. In the summer of 2023, for instance, the WFP reduced by one-third the value of its cash assistance and excluded approximately 50,000 individuals living in host communities from its program.

One way to estimate the poverty impact of such a change is to assume that the 50,000 individuals, approximately the 10 percent of households with the lowest level of poverty among recipients living in host communities, receive zero assistance (that is, they reduce their per capita consumption by JD 23), whereas other recipients of WFP food assistance, whether living in camps or outside of them, have their per capita consumption reduced by one-third, that is, JD 8.

If the cuts were implemented in this way, poverty can be expected to have increased by 8 percentage points, to 66 percent, as a result of the decline in cash assistance (figure B4.1.1).

FIGURE B4.1.1

Impact of reduced food assistance on poverty among Syrian refugees, 2023

(percent)

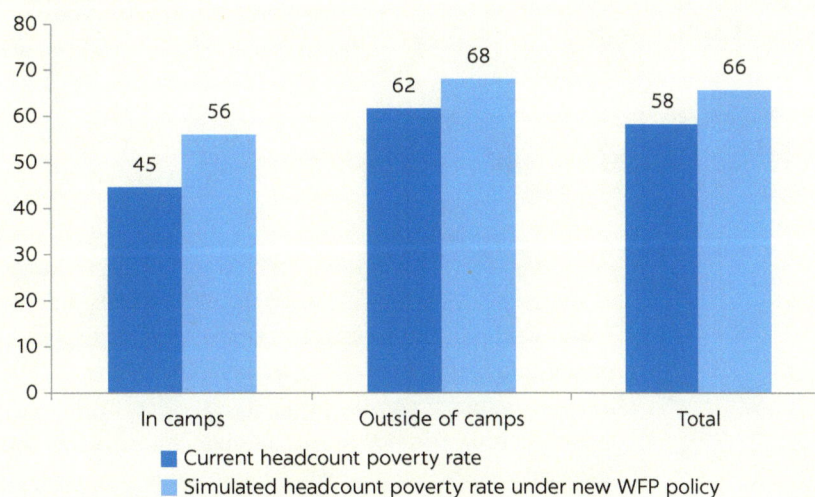

Source: Original figure for this publication using data from UNHCR 2021b.
Note: WFP =World Food Programme.

received by refugees residing outside of camps has less value than that received by those living in camps, as shown by a comparison of the average amount of cash assistance for each decile for those living in camps (panel a) with that for those living in host communities (panel b). Third, current levels of assistance are insufficient to bring all refugees' income up to the poverty line, particularly those in the lower deciles of preassistance consumption: the relatively poorer refugees.

With respect to targeting efficiency, from one perspective, assistance is currently well targeted. Across the consumption deciles in figure 4.10, for both refugees residing in camps and those living in host communities, those with lower

FIGURE 4.10

Per capita preassistance consumption and assistance among Syrian refugees by location and household consumption decile

(Jordanian dinars)

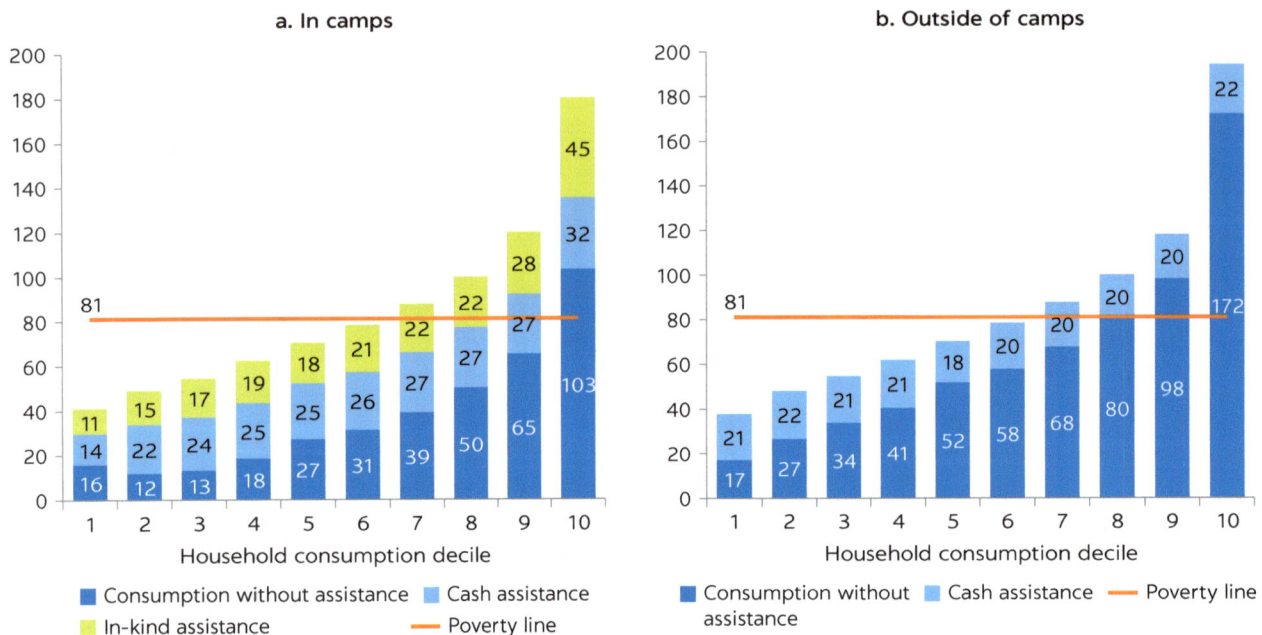

a. In camps

b. Outside of camps

Legend: Consumption without assistance, Cash assistance, In-kind assistance, Poverty line

Source: Original figure for this publication using data from UNHCR 2021b.
Note: For refugees living in camps, the poverty line does not cross consumption in the fourth decile (poverty incidence among those in camps is 42 percent) because the deciles are defined for all Syrian refugees, not just those living in camps.

preassistance levels of income receive a *proportionally* larger share of assistance. For the very poorest households, assistance exceeds their earned income.

Yet considered in an *absolute* sense, assistance could be better targeted. Among refugees living in camps, the poorest beneficiaries—those with very low preassistance consumption levels—receive the least in assistance. As household preassistance consumption increases, so does the amount of assistance received: those whose preassistance consumption is already above the poverty line receive *three times* the amount of assistance that refugees in the poorest decile receive. These very poor refugees remain far below the poverty line even after they receive assistance. This is unfortunate, because within the camps, there are sufficient resources available to lift all refugees out of poverty (figure 4.10).

It is tempting to speculate that the differences in amounts of assistance received are related to the fact that some households do not access any aid program, whereas others are able to access multiple ones. The 2021 Vulnerability Assessment Framework survey did not collect information on the number of assistance programs refugees accessed, but the finding that the amount received in assistance increases for less poor households suggests that extremely vulnerable refugees may lack access to (mobile) phones or be exposed to constant displacement and hence find it more difficult to access the humanitarian system than less poor refugees.

For households residing in host communities, very little targeting according to wealth seems to take place, and the average assistance received is almost uniform across the wealth distribution.

There is another way, however, to consider the data in figure 4.10. Assuming no redistribution of assistance, the space between the poverty line and the bars in the two panels is the minimum amount in assistance that would be needed to bring all refugees' incomes up to the poverty line. Interpreting the figure in this way makes it evident that redistributing assistance from the wealthiest to the poorest would go a long way toward eliminating poverty among those living in camps. Yet for the majority of refugees, who live in host communities, such a redistribution would be inadequate to accomplish this goal. Even under the unrealistic assumption of perfect targeting, more resources are needed to eliminate poverty among Syrian refugees in Jordan.

Does assistance reduce poverty efficiently?

Although humanitarian assistance reduces poverty among refugees in a way that is noteworthy, this is not necessarily evidence of its economic efficiency. The humanitarian cash assistance program for Syrian refugees in Jordan has as its core mandate to provide life-saving cash, so as long as refugees remain alive, it fulfills this mandate. Yet globally, Sustainable Development Goal 1 states that all human beings should live a life free of poverty, which the current assistance programs do not accomplish. This perspective allows analysis of how efficiently resources are used, by establishing the degree to which poverty could have been reduced had assistance been allocated in the most effective manner possible.

Efficiency is a challenging concept in this regard, however. If the priority is to reduce monetary poverty among refugees as much as possible, an antipoverty program that provides cash assistance equal to each refugee household's poverty gap[11] is the optimal program. Ranking all households from poorest to richest and closing the poverty gap for those closest to the poverty line would be one way to do this, one that would maximize the number of households lifted out of poverty, given available funds. For households very close to the poverty line, it would cost little. Then the program would move to the next household, and then the next, until all resources had been distributed.

Such an antipoverty program would be optimal from the perspective of reducing the total number of poor refugees, but if resources are inadequate to cover all refugees, it will ignore the most destitute among them, who are the last in line to receive assistance. An alternative program that takes into account depth of poverty would use the same ranking of households but would instead start providing assistance to the household farthest removed from the poverty line, then gradually work its way toward less destitute households.

The following analysis evaluates the effectiveness of current UNHCR and WFP cash assistance programs for Syrian refugees in Jordan by comparing performance across three dimensions: a program's ability to reduce the incidence of poverty, how much it reduces refugees' poverty gap, and its ability to reduce the rate of severe poverty (poverty severity), calculated as the square of the poverty gap, which gives greater weight to households farther below the poverty line. In combination, these three measures of poverty allow the performance of different assistance programs to be compared (see Foster, Greer, and Thorbecke 1984).

This subsection compares four different scenarios involving the existing cash assistance programs for Syrian refugees in Jordan, which provided an average total of JD 49.5 to each camp dweller and on average JD 22.1 to the 93 percent of 2021 Vulnerability Assessment Framework survey respondents who received cash assistance.[12] In scenarios 1 and 2, aid organizations disburse assistance such that all refugees receive in assistance exactly the amount of their poverty gaps, which thus helps them to escape poverty. In scenario 1, these organizations make refugees closest to the poverty line the priority in distributing assistance, whereas in scenario 2, they give precedence to those farthest from the poverty line. Disbursement stops, in each scenario, as soon as the cumulative assistance amount equals the amount the organizations spend under the program, JD 17.3 million ($24.5 million) per month.[13]

Even with perfect targeting, in which assistance would reach only poor refugee households, with no refugee receiving more than the amount needed to reach the poverty line, JD 17.3 million would be insufficient to eliminate poverty among refugees, which would require at least JD 21.4 million according to 2021 data.[14] Indeed, in scenario 1, aid organizations would have reached only 73 percent of the refugee population (providing an average JD 37 in assistance) in 2021; in scenario 2, they would have reached an even smaller share of refugees, 48 percent, as the average amount in assistance was higher (JD 55).

Scenarios 1 and 2 indicate what gains perfect targeting might realize. In reality, however, it is nearly impossible to offer households the exact amount of assistance they need to bring their incomes up to the poverty line. Not only would it be costly to collect the information required to do this, but in practice, refugees would likely provide strategic responses to questions asked to gather this information, in order to maximize their benefits, which would affect the accuracy of the information collected. With this in mind, this subsection presents two additional scenarios: scenario 3, in which aid organizations provide only one fixed amount to poor households, and scenario 4, in which these organizations provide two different amounts (a base amount and a top-up for the most destitute). In scenario 3, all poor households (78 percent of all refugees, as of 2021) would receive JD 34 per capita per month. In scenario 4, the amount of assistance would vary, with the poorest 40 percent of refugees in 2021 receiving a monthly JD 40 and the remaining poor refugees receiving JD 29 per month.

Table 4.4 summarizes results for the four scenarios. Scenarios 1 and 2 demonstrate what would be theoretically possible if assistance were optimally distributed. Rather than the recorded 2021 poverty rate of 58 percent, providing those closest to the poverty line with amounts of assistance equal to their poverty gap could reduce the poverty rate to as little as 8 percent. A program that achieved the latter rate would not, however, give priority to those most in need—those with the largest poverty gaps—and as a consequence, scenario 1 would result in the highest rate of poverty severity: 7 percent. By contrast, an assistance program that focused on the very poorest by transferring to them the amount of their poverty gaps would be less effective in reducing poverty overall. Assistance administered in this way would lift 28 percent (the difference between the 58 percent rate in 2021 and the 30 percent rate such assistance would achieve under scenario 2) of poor refugees out of poverty. But by its design, scenario 2 would reduce the rate of severe poverty most effectively, bringing it down to 2 percent. Scenarios 1 and 2 would not change the poverty gap, obviously, as how resources are distributed does not affect the gap, as long as people below the poverty line benefit.

Scenarios 3 and 4 make assistance provision a bit more realistic by having aid programs offer fixed amounts to poor refugees. In both scenarios, the programs would perform as expected: offering a flat amount to all refugees would reduce the poverty incidence by more, and poverty severity by less, than a program that

TABLE 4.4 Poverty rates among Syrian refugees and targeting efficiency under different targeting options
(percent)

SCENARIO	POVERTY INCIDENCE	POVERTY GAP	POVERTY SEVERITY (POVERTY GAP SQUARED)	TARGETING EFFICIENCY
Poverty rate without assistance	78	40	26	n. a.
Poverty rate with current assistance (baseline)	58	17	6	71
Scenario 1 (those closest to the poverty line receive, on average, JD 37)	8	7	7	100
Scenario 2 (those farthest from the poverty line receive, on average, JD 55)	30	7	2	100
Scenario 3 (fixed assistance of JD 34 for poor only)	49	13	5	83
Scenario 4 (varying assistance: JD 29 to poor; bottom 40 percent receive top-up of JD 11)	55	11	3	90

Source: Original table for this publication using data from UNHCR 2021b.
Note: n. a. = not applicable.

offered more to the poorest refugees, because there would be less "leakage," in the sense that the amount of a refugee's postassistance consumption exceeded the poverty line.

The last column of table 4.4 presents the scenarios' targeting efficiency; it measures how much of the assistance provided would go toward alleviating poverty.[15] Since in scenarios 1 and 2, aid organizations allocate all resources to poor households and no household receives more than enough to reach the poverty line, leakage is zero and targeting efficiency 100 percent. In scenarios 3 and 4 poor households may receive more in assistance than the amount that separates them from the poverty line, leading to some leakage.

As table 4.4 quantifies, scenario 4 has a higher targeting efficiency than scenario 3. Both programs perform considerably better than the current assistance programs (which operate in the real world and confront the real inability to identify perfectly who is poor and who is not). A case can therefore be made for varying the amount of assistance provided, offering more to the most destitute refugees. After all, not only does scenario 4 reduce the poverty incidence more than scenarios in which a fixed amount is provided, but it results in less leakage (that is, it is more efficient) and benefits the most destitute refugees more (as measured by poverty severity).

To summarize, then, although the UNHCR's cash assistance and the WFP's food assistance program have a considerable impact on reducing poverty, poverty levels among Syrian refugees in Jordan remain high. The results presented here demonstrate that if it were possible to perfectly identify poor refugees and rank them from poorest to least poor, poverty could be reduced much more. Yet perfect targeting is unrealistic, and in practice, aid programs have to rely on somewhat crude proxy means tests.

It is also evident from figure 4.10 that the current assistance programs are not necessarily the most efficient ones possible. Varying the amount of assistance provided to the most destitute and less poor refugees might yield better results. The next question is whether enhancing the targeting algorithm humanitarian organizations use might help.

Estimating the shortfall in assistance

The available data—in particular, the first two rows of table 4.4—make it possible to estimate how much additional assistance would be needed to bring the income of all Syrian refugees in Jordan up to the poverty line. In the case in which refugees earn no income, the total amount of assistance required to bring refugees up to the poverty line in 2021 would have equaled the annual amount of the poverty line, or 12 times JD 81 ($113), multiplied by the number of refugees (662,000 in that year), or $899 million per year.

In reality, of course, Syrian refugees in Jordan do earn incomes. How much? As shown earlier in the chapter, preassistance consumption can serve as a proxy for income earned. Table 4.4 shows that the preassistance poverty gap in 2021 was 40 percent, suggesting that these refugees earned $539 million per year (0.6 × $899 million). Then the assistance needed to bring all refugees up to the poverty line in 2021 would have been the balance, or $360 million per year.

In 2021, UNHCR and WFP provided $299 million in cash assistance (table 4.1) plus $27 million (JD 23 per month × 12 × number of refugees in camps) in in-kind assistance for housing and utilities for refugees living in camps, for a total of $326 million in assistance. Because moving from preassistance consumption to postassistance consumption would reduce the 2021 poverty gap by 23 percent (from 40 percent to 17 percent), $206 million (0.23 × $899 million) of this amount effectively reduced poverty. Then the difference between $326 million and $206 million was a $120 million leakage of assistance to the nonpoor, implying a 2021 targeting efficiency of about 63 percent ($206 million/$326 million) (figure 4.11).

As noted earlier, the total amount of assistance needed to bring all refugees' incomes up to the poverty line in 2021, taking into account that refugees did earn incomes, would have been $360 million, assuming perfect targeting. But targeting efficiency isn't perfect, and with a targeting efficiency of 63 percent,

FIGURE 4.11

Assistance needed to bring incomes of all UNHCR-registered Syrian refugees up to poverty line, 2021

(million US dollars)

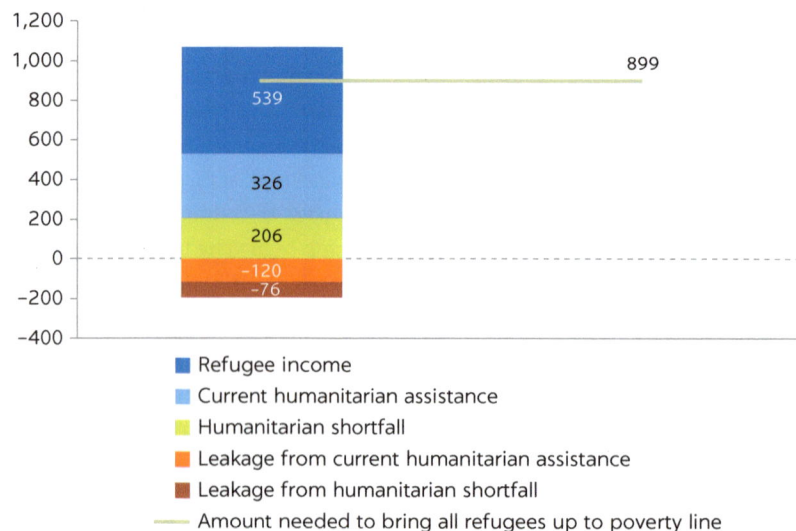

- Refugee income
- Current humanitarian assistance
- Humanitarian shortfall
- Leakage from current humanitarian assistance
- Leakage from humanitarian shortfall
- Amount needed to bring all refugees up to poverty line

Source: Original figure for this publication using data from UNHCR 2021b.
Note: UNHCR = United Nations High Commissioner for Refugees.

effectively $570 million would have been required (because $570 million × 0.63 = $360 million). Since $326 million was provided, it follows that there was a shortfall of $244 million.

IMPROVING TARGETING

Along with other factors, the ability of humanitarian assistance to accurately identify poor refugees affects its targeting performance. At the time of publication, aid organizations were using an outdated proxy means test to identify whether potential beneficiaries are eligible for assistance. A new proxy means test model might have greater targeting accuracy.

This section explores two approaches that might improve the performance of assistance targeting. It first examines what an updated proxy means test could contribute, then shifts the focus to inclusion of such a test in national social protection programs.

Updating the proxy means test

Humanitarian aid organizations use proxy means tests to determine which households are eligible for assistance.[16] Such tests aim to predict the welfare levels of potential aid beneficiaries when detailed measurements of actual consumption, expenditure, or income are unavailable or too costly or difficult to obtain. As the name suggests, proxy means tests use readily available proxies for consumption (that is, observable characteristics that are correlated with consumption) to predict welfare among an entire population of refugees, implying that the proxies need to be available for all refugees. In the case of Syrian refugees in Jordan, each proxy indicator is weighted according to econometric (regression) analysis of refugee consumption obtained from the 2021 Vulnerability Assessment Framework survey, using variables found in the refugee population registration database to explain consumption.

The existing proxy means test model employed for Syrian refugees in Jordan, developed in 2014, uses a formula comprising 10 variables related to household composition, employment, location, and housing, as well as subjective assessment by an enumerator who visits the refugee household for whom the test calculation is being performed. Since 2014, numerous changes have likely altered the relationship between the proxy means test indicators and consumption. Prices of consumption goods have changed, and so has the policy environment. For instance, in 2014, Syrian refugees barely had access to work permits, but the Jordan Compact changed this. Household characteristics such as the age of getting married and the likelihood of sending children to school, which are relevant in household welfare calculation, have also changed. Hence, updating to reflect refugees' changed demographic and economic situations could benefit the model.

In addition, the 2014 proxy means test is estimated using household consumption derived from a list of only 15 items. The 2021 Vulnerability Assessment Framework survey's consumption module—which can also be characterized as a proxy means test—uses a much more extensive list of 98 consumption items, which allows household welfare status to be more accurately evaluated. The 2021 proxy means test model also improves upon the 2014 model by using preassistance consumption. By not excluding assistance received, the 2014 proxy means test introduces biases against current beneficiaries, who appear better off than they really are.[17]

The narrow distribution of preassistance consumption (shown in figure 4.8), coupled with the near-universal (preassistance) poverty (91 percent, as noted earlier in the chapter) among Syrian refugees residing in Jordan's refugee camps, has implications for aid targeting. First, in a situation in which almost all potential aid recipients are poor, targeting makes less sense, and it is probably more efficient to distribute assistance uniformly to all and in so doing, save the administrative and transaction costs associated with targeting. Moreover, when the distribution of consumption is as narrow as figure 4.8 shows, it is technically unrealistic to expect an accurate targeting formula. Indeed, the 2021 proxy means test for those living in camps has low explanatory power (23 percent, about half the explanatory power of the proxy means test for those living outside of camps), with only household size and composition and shop ownership showing up as statistically significant proxies for refugee need. Because a proxy means test based on such a regression is unlikely to be very accurate, the remainder of this chapter uses no proxy means test for camp settings.

The updated proxy means test model for out-of-camp residents includes many of the variables that are reported as correlating with poverty, as discussed in chapter 3. Table 4.5 shows key differences between the 2014 and 2021 proxy means test models for those living outside of camps. The 2021 model includes 20 variables; covers more diverse aspects that correlate with refugee welfare, such as asset ownership and disability, that were not included in the 2014 model; and avoids subjective variables.

How do the two models stack up in terms of targeting efficiency? Table 4.6 compares, for Syrian refugees living in host communities, the poverty incidence as measured by the 2021 Vulnerability Assessment Framework survey data, with poverty incidence predicted by the two proxy means test models. Using the data from that survey, the table categorizes individuals into three groups according to whether their observed and predicted poverty levels coincide. The 2014 proxy means test categorizes 77 percent of refugees correctly as poor or nonpoor. The 2021 proxy means test does only slightly better: it categorizes 80 percent of refugees correctly. But the 2014 proxy means test incorrectly identifies 22 percent of nonpoor refugees as poor and hence eligible for assistance, whereas the 2021

TABLE 4.5 **Comparison of 2014 and 2021 proxy means test models**

	2014 MODEL	2021 MODEL
Number of variables	10	20
Includes subjective variables?	Yes	No
Includes location variable?	Yes	Yes
Includes employment variable?	Yes	Yes
Includes housing quality?	Yes	Yes
Includes ownership of assets?	No	Yes
Includes family characteristics?	Yes	Yes
Includes vulnerability and disability variable?	No	Yes
Welfare indicator: consumption net of assistance?	No	Yes
Eligibility decision based on poverty line?	No	Yes

Source: Original table for this publication using proxy means test models.

TABLE 4.6 Targeting efficiency of 2014 and 2021 proxy means test models, refugees living outside of camps
(percent)

	2014 MODEL	2021 MODEL
Poor and nonpoor correctly identified	77	80
Nonpoor identified as poor: leakage (inclusion error)	22	13
Poor not identified as poor (exclusion error)	3	13

Source: Original table for this publication using data from UNHCR 2021b.

test does better in this regard, identifying only 13 percent of the nonpoor as poor. By contrast, the 2014 proxy means test is more accurate in identifying the poor, classifying only 3 percent of poor people as nonpoor, against 13 percent for the 2021 test. Based on these performance indicators, it is hard to judge which proxy means test model performs better: if the criterion is leakage of assistance to the nonpoor, the 2021 test may be preferred; if the criterion is ensuring that all poor are identified as beneficiaries, the 2014 model would be a better choice.

Another way to compare the two tests is by evaluating their performance in reducing poverty relative to that in the baseline. In this case the amount of assistance provided to refugees residing in camps remains unchanged, as no new proxy means test is employed for these refugees. Thus, as in the baseline, camp dwellers receive JD 49.5 per person, or a total of JD 6,465,600, per month. The balance of JD 10,880,193 (recall that the total aid provided to those living in camps each month in 2021 was JD 17.3 million) is distributed among those identified as poor by the 2021 proxy means test. In the baseline, each household receives assistance of JD 22 per person, but because the 2021 proxy means test reduces leakage, this amount can be raised to JD 27 so that the full available amount is distributed. Note that this scenario changes two aspects of the baseline scenario: it provides a fixed amount per refugee (as in scenarios 3 and 4) *and* it changes the targeting formula. The results, presented in table 4.7, show that the 2021 proxy means test is able to reduce the poverty incidence slightly, from 58 percent to 57 percent, and the poverty gap slightly, from 17 percent to 15 percent.

Inclusion in national social protection programs

So far the discussion in this chapter has considered only assistance provided by humanitarian agencies. But what if assistance were provided not by UNHCR or WFP or any of the other agencies that currently provide it, but instead by the government of Jordan. This is a truly hypothetical scenario, because even if existing national social assistance programs in Jordan were modified to make them suitable for refugees, the government of Jordan might find it unattractive to take on the financial obligation associated with extending them to refugees unless it had (multiyear) financial guarantees from donors. But assuming such an obstacle could be overcome, how would it affect poverty rates if Syrian refugees in Jordan were eligible for the same package of direct assistance as Jordanians?

Jordan has multiple social assistance programs. The main cash transfer program is the National Aid Fund, an unconditional transfer that targets beneficiaries without income and people belonging to especially vulnerable

TABLE 4.7 Poverty rates among Syrian refugees and targeting efficiency under different targeting options
(percent)

SCENARIO	POVERTY INCIDENCE	POVERTY GAP	POVERTY SEVERITY (POVERTY GAP SQUARED)	TARGETING EFFICIENCY
Poverty rate without assistance	78	40	26	n. a.
Poverty rate with current assistance (baseline)	58	17	6	71
Scenario 5 (current assistance allocated using 2014 proxy means test formula)	59	17	8	71
Scenario 6 (current assistance allocated using 2021 proxy means test formula)	57	15	6	77

Source: Original table for this publication using data from UNHCR 2021b.
Note: n. a. = not applicable.

groups (for example, families taking care of orphaned children, elderly individuals, persons with disabilities, families headed by divorced or abandoned women, women with young children, and families whose breadwinner is in prison). Beneficiaries receive a monthly cash transfer of approximately JD 45 per person (up to a maximum of JD 180 per family) depending on income, assets, and family characteristics. In 2018, the National Aid Fund expanded the reach of its cash transfers; a new transfer program for the poor—Takaful—was launched in May 2019 as part of Jordan's National Social Protection Strategy for 2019–25.

In addition, Jordan's Zakat fund provides an unconditional cash transfer of JD 30 per household per month plus JD 5 per household member for households living on an income below the extreme poverty line. Finally, Jordan has had, since January 2018, a cash compensation scheme ("bread compensation") that replaced a previous flour subsidy with a small cash transfer of JD 27 per person per year; the transfer is provided to Jordanian households with annual earnings under JD 18,000 per year and National Aid Fund beneficiaries. This transfer reaches nearly 80 percent of Jordan's population.

To explore what would happen to poverty among Syrian refugees in Jordan if refugees were included in Jordan's national social protection systems, two additional scenarios are evaluated. In scenario 7, the government of Jordan distributes the available aid amount (JD 17.3 million, the amount provided in 2021 in aid to refugees living in camps) as follows: refugees whose preassistance consumption is less than the refugee food poverty line (82 percent of refugees; see chapter 3) receive cash transfers under the National Aid Fund. This costs the government JD 15.4 million. The remaining JD 1.9 million amount is distributed from the Zakat fund to households under the refugee poverty line, starting with the poorest, until the money has run out. In this scenario, only 19 percent of the refugee population would receive transfers from the Zakat fund, and no resources would remain to provide bread subsidies. Scenario 8 assumes no budget constraint. Assistance is distributed following the same logic as in scenario 7: extremely vulnerable refugees with preassistance consumption less than the refugee food poverty line receive transfers from the National Aid Fund. Refugees with preassistance consumption below the refugee poverty line receive transfers from the Zakat fund, and all refugee households receive bread subsidies. This package has a higher cost: JD 19.4 million per month.

TABLE 4.8 **Poverty rates among Syrian refugees and targeting efficiency under different targeting options**
(percent)

SCENARIO	POVERTY INCIDENCE	POVERTY GAP	POVERTY SEVERITY (POVERTY GAP SQUARED)	TARGETING EFFICIENCY
Poverty rate without assistance	78	40	26	n. a.
Poverty rate with current assistance (baseline)	58	17	6	71
Scenario 7 (Jordanian assistance programs with budget constraint)	54	15	6	77
Scenario 8 (Jordanian assistance programs without budget constraint)	40	7	2	72

Source: Original table for this publication using data from UNHCR 2021b.
Note: n. a. = not applicable.

Table 4.8 presents the results. In scenario 7, Jordan's national protection system performs better than the baseline (that is, current assistance) and would reduce poverty from the 2021 rate of 58 percent to 54 percent and the poverty gap from 17 percent in 2021 to 15 percent. In comparison with the new 2021 proxy means test (scenario 6), Jordan's national program performs better too, though the difference is small. However, relative to scenario 4, which offers a higher amount to the poorest refugees and less to other poor refugees, Jordan's national program would perform worse. A simple program that offers more to the poorest refugees affects in particular the poverty gap and poverty severity more.

Results shift, and quite dramatically, actually, in scenario 8, when the budget constraint is dropped and all refugees who are eligible receive assistance through Jordan's national protection system. The poverty incidence drops to 40 percent—still more than twice the national average, but a huge improvement over the 2021 situation—and the poverty gap and poverty severity drop considerably, suggesting that the program effectively reaches the poorest refugees. Spending JD 2.1 million per month more achieves a noteworthy additional reduction in poverty, even though spending becomes less efficient—naturally, as it becomes increasingly hard to avoid leakage.

Of course, these results assume, again, perfect targeting of the (food) poor, something that proxy means tests are unable to achieve.

One conclusion that can be drawn from this exercise is that unless current transfer amounts are increased, the scope of Jordan's current transfer program is not suited to address the depth of poverty Syrian refugees there face. This is unsurprising, given the shortfall in income that these refugees experience, which is considerably greater than the shortfall Jordanian households experience.

CONCLUSION

For most Syrian refugees in Jordan living in refugee camps, cash and in-kind assistance are the main source of income. For many of refugees living in host communities, cash assistance remains important as well. More than a decade after most Syrians arrived in Jordan, and more than seven years after the conclusion of the Jordan Compact, the continued dependence on this assistance reflects the challenges these refugees face in becoming more self-reliant.

This chapter has taken a closer look at the assistance provided to these refugees and shows a mixed picture. From one perspective, existing assistance fails, as a large fraction of refugees remain poor. Assistance is thus unable to achieve its key objective of providing protection against poverty to the most vulnerable, because there is not enough assistance to meet the needs of all refugees and assistance could be provided more efficiently.

With respect to the first reason, the chapter estimates that to alleviate poverty, assistance would have to increase from the 2021 amount of $326 million to at least $360 million, under the strong assumption of perfect targeting. But if the 2021 targeting efficiency is maintained (63 percent), $570 million a year would be needed.

There also seems to be scope to improve the efficiency with which assistance is provided. First, the way amounts of assistance are determined leaves room for improvement. Relative to a minimum expenditure basket or survival minimum expenditure basket, the poverty line appears to be a more robust way of setting minimum amounts of assistance. Yet poverty lines would be even more useful if they took into account adult equivalence and economies of scale. How to make this change rigorously, and in a refugee setting, is an area on which future research could shed light.

Efficiency can also be improved in other areas, starting with the data recorded in RAIS, which could be more complete and up to date. The chapter's analysis also suggests that Syrian refugees in Jordan have unequal access to assistance, with some refugees receiving (much of) it and others very little or nothing at all. Among those living in camps, for instance, some refugees receive four times as much cash assistance as the most deprived.

Although there are avenues for improving the efficiency of the existing assistance programs, probably the biggest potential gains fall outside the scope of the humanitarian sector. In addition to enhancing efficiency and increasing the amount of cash assistance, the focus of attention should shift toward ways to reduce refugees' need for assistance by increasing their income-earning capacity.

NOTES

1. For 84 percent of refugees living in Jordanian refugee camps, assistance is their main source of income. Among refugees living in host communities, cash assistance is the main source of income for 54 percent.
2. For these reasons, the data presented in the chapter may differ from those in the official reports of each aid organization.
3. As explained in chapter 3, "cases" are registration groups used in the UNHCR registration database; for the purposes of this chapter's analysis, a case is assumed to be synonymous with a household, though in practice this may not be accurate in all instances.
4. Not included here is in-kind assistance to refugees, the value of which, as previously noted, RAIS does not record. In-kind assistance covers free shelter, water, and electricity, as well as health assistance, employment training, education, and direct employment through incentive-based volunteer programs.
5. Since this chapter was written, the value has decreased to $21 (JD 15) per person per month.
6. As with that provided to those living in camps, the value for those living in host communities was reduced starting in summer 2023 to a unified $21 (JD 15) per person per month.
7. For the first time in 2023, no seasonal assistance was provided.
8. For comparison, the cost of the minimum expenditure basket has to be expressed in per capita terms. This is calculated by weighting the different amounts for each household size in the minimum expenditure basket by the fraction at which households of that size occur

in the total number of households, then summing the results and expressing the final total in per capita terms.

9. To calculate preassistance consumption, data from RAIS on cash assistance received is merged into consumption data from the 2021 Vulnerability Assessment Framework survey. Chapter 3 estimates the value of in-kind assistance (shelter and utilities), and those estimates are used here. Preassistance consumption is then calculated by deducting the value of in-kind and cash assistance from total consumption.

10. If Y reflects income refugees earn, A assistance they receive, C their consumption, and S their savings, then $Y + A = C + S$. Assuming S is zero, this identity can be rewritten as $Y = C - A$; in other words, refugee earned income equals preassistance consumption.

11. Represented by the difference between consumption without assistance and the poverty line.

12. The fact that 93 percent of 2021 Vulnerability Assessment Framework survey respondents indicated they received cash assistance suggests that the survey oversampled refugees who were beneficiaries of cash assistance and undersampled those who were not. This is an important limitation of the data that future rounds of the survey would need to address.

13. The analysis calculates the cumulative value of assistance received by all 2021 Vulnerability Assessment Framework survey respondents (living in and outside of camps) who received any or all of the three types of assistance used in calculating household consumption: multipurpose cash assistance, food, or camp in-kind assistance. The various scenarios remove the assistance households received, then redistribute it according to the particular scenario.

14. This amount is calculated by taking the poverty gap of 40 percent of a "poverty without assistance" scenario and multiplying it by the refugee poverty line (JD 81) and the number of refugees registered with UNHCR as of 2021 (662,000).

15. Targeting efficiency is determined by dividing the monetary value of the decline in the poverty gap between poverty without assistance and the scenario at hand (based on 662,000 refugees and a refugee poverty line of JD 81) by the assistance provided.

16. In a typical UNHCR response to emergencies, however, categorical targeting of in-kind assistance is often the preferred methodology.

17. The 2021 and 2014 proxy means tests also have different eligibility cutoffs. In 2014, the cutoff was an arbitrary number; the 2021 proxy means test uses the poverty line as cutoff.

REFERENCES

Deaton, Angus. 2003. "Household Surveys, Consumption, and the Measurement of Poverty." *Economic Systems Research* 15 (2): 135–59. https://doi.org/10.1080/0953531032000091144.

Foster, James, Joel Greer, and Erik Thorbecke. 1984. "A Class of Decomposable Poverty Measures." *Econometrica* 52 (3): 761–66. https://doi.org/10.2307/1913475.

UNHCR (United Nations High Commissioner for Refugees). 2019. "Minimum Expenditure Basket 2019." Guidance Note, UNHCR Interagency Coordination Unit, Geneva.

UNHCR (United Nations High Commissioner for Refugees). 2021a. "Minimum Expenditure Basket 2021." UNHCR, Geneva.

UNHCR (United Nations High Commissioner for Refugees). 2021b. "Vulnerability Assessment Framework Population Survey for Refugees in Host Communities: Jordan, 2021" (data set). UNHCR, Geneva.

UNHCR (United Nations High Commissioner for Refugees). 2022. "Multi-purpose Cash Assistance: Mid-year Post Distribution Monitoring Report; Jordan—June 2022." Geneva, UNHCR.

UNHCR (United Nations High Commissioner for Refugees). 2023. "Refugee Assistance Information System (RAIS)" (data set). UNHCR, Geneva.

World Bank. 2023. "Welfare in Forcibly Displaced Populations: From Measuring Outcomes to Building and Leveraging Harmonized Data to Improve Welfare among Forcibly Displaced Populations and Their Hosts; A Technical Brief Series." Issue Brief 3, Poverty and Equity Global Practice, World Bank, Washington, DC.

5 Labor Market Outcomes

CÉLINE FERRÉ AND SILVIA REDAELLI

MAIN MESSAGES

This chapter explores how Syrian refugees navigate the Jordanian labor market. It starts by acknowledging that the labor market characteristics of Syrian refugees differ substantially from those of other labor market participants, Jordanians, and labor migrants. These differences are insufficient, however, to explain variances observed in labor market participation, sector of employment, degree of informality, type of occupation, and number of hours worked.

The chapter finds that Syrians earn low wages not only because of differences in personal characteristics, but also because of policy decisions and unequal treatment. Increasing refugees' earnings requires investing in their human capital, as well as changing labor market policies and creating a level playing field between Syrians and other participants in the labor market.

INTRODUCTION

The previous chapter concluded by suggesting that one way to decrease refugees' need for assistance would be to increase their financial autonomy. This chapter delves more deeply into Jordan's labor market and how Syrian refugees[1] navigate it.

Most Syrians in Jordan did not arrive as economic migrants, but as people who fled a war in their home country. This of course does not mean that refugees should be treated as people who are unable to work (many have also worked in the Syrian Arab Republic), but as Stark (2004) discusses, refugee flows, being group movements, often bring a specific policy response that includes not only the option to receive humanitarian assistance and the creation of camps, but also the introduction of specific (labor market) rules and regulations.

Not only do Syrians have different motivations from other foreign immigrants in Jordan, their personal characteristics contrast with those of other foreign immigrants, the majority of whom (52 percent) came to seek work or as dependent family members (figure 5.1).

FIGURE 5.1

Distribution of non-Jordanians by reason for moving to Jordan

(percent)

a. Syrians

As a dependent
family member
10

Other
2

For work, or to
look for work
1

As asylum
seekers
1

As refugees
86

b. Other foreigners

Other 2

As a dependent
family member
24

As refugees
19

As asylum
seekers
2

To study
1

For work, or to
look for work
52

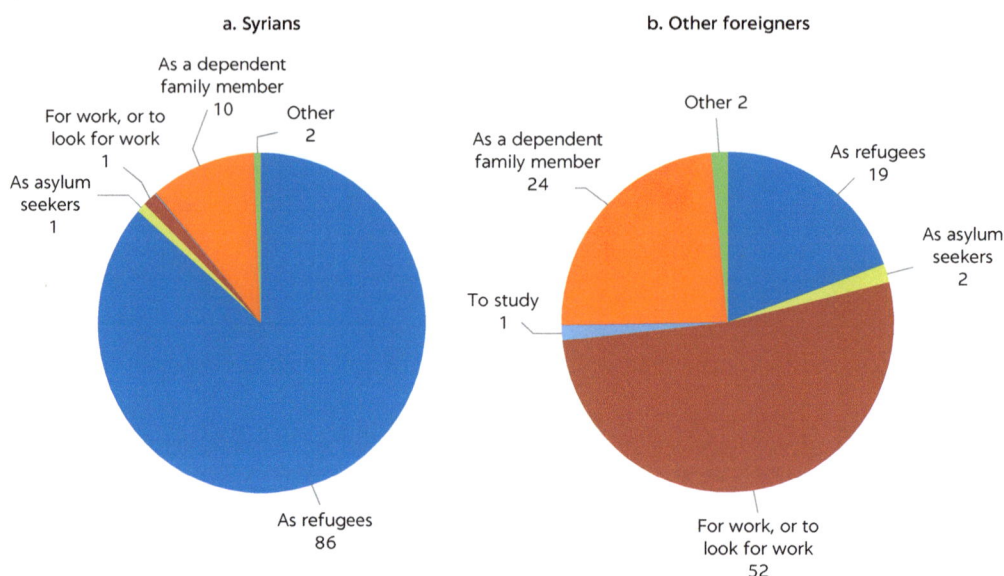

Source: Original figure for this publication using data from Jordan Department of Statistics 2019.

Unsurprisingly, the family composition of Syrian refugees is also different from those of other labor migrants and Jordanians. Overall, the Syrian population in Jordan has a dependency ratio of 0.91,[2] meaning that for every 100 people of working age, there are 91 not of working age, either below the age of 15 or above the age of 64. By contrast, Jordanians have a dependency ratio of 0.53 and other foreigners only 0.40. In addition, the Syrian population's demographic structure population shows a substantial male deficit, particularly in the 25–35 age group, which can reflect different migration choices among prime-aged men, an excess of conflict-induced mortality in this age group, or both (World Bank 2022).

As a result, Syrians have a smaller presence in Jordan's male working-age population than other foreigners. Differences in population structure translate into differences in the incidence of Syrians and other foreigners in Jordan's working-age population and across more narrowly defined age groups (see figure 5.2). The underrepresentation of Syrians is even more striking when one looks at the subgroup of prime-aged men, which is typically the most active in the labor market. Among men in the 25–54 age group, Syrians account for a mere 13 percent of the population, whereas other foreigners make up 28 percent. This difference holds even after the personal characteristics of Syrian refugees (education, skills, age profile), which differ from those of Jordanians and non-Syrian immigrants, are taken into account, as this chapter does.

The chapter's main objective is to profile labor market outcomes of Syrians living in Jordan and to compare them with those of Jordanians as well as non-Jordanians.[3] To allow comparison of non-Jordanians and Jordanians, and in contrast to that in previous chapters, the analysis uses the Jordan Labor Force Survey 2019, implemented by the Department of Statistics, which covered about 16,500 households. The survey employed a multistage cluster-stratified sampling methodology using Jordan's 2015 census as a sampling frame: as such, it is representative at the national, regional, governorate, and urban or rural levels, as well as for both the Jordanian and non-Jordanian populations. It is one of the

FIGURE 5.2

Nationality of males in Jordan as share of age group

(percent)

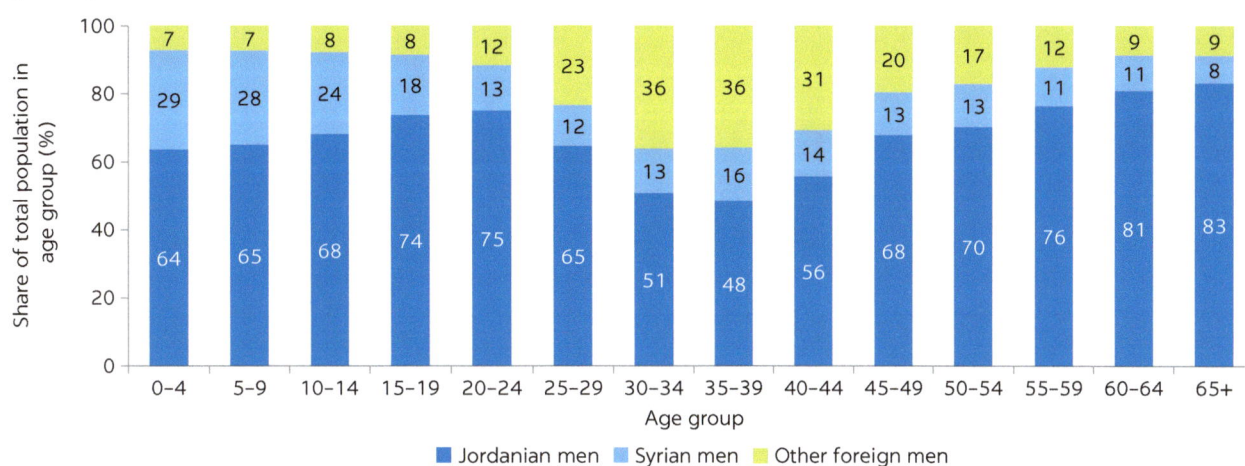

Source: Original figure for this publication using data from Jordan Department of Statistics 2019.

few surveys in Jordan whose data have been made available that is inclusive and representative of refugees[4] as well as other foreign nationals living in Jordan.

The chapter is structured as follows. The next section reviews the policies governing Syrians' access to Jordan's labor market. This review is followed in the second section by a discussion of Syrian refugees' labor market performance. Both sections compare characteristics and outcomes of Syrians versus other foreign nationals and hosts to identify challenges and opportunities specific to the Syrian population living in Jordan. The third section summarizes the evidence presented in the chapter and suggests additional lines of inquiry. Conclusions follow in the final section.

LABOR MARKET REGULATIONS

Until the beginning of the Syrian civil war, Syrians could enter Jordan with no restrictions, and many Syrians moved there to settle, start a business, or get a job. Since the start of the conflict, however, Syrians have had much more limited access to Jordan's labor market.

As the influx of Syrian refugees escalated, through the beginning of 2016, Jordan increasingly restricted access to its labor market. According to the labor law enforced at the time, migrant workers—irrespective of nationality—could work in Jordan only if they had competences not found among Jordanian natives or if they applied to positions for which demand exceeded supply. Employers had to request work permits for each new hire through a cumbersome process, and employees were not allowed to change jobs during the time their work permits were valid. As a consequence, up until 2016, as few as 3,000 Jordanian work permits were issued annually to Syrians.

Adoption of the Jordan Compact in 2016 eased labor market access for Syrian refugees. In March 2016, the government of Jordan and the European Union (EU) concluded an agreement under which the EU would provide Jordan with

BOX 5.1

The asset framework and refugee earning capacity

The asset framework (Attanasio and Székely 2001; Bussolo and López-Calva 2014; Carter and Barrett 2006; López-Calva and Rodríguez-Castelán 2016), summarized in figure B5.1.1, illustrates what drives refugees' ability to earn an income. The assets households own, the intensity with which they use those assets, and the returns to the assets primarily determine households' income and consumption possibilities.[a] Productive assets include human capital (education, capacity to work), physical capital (land, machines), and financial capital (savings, financial assets). Besides productive assets, households can also leverage social capital to support their income generation capacity (for example, by using their social networks to find jobs).[b]

Refugees' overall asset endowment determines their income-generating potential. How much income they earn depends in turn on whether they put physical assets to productive use, how intensively they use their assets (for example, how many hours they work), and the remuneration (wages, interest) they receive.

At the macro level, government policies (for example, labor market, health, education, and welfare policies) and institutions (property rights and markets), as well as the overall risk environment (that is, how much households are exposed and vulnerable to shocks) affect refugee welfare and its determinants.

The asset framework applies to refugees, just as it does to anyone else, but refugees are a special case, because unlike citizens of their host countries, they have a severely diminished productive asset base, and their main asset is their capacity to work (human capital).

FIGURE B5.1.1

Asset framework applied to refugees

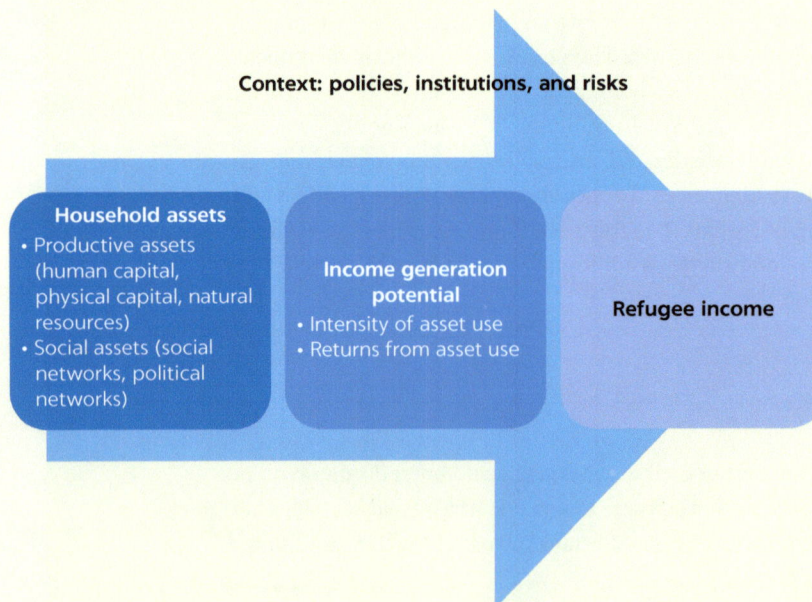

Context: policies, institutions, and risks

Household assets
- Productive assets (human capital, physical capital, natural resources)
- Social assets (social networks, political networks)

Income generation potential
- Intensity of asset use
- Returns from asset use

Refugee income

Source: Original figure for this publication.

[a] For ease of exposition, savings are ignored.
[b] Households can also benefit from location assets, such as water bodies in which they fish or forests in which they forage.

FIGURE 5.3
Work permits issued
(number)

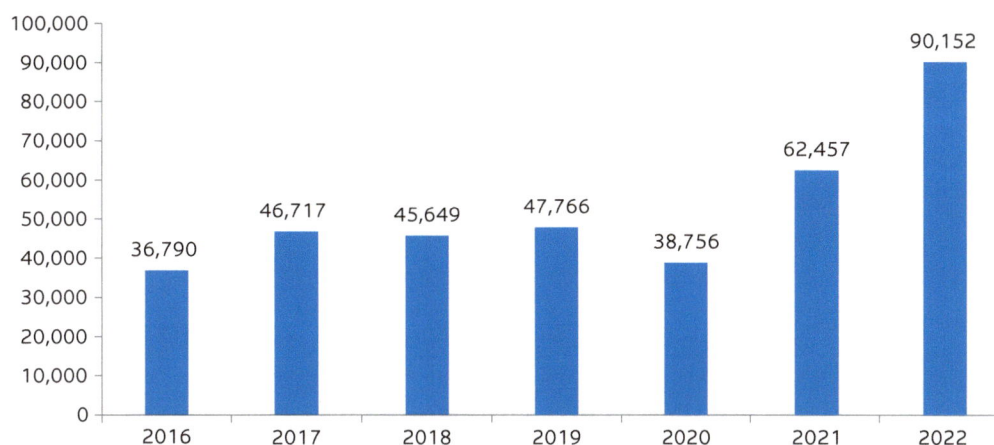

Source: Original figure for this publication using data from Jordan Ministry of Labor 2023.

major grants, concessional loans, and exemptions to trade barriers to stimulate jobs and investments; the government of Jordan, for its part, agreed to issue up to 200,000 work permits to Syrian refugees registered with the United Nations High Commissioner for Refugees. The compact restricts the issuance of work permits, however, to specific sectors such as manufacturing, construction, agriculture, care work, and the food industry. Refugees are permitted to work mainly in manufacturing, construction, agriculture, and the hospitality sector, whereas other sectors are closed to non-Jordanians. Jordan's migrant worker sector-based quota system, which regulates the maximum percentage of foreign workers in a particular sector, governs the sectors open to Syrians. Quotas under this system range from 5 to 70 percent, depending on the sector (ILO 2015).

The Jordanian authorities increasingly streamlined regulations governing work permits for Syrian refugees as defined under the compact over time. In April 2016, for example, registration fees for the issuance of work permits were waived. At the end of 2017, the government allowed bulk issuance of flexible work permits through cooperatives in the agricultural and construction sectors; this was later extended to all sectors open to foreign workers. Since December 2020, foreign workers have been allowed to move freely between jobs and work for different employers within the sector for which they have been issued a work permit. In July 2021, social security registration became mandatory for flexible work permit holders. As of December 31, 2023, a cumulative total of 370,000 work permits had been issued (see figure 5.3). Beyond the increased flexibility in regard to work permits, at the end of 2018, Syrians were further allowed to open and operate home-based businesses.

SYRIA'S LABOR MARKET PERFORMANCE

Labor market outcomes

Syrians in Jordan generally have poor labor market outcomes, but labor market outcomes for Syrians are only slightly worse than those for Jordanians. Among Jordanians, 30 percent of those of working age (that is, 15–64 years old) are employed (versus 24 percent for Syrians), 7 percent are unemployed (as compared with 11 percent of Syrians), and 63 percent do not participate in the labor force at all (65 percent for Syrians).

Relative to those of other foreigners, however, the majority of whom come to Jordan through migrant recruiting schemes, Syrian labor market outcomes in Jordan are dismal. As many as 68 percent of other foreigners in Jordan are employed, almost three times the percentage of Syrians. Only 3 percent of other foreigners are unemployed, and less than a third of other foreigners are out of the labor force entirely (compared with almost two-thirds among Syrians) (figure 5.4).

Although differences in labor market outcomes according to nationality are striking, the largest differences in labor market outcomes are those related to gender. Relative to Syrian men, Syrian women in Jordan are much less likely to be employed and more likely to be inactive in the labor market. The patterns described previously for Syrians as a whole hold also for Syrian women, and the labor outcomes of female Syrians are closer to those of Jordanians than those of other foreigners. The percentage of women inactive in the labor market is highest among Syrians (96 percent), followed by Jordanians (85 percent), and non-Jordanians (72 percent). Only 3 percent of Syrian women are employed, compared with 26 percent of non-Jordanian women and 11 percent of Jordanian women.

Multivariate analysis confirms the role of gender, age, and education as important correlates of labor market outcomes among Syrians. Here, a linear probability model is estimated to better explore correlates of the probability of being employed, unemployed, or active in the labor force. Figure 5.5 plots conditional differences (blue dots) and 90 percent confidence intervals yellow dots (lower bound) and red dots (upper bound) for various labor market outcomes among Syrians. The dependent variable is, alternatively, a dummy for whether an individual is employed (panel a), unemployed versus

FIGURE 5.4

Labor market outcomes of working-age population by gender and nationality

(percent)

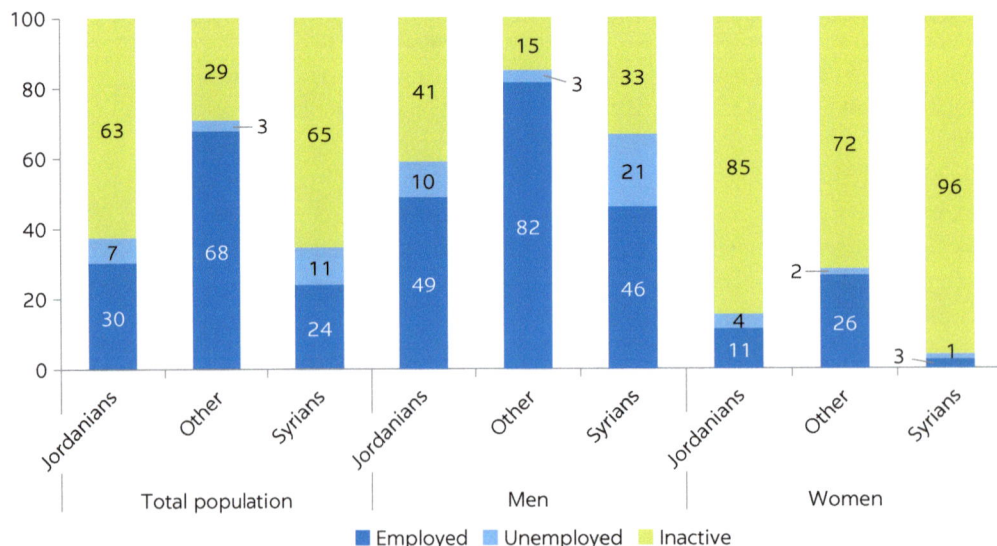

Source: Original figure for this publication using data from Jordan Department of Statistics 2019.
Note: Working-age population is defined as those ages 15–64.

FIGURE 5.5

Determinants of labor market outcomes among Syrians in Jordan

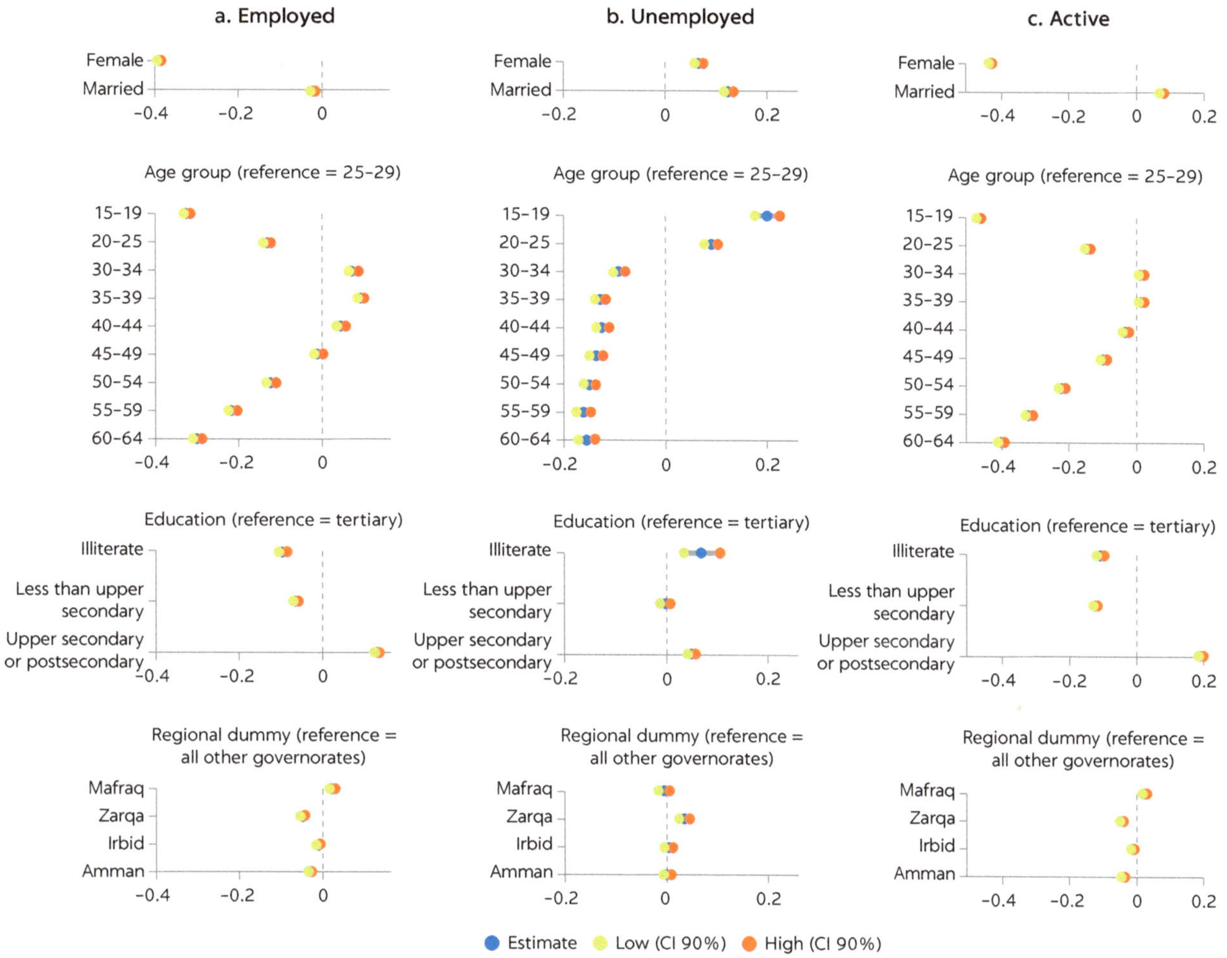

Source: Original figure for this publication using data from Jordan Department of Statistics 2019.
Note: CI = confidence interval.

employed (panel b), or active (employed or unemployed) versus inactive in the labor force (panel c). Controls include gender, age group, civil status, education, and five regional dummies. The sample comprises Syrians 15–64 years of age.

Gender turns up as the strongest predictor of labor market participation and employment among Syrians in Jordan: Syrian women are 44 percentage points less likely to be active in the labor market than Syrian men and 39 percentage points less likely to be employed. Marital status also plays a significant role: a married individual (of either gender) is 8 percentage points more likely to be active than someone who is not married. Older age groups are significantly less likely to be active in the market or employed than younger age groups: for instance, individuals ages 50–54 are 22 percentage points less likely to be active than 25–29-year-olds and 12 percentage points less likely to be working. Education is also important: illiterate individuals and those with less than upper-secondary education are much less likely to be employed and active than those with at least upper-secondary education.

Labor market participation

Much of the difference in labor market outcomes among Jordanians, Syrians, and other foreigners can be ascribed to differences in labor market participation. Syrian men with less than upper-secondary education participate less in the labor force and have higher unemployment rates than those with higher levels of education attainment (figure 5.6). Age is another important correlate of labor market outcomes, with activity and employment rates showing a marked decline after the age of 40, possibly reflecting limited labor market opportunities for relatively older workers.

Inactivity in the labor market may sometimes mean unemployment or nonparticipation, or it may be related, in other instances, to ongoing pursuit of education. A combination of the first two factors accounts for Syrians' high level of labor market inactivity (figure 5.7). Among Syrians between the ages of 15 and 29, 58 percent are neither in employment, nor in education or training. This contrasts sharply with Jordanians and foreigners other than Syrians; only 38 percent of Jordanians are not in employment, education, or training, and the share drops to 23 percent among other foreigners. Smaller shares of Jordanians and foreigners other than Syrians are not in employment, education, or training at a younger age because when they are younger, they are more likely than Syrians to be in school (more so for Jordanians), and when they are older, they are more likely than Syrians to be employed (more so for other foreigners).

Sector of employment

Public sector jobs in Jordan are reserved for Jordanians. Not surprisingly, then, 92 percent of Syrians who are working and 98 percent of other foreign workers are employed in the private sector, compared with 58 percent of Jordanians.

FIGURE 5.6

Labor force participation among working-age Syrian men in Jordan by education level and age
(percent)

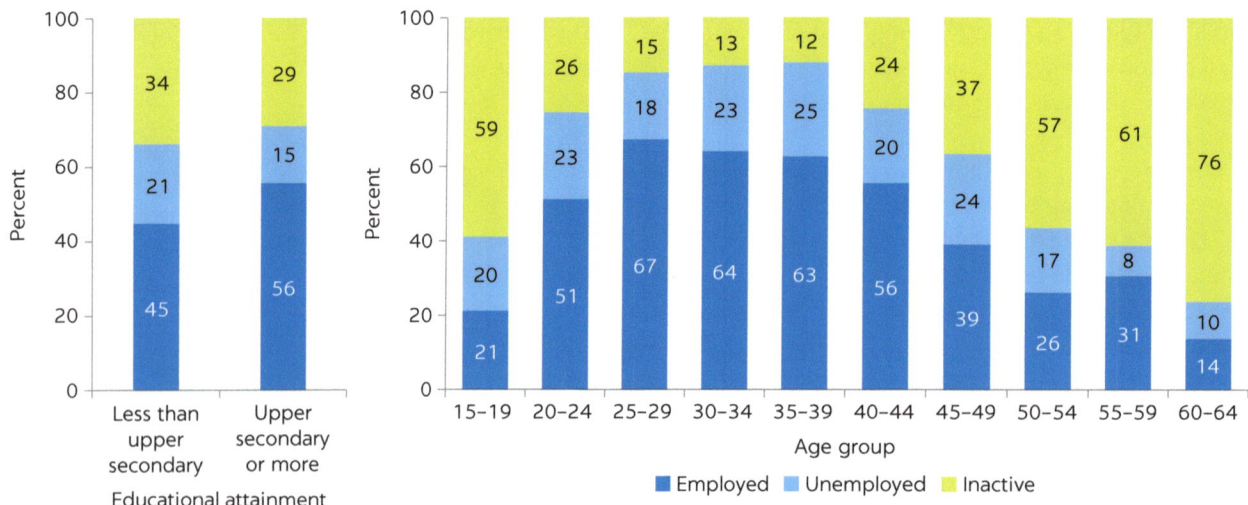

Source: Original figure for this publication using data from Jordan Department of Statistics 2019.
Note: Working-age population is defined as those ages 15–64.

FIGURE 5.7

Share of working-age population not in employment, education, or training by nationality

(percent)

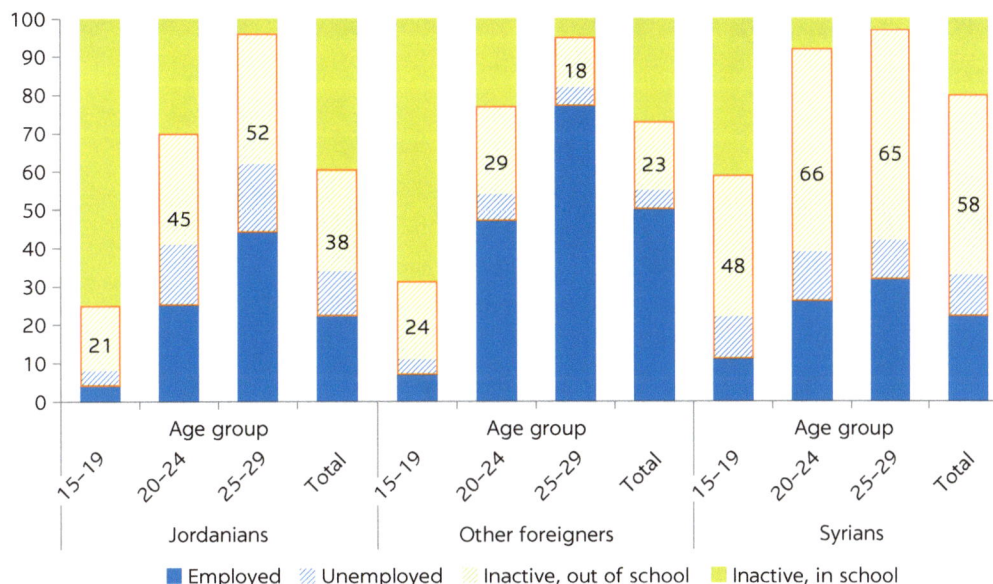

Source: Original figure for this publication using data from Jordan Department of Statistics 2019.
Note: Working-age population is defined as those ages 15–64. Number labels in the figure reflect total percentage of those neither in employment, nor in education or training (those unemployed plus those inactive in the labor market and out of school).

Immigrants have a relatively low rate of self-employment: only 12 percent among Syrians and 7 percent among other foreigners. But the Jordanian population also has a low self-employment rate (15 percent), possibly reflecting constraints specific to the Jordanian labor market.

Syrians in Jordan are mostly employed in construction, manufacturing, and trade-related activities. Other foreigners, by contrast, work in administrative services and as domestic workers, whereas Jordanians are mostly engaged in public administration, wholesale and retail, manufacturing, and other services (figure 5.8).

Overall (figure 5.9), Syrians in Jordan have the highest incidence of employment in jobs provided by international organizations (55 percent),[5] construction (33 percent), and accommodation and food services (30 percent). Employment in these sectors is open to non-Jordanians, and thus the sectors are particularly desirable to Syrian refugees.

Informality

Syrians in Jordan are disproportionately employed informally. When type of contract is the criterion for judging informality, only 8 percent of Syrians in Jordan have a written and open-ended contract (and thus the other 92 percent would be considered informally employed), as opposed to 57 percent of Jordanians. When informality is defined based on social and health contributions, however, almost all are employed informally: only 1 percent of employed Syrians contribute to the social security and health insurance funds. Jordanians contribute at much higher rates: 56 percent to both funds and 11 percent to social security only.

FIGURE 5.8

Distribution of employment among working-age population across sectors by nationality
(percent)

a. Jordanians

Sector	Percent
Public administration	27.4
Wholesale and retail	14.7
Manufacturing	9.4
Other industries	6.8
Construction	4.9
Accommodation, food service	3.2
Professional, scientific	2.9
Other services	2.4

b. Syrians

Sector	Percent
Construction	25.1
Manufacturing	18.3
Other services	17.2
Wholesale and retail	16.0
Accommodation, food service	10.3
Agriculture, forestry, fishing	5.2
Administration	3.2
Household activities	3.2
Other industries	1.4
Public administration	0.0

c. Other foreigners

Sector	Percent
Administration	37.7
Household activities	30.7
Construction	8.6
Agriculture, forestry, fishing	5.9
Other services	5.6
Wholesale and retail	4.2
Manufacturing	4.1
Accommodation, food service	2.1
Public administration	0.5
Other industries	0.5

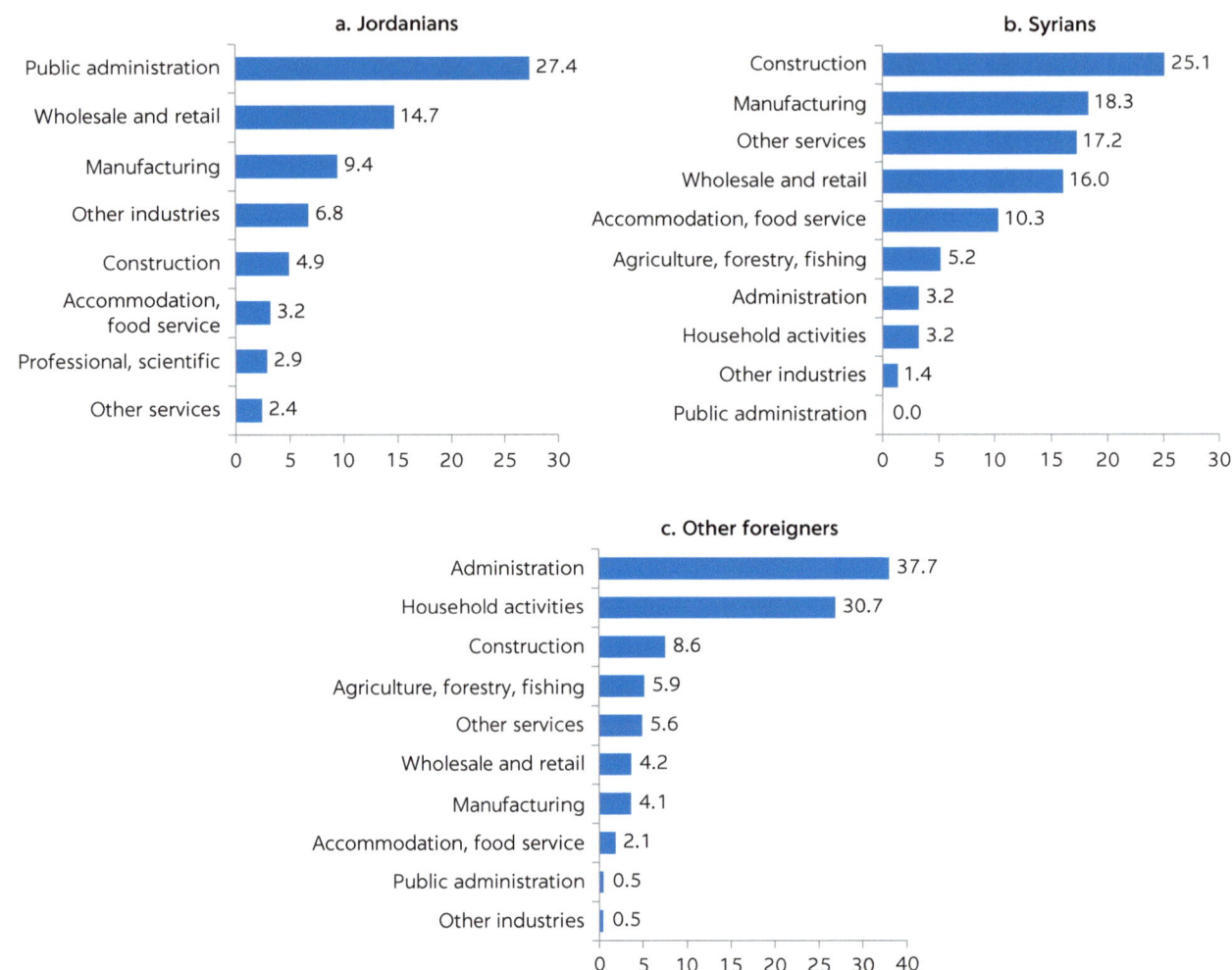

Source: Original figure for this publication using data from Jordan Department of Statistics 2019.
Note: Working-age population is defined as those ages 15–64.

Not surprisingly, then, a majority of Syrian workers lack social security coverage (figure 5.10), even though Jordan's social security law does not discriminate by nationality and coverage for non-Jordanian employees is required. Syrians do, however, have informality rates close to those observed among other foreigners.

One reason Syrians in Jordan have higher rates of informality is that as previously noted, Jordanians have exclusive access to (formal) public sector jobs. Syrians, by contrast, are forced to work in a limited number of sectors. If the analysis limits itself to sectors in which the majority of Syrians are employed, does it still show Syrians are more likely to work informally? When the analysis is restricted to the five sectors in which Syrians are most often employed—construction, manufacturing, wholesale and retail, food and accommodation, and agriculture—the share of Syrians in informal jobs remains unchanged, whereas the share of Jordanians engaged in informal jobs increases: only 23 percent of Jordanians in these five sectors have a written and open-ended contract (as compared with 57 percent when the sample is not restricted).

FIGURE 5.9

Sectors among working-age population with highest concentration of Syrian labor
(percent)

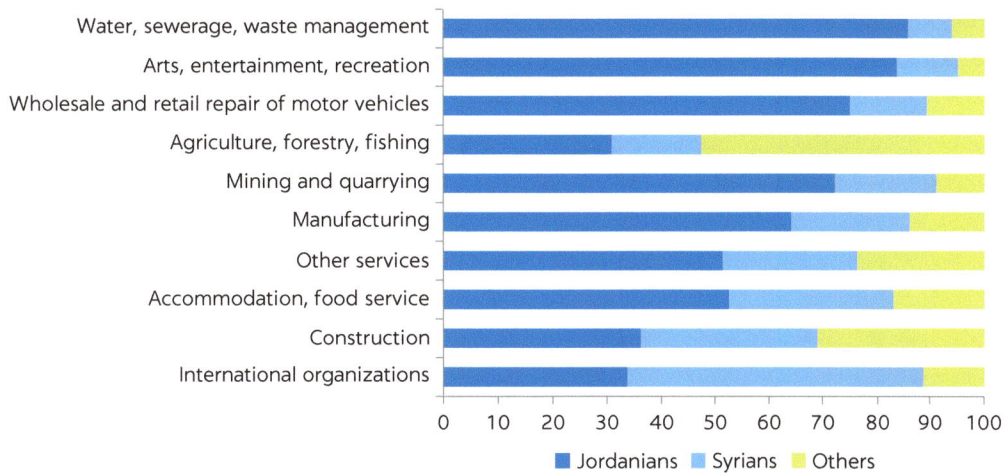

Source: Original figure for this publication using data from Jordan
Department of Statistics 2019.
Note: Working-age population is defined as those ages 15–64.

FIGURE 5.10

Share of workforce in informality
(percent)

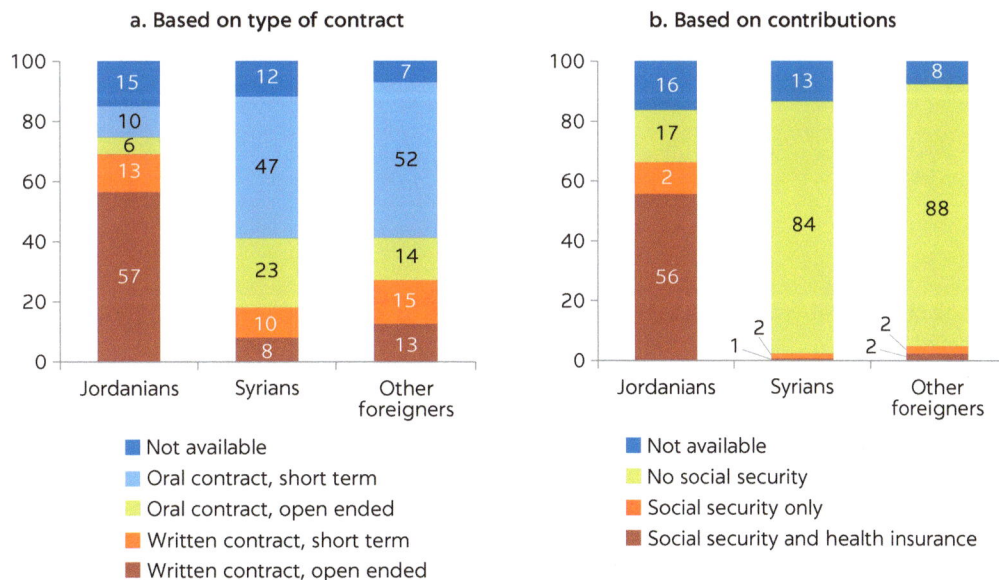

Source: Original figure for this publication using data from Jordan Department of Statistics 2019.

Similarly, 17 percent of Jordanians in these five sectors make both social security and health fund contributions, as opposed to 56 percent of the entire Jordanian sample (figure 5.11). So not only are Syrians in Jordan more likely to be employed in sectors with relatively higher incidences of informality, but within these sectors, they are more likely than Jordanians to be employed informally.

Relative to Jordanians and foreigners from other countries, Syrians in Jordan have lower levels of education. They are more likely to be illiterate, or to have less than upper-secondary education, than both Jordanians and other foreigners, and they are less likely to have higher levels of education (as was shown in chapter 2). These education differentials carry over into jobs, and in the sectors within which they are authorized to work, Syrians are more likely than Jordanians or other foreigners to be employed in lower-level occupations: 16 percent are employed as low-skilled blue collar workers and 44 percent as high-skilled blue collar workers (crafts and related trade workers) (figure 5.12).

FIGURE 5.11

Share of working-age population in informality, selected sectors

(percent)

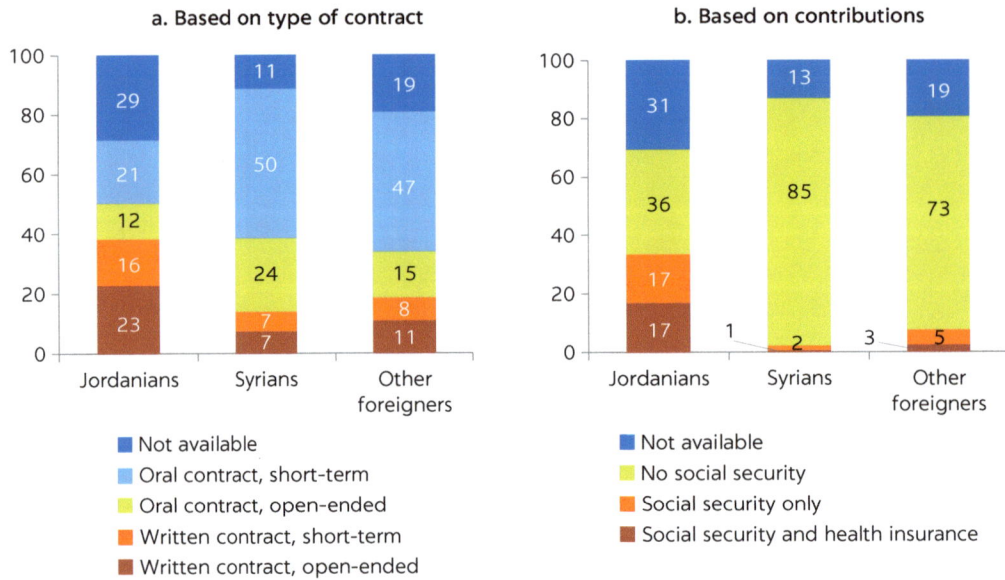

a. Based on type of contract

b. Based on contributions

Legend (a):
- Not available
- Oral contract, short-term
- Oral contract, open-ended
- Written contract, short-term
- Written contract, open-ended

Legend (b):
- Not available
- No social security
- Social security only
- Social security and health insurance

Source: Original figure for this publication using data from Jordan Department of Statistics 2019.
Note: Working-age population is defined as those ages 15–64. Sample for the figure is restricted to non-public-sector firms in the following sectors of activity in revision 2 of the Statistical Classification of Economic Activities in the European Community (NACE): construction, manufacturing, wholesale and retail, food and accommodation, and agriculture.

FIGURE 5.12

Distribution of employment by nationality across types of occupations

(percent)

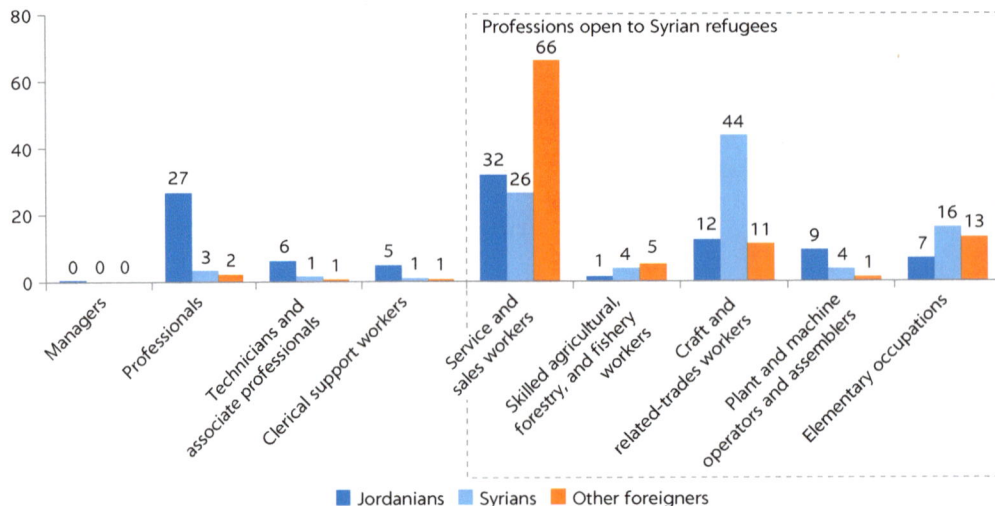

Legend: Jordanians, Syrians, Other foreigners

Source: Original figure for this publication using data from Jordan Department of Statistics 2019.

Only 26 percent of Syrians in Jordan are engaged in low-skilled white-collar work (services and sales).

EXPLAINING THE POOR PERFORMANCE OF SYRIANS IN THE LABOR MARKET

An important policy question is whether the observed differences in labor market outcomes between Jordanians and Syrians and other foreigners and Syrians stem from different personal characteristics, unequal treatment in the labor market, or a combination of these two factors. Disentangling the importance of each factor requires controlling for the lower educational attainment of Syrian workers compared with those of Jordanians and other foreigners while also controlling for other characteristics like age and location (figure 5.13).

To investigate whether different socioeconomic characteristics explain differential labor market outcomes for Syrians, figure 5.14 shows the results of a regression analysis that compares Syrians' labor market outcomes with those of Jordanians and foreigners other than Syrians. Baseline estimates are obtained from linear probability regressions that include a dummy for nationality only. Conditional estimates further control for gender, age group, civil status, education, and regional dummies. In the models comparing Syrians with other foreigners, year of arrival and squared year of arrival are included as additional controls. The sample comprises individuals ages 15–64.

The results show that some of the differences in labor market outcomes arise from differences in personal characteristics, but not all. For instance, conditioning on observable characteristics reduces Syrians' disadvantage in terms of labor market outcomes compared with Jordanians and other foreigners in an important way, but it does not eliminate it (the red dots in the figure remain different

FIGURE 5.13

Educational attainment among working-age population

(percent)

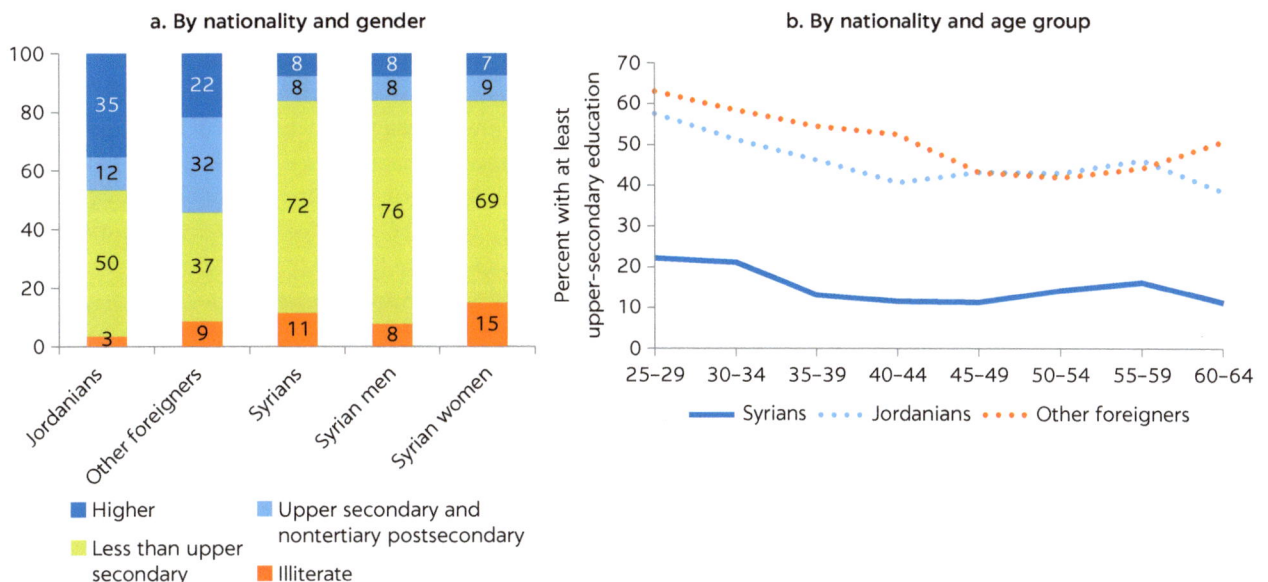

a. By nationality and gender

b. By nationality and age group

Legend: Higher / Upper secondary and nontertiary postsecondary / Less than upper secondary / Illiterate

Syrians • • • • Jordanians • • • • Other foreigners

Source: Original figure for this publication using data from Jordan Department of Statistics 2019.
Note: Working-age population is defined as those ages 15–64.

FIGURE 5.14

Probability gaps in labor market participation between Jordanians and Syrians and other foreigners and Syrians

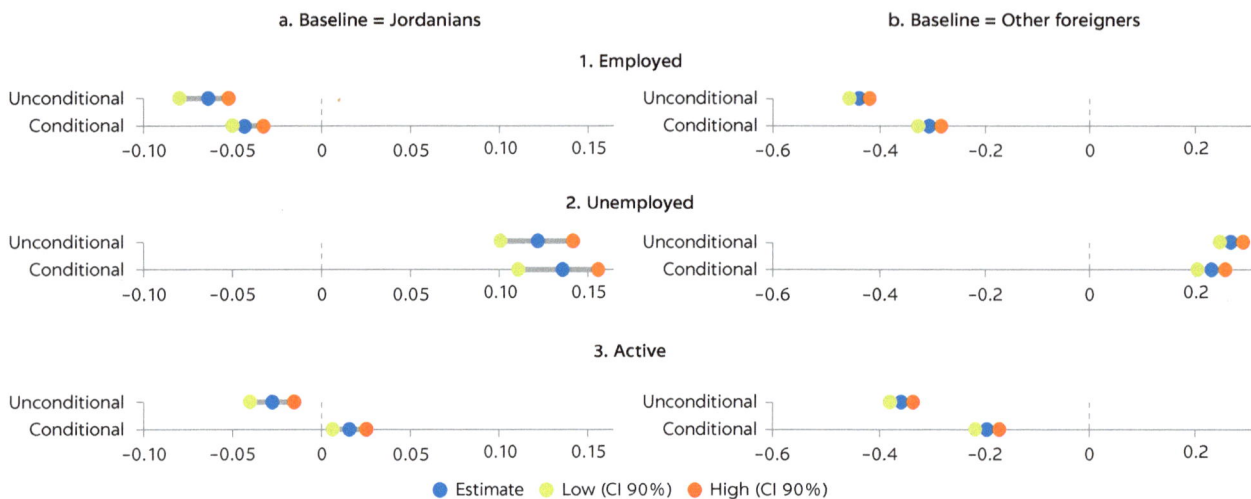

Source: Original figure for this publication using data from Jordan Department of Statistics 2019.
Note: The figure captures both unconditional and conditional differences and 90 percent confidence intervals for various differences in labor market outcomes between Jordanians and Syrians, on the one hand, and other foreigners and Syrians, on the other. The dependent variable is, alternatively, a dummy for whether the individual is employed (row 1), the individual is unemployed (row 2), and the individual is active in the labor market (employed or unemployed) (row 3). CI = confidence interval.

from zero with statistical significance), with one exception: when observable differences are controlled for, Syrians are more likely to be active in the labor market, compared with Jordanians.

Another interesting finding relates to the comparative risk of unemployment Syrians face. Controlling for differences in observable characteristics reduces the unemployment gap between other foreigners and Syrians but increases that between Jordanians and Syrians, suggesting that Jordan's labor market generally favors Jordanians.

The finding that Syrians in Jordan tend to be discriminated against in the labor market and are more likely to be unemployed even though they are more likely to be active in the labor market carries over into wages. Working Syrians are more likely to be engaged in low-paying jobs: 73 percent of Syrians earn less than JD 300 per month, including 28 percent who earn less than JD 200. The rate among foreigners other than Syrians is roughly comparable, at 69 percent, but Jordanians have a much lower rate, at 23 percent among Jordanians (figure 5.15, panel a). Syrians remain more likely to earn low wages even when the analysis focuses on sectors with high rates of Syrian employment: 70 percent of Syrians earn less than JD 300 per month, as compared with 40 percent among Jordanians and 55 percent among foreigners other than Syrians (figure 5.15, panel b).

As was found earlier in regard to labor market outcomes, differences in the sociodemographic and employment profiles of Syrians in Jordan do not fully account for the higher incidence of low pay among them. Multivariate analysis confirms the role of nationality as an important correlate of low pay, defined as the probability of earning less than JD 300 per month (see figure 5.16).[6] As in the regressions discussed earlier in the chapter, unconditional estimates are obtained from linear probability regressions that include a dummy for nationality only.

FIGURE 5.15

Earnings distribution among employed working-age population, by nationality

(percent)

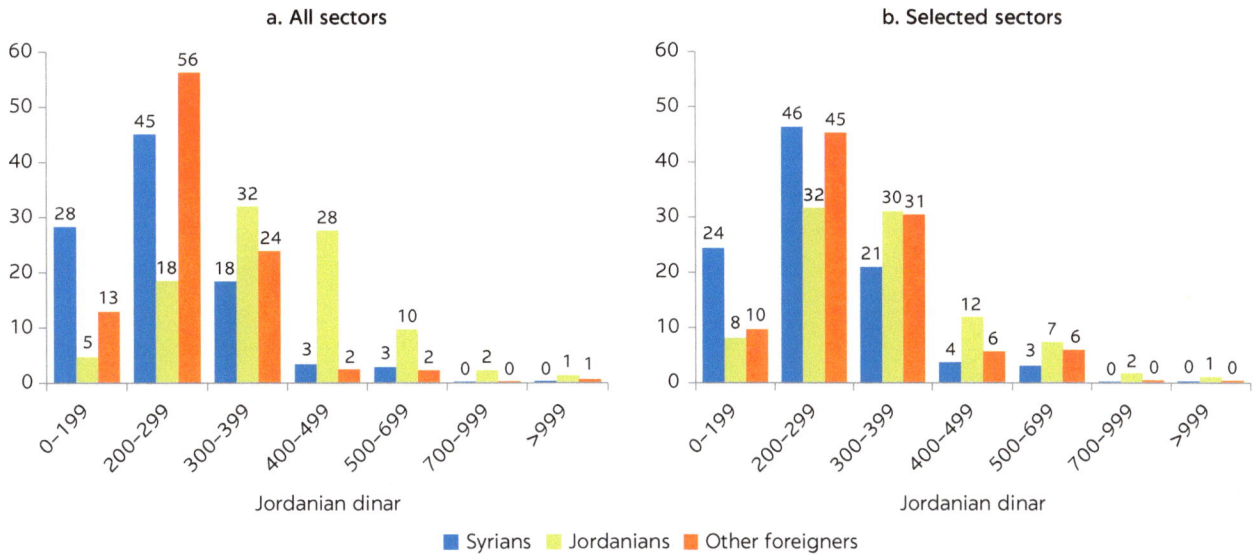

a. All sectors

b. Selected sectors

■ Syrians ■ Jordanians ■ Other foreigners

Source: Original figure for this publication using data from Jordan Department of Statistics 2019.
Note: Working-age population is defined as those ages 15–64. In panel b, the sample is restricted to firms not in the public sector that are in the following sectors of activity in revision 2 of the Statistical Classification of Economic Activities in the European Community (NACE): construction, manufacturing, wholesale and retail, food and accommodation, and agriculture.

FIGURE 5.16

Difference in probability of receiving low pay (< JD 300) between working-age Jordanians and Syrians and between other foreigners who are working and working-age Syrians

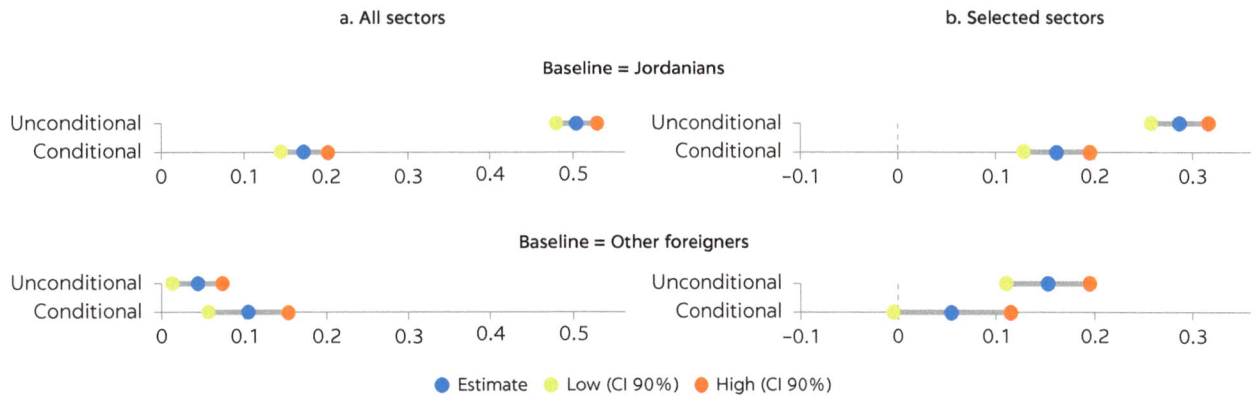

a. All sectors

b. Selected sectors

● Estimate ● Low (CI 90%) ● High (CI 90%)

Source: Original figure for this publication using data from Jordan Department of Statistics 2019.
Note: Working-age population is defined as those ages 15–64. The figure captures unconditional and conditional differences and 90 percent confidence intervals for the differences in the probability of receiving a monthly pay below JD 300 between Syrians and natives, on the one hand, and Syrians and other foreigners, on the other hand. CI = confidence interval.

To estimate conditional gaps, the regressions further control for the same variables as the earlier regressions (gender, age group, civil status, education, regional dummies, and years since arrival and years squared for the model with other foreigners), as well as type of occupation (by International Standard Classification of Occupations [ISCO]-08 one-digit code), sector of activity (by Statistical Classification of Economic Activities in the European Community [NACE], revision 2 one-digit code), an indicator of informality, and number of hours worked. Panel b restricts the regression to firms that are not in the public sector and sectors of activity accessible to Syrian refugees (construction, manufacturing, wholesale and retail, food and accommodation, and agriculture).

After controls are included in the model, the results show that Syrians in Jordan are 17.2 percent more likely than Jordanians and 10.5 percent more likely than foreigners other than Syrians to receive low pay, suggesting wide disparities between Syrians and both groups. Although Jordan's minimum wage applies to those of all nationalities, wage discrimination with respect to Jordanians persists when the sample is restricted to non-public-sector firms that have a large incidence of Syrian labor, but that with respect to other foreigners loses statistical significance.

CONCLUSION

The Jordanian labor market has witnessed significant increases in the presence of foreign workers over the last two decades, and many of those workers are from Syria.

Unlike the vast majority of foreigners of other nationalities residing in Jordan, Syrians are not economic migrants, and hence Syrians in Jordan are less likely to be self-selected based on characteristics positively correlated with economic outcomes in the host country. Chapter 2 highlighted that the sociodemographic profile of the Syrian population differs profoundly from that of its host country and of other foreigners in Jordan: the Syrian population is significantly younger and less educated. Syrians also have higher dependency ratios than both groups and have been in Jordan for a shorter period than other migrants.

Although the Jordanian government has tried to ease access to the labor market for Syrian refugees, labor market outcomes of the broader Syrian population remain challenging. A high incidence of unemployment and extremely low levels of female labor force participation are the main challenges. An additional concern is the high share of Syrians ages 15 to 29 who are not in employment, education, or training.

The analysis in this chapter indicates that socioeconomic differences do not fully account for the poorer labor market performance of Syrians compared with that of Jordanians and other foreigners. Syrians are less likely to be employed and more likely to earn a low wage than should be expected given their personal and other characteristics. Syrians are subject to constraints in the labor market that Jordanians and other foreigners do not face, or face to a lesser degree, as well as unequal treatment.

Additional elements of vulnerability emerge from analysis of Syrians who are employed. The evidence suggests a significant degree of labor market segmentation between Jordanians and Syrians and, to a lesser extent, between foreigners of other nationalities and Syrians. The Syrian workforce is predominantly male and unskilled, which explains the concentration of Syrian workers in low-skill jobs in a small number of sectors, notably construction, manufacturing, wholesale and retail, agriculture, and food and accommodation.[7] The higher incidence of informality among Syrian workers is another striking element of their vulnerability. In fact, not only are Syrians in Jordan more likely to work in sectors of the Jordanian economy in which informality is most common, but within these sectors, they are also more likely to work informally than Jordanian workers.

In combination, these and other factors (differences in sociodemographic characteristics, sectors of employment, occupations, formality, and number of hours worked) contribute to low wages: Syrians are more likely than Jordanians and foreigners of other nationalities to be working for less than JD 300 per month.

The flip side of these low wages is that Syrian refugees are more dependent on assistance for their survival than Jordanians or other foreigners. Yet as chapter 4 demonstrated, the amount of assistance provided is inadequate to ensure that all refugees attain an acceptable minimum standard of living. Mindful that earnings and assistance can substitute for one another, the next chapter explores how Jordan, by allowing refugees to work, creates a global public good by reducing the amount of money needed for assistance.

ANNEX 5A. ADDITIONAL TABLES

TABLE A5.1 Conditional regressions for probability gaps in labor market outcomes

	BASELINE = JORDANIANS			BASELINE = OTHER FOREIGNERS		
	EMPLOYED	UNEMPLOYED	ACTIVE	EMPLOYED	UNEMPLOYED	ACTIVE
Syrian	−0.043*** (0.01)	0.136*** (0.01)	0.016** (0.01)	−0.307*** (0.01)	0.232*** (0.02)	−0.196*** (0.01)
Female	−0.400*** (0.00)	0.066*** (0.01)	−0.472*** (0.00)	−0.472*** (0.01)	0.005 (0.02)	−0.597*** (0.01)
Married	−0.022*** (0.00)	0.126*** (0.01)	0.074*** (0.00)	−0.042** (0.01)	0.038** (0.01)	−0.012 (0.01)
Age groups (baseline = ages 25–29)						
15–19	−0.299*** (0.01)	0.152*** (0.02)	−0.430*** (0.01)	−0.298*** (0.02)	0.184*** (0.04)	−0.313*** (0.02)
20–24	−0.121*** (0.01)	0.078*** (0.01)	−0.131*** (0.01)	−0.119*** (0.02)	0.050* (0.02)	−0.094*** (0.02)
30–34	0.051*** (0.01)	−0.070*** (0.01)	0.009 (0.01)	−0.002 (0.02)	0.022 (0.02)	0.009 (0.02)
35–39	0.072*** (0.01)	−0.093*** (0.01)	0.021*** (0.01)	−0.016 (0.02)	0.023 (0.02)	−0.000 (0.02)
40–44	0.032*** (0.01)	−0.098*** (0.01)	−0.026*** (0.01)	−0.051* (0.02)	0.022 (0.02)	−0.045* (0.02)
45–49	−0.029*** (0.01)	−0.094*** (0.01)	−0.093*** (0.01)	−0.128*** (0.02)	0.058* (0.02)	−0.113*** (0.02)
50–54	−0.134*** (0.01)	−0.106*** (0.01)	−0.212*** (0.01)	−0.207*** (0.02)	0.064* (0.03)	−0.206*** (0.02)
55–59	−0.211*** (0.01)	−0.137*** (0.01)	−0.304*** (0.01)	−0.253*** (0.03)	0.011 (0.03)	−0.279*** (0.03)
60–64	−0.299*** (0.01)	−0.102*** (0.02)	−0.388*** (0.01)	−0.383*** (0.03)	0.104 (0.06)	−0.403*** (0.03)
Education (baseline = less than upper secondary)						
Illiterate	−0.073*** (0.01)	0.046 (0.03)	−0.090*** (0.01)	0.055*** (0.02)	−0.019 (0.02)	0.035* (0.02)
Upper secondary or postsecondary	−0.058*** (0.00)	−0.013 (0.01)	−0.113*** (0.00)	0.002 (0.01)	−0.017 (0.01)	−0.034** (0.01)
Tertiary	0.132*** (0.00)	0.045*** (0.01)	0.195*** (0.00)	−0.096*** (0.02)	0.035* (0.02)	−0.074*** (0.02)

continued

TABLE A5.1., *continued.,*

	BASELINE = JORDANIANS			BASELINE = OTHER FOREIGNERS		
	EMPLOYED	**UNEMPLOYED**	**ACTIVE**	**EMPLOYED**	**UNEMPLOYED**	**ACTIVE**
Region (baseline = all other governorates)						
Mafraq	−0.002	0.034***	0.018***	−0.063***	0.129***	−0.000
	(0.00)	(0.01)	(0.00)	(0.01)	(0.02)	(0.01)
Zarqa	−0.053***	0.053***	−0.043***	−0.103***	0.115***	−0.062***
	(0.00)	(0.01)	(0.00)	(0.02)	(0.03)	(0.01)
Irbid	−0.013***	0.003	−0.016***	−0.024	0.016	−0.010
	(0.00)	(0.01)	(0.00)	(0.01)	(0.02)	(0.01)
Amman	−0.030***	0.001	−0.037***	−0.025*	0.027**	−0.008
	(0.00)	(0.01)	(0.00)	(0.01)	(0.01)	(0.01)
Year of arrival				−0.303	−0.005	−0.550**
				(0.21)	(0.16)	(0.20)
Squared year of arrival				0.000	0.000	0.000**
				(0.00)	(0.00)	(0.00)
Constant	0.601***	0.134***	0.719***	303.581	5.338	550.912**
	(0.01)	(0.01)	(0.01)	(205.89)	(161.23)	(196.09)
R-squared	0.316	0.121	0.412	0.497	0.194	0.533
N	153,467	59,269	153,467	12,152	5,953	12,152

*p < .05 **p < .01 ***p < 001

TABLE A5.2 Conditional regressions for probability of receiving low pay (<JD 300) by nationality

	ALL SECTORS		SELECTED SECTORS	
	BASELINE = JORDANIANS	**BASELINE = OTHER FOREIGNERS**	**BASELINE = JORDANIANS**	**BASELINE = OTHER FOREIGNERS**
Syrians	0.172***	0.105***	0.161***	0.055
	(0.02)	(0.03)	(0.02)	(0.04)
Female	0.118***	0.002	0.202***	0.131*
	(0.01)	(0.03)	(0.02)	(0.06)
Married	0.077***	0.008	0.159***	0.083*
	(0.01)	(0.03)	(0.02)	(0.04)
Age groups (baseline = ages 25–29)				
15–19	0.133***	0.119**	0.081**	0.048
	(0.02)	(0.04)	(0.03)	(0.06)
20–24	0.033**	0.013	0.035	−0.027
	(0.01)	(0.04)	(0.02)	(0.06)
30–34	−0.015	0.006	−0.031	−0.008
	(0.01)	(0.03)	(0.03)	(0.05)
35–39	−0.040***	0.059	−0.067*	−0.003
	(0.01)	(0.03)	(0.03)	(0.05)
40–44	−0.030*	0.058	−0.024	0.046
	(0.01)	(0.04)	(0.03)	(0.05)
45–49	−0.049***	−0.006	−0.074*	0.021
	(0.01)	(0.05)	(0.03)	(0.07)
50–54	−0.041**	0.017	−0.054	0.072
	(0.02)	(0.05)	(0.04)	(0.07)
55–59	−0.014	0.020	−0.014	0.083
	(0.02)	(0.08)	(0.05)	(0.10)
60–64	−0.027	−0.001	−0.084	−0.197
	(0.03)	(0.10)	(0.07)	(0.16)

continued

TABLE A5.2., *continued.,*

	ALL SECTORS		SELECTED SECTORS	
	BASELINE = JORDANIANS	BASELINE = OTHER FOREIGNERS	BASELINE = JORDANIANS	BASELINE = OTHER FOREIGNERS
Education (baseline = less than upper secondary)				
Illiterate	0.121***	−0.052	0.126**	−0.001
	(0.03)	(0.04)	(0.05)	(0.05)
Upper secondary or postsecondary	−0.033**	−0.034	−0.065*	−0.100*
	(0.01)	(0.02)	(0.03)	(0.04)
Tertiary	−0.075***	−0.089*	−0.101***	−0.144*
	(0.01)	(0.04)	(0.03)	(0.06)
Region (baseline = all other governorates)				
Mafraq	0.039***	0.160***	0.077***	0.123***
	(0.01)	(0.03)	(0.02)	(0.03)
Zarqa	0.064***	0.155***	0.091***	0.154***
	(0.01)	(0.04)	(0.02)	(0.04)
Irbid	0.034***	0.078*	0.079***	0.052
	(0.01)	(0.03)	(0.02)	(0.04)
Amman	−0.017*	0.064*	−0.038*	0.067
	(0.01)	(0.03)	(0.02)	(0.03)
Social contributions (baseline = social security and health insurance)				
Social security only	0.235***	0.064	0.091***	0.051
	(0.01)	(0.08)	(0.02)	(0.10)
None	0.356***	0.293***	0.250***	0.381***
	(0.01)	(0.06)	(0.02)	(0.09)
Number of hours worked (baseline = 35 to 48)				
Less than 35 hours	0.048***	−0.008	0.090**	−0.014
	(0.01)	(0.04)	(0.03)	(0.05)
More than 48 hours	−0.024*	0.090***	−0.007	0.063*
	(0.01)	(0.03)	(0.02)	(0.03)
Year of arrival		−1.330***		−1.704***
		(0.34)		(0.42)
Squared year of arrival		0.000***		0.000***
		(0.00)		(0.00)
Sector fixed effects	Yes	Yes	Yes	Yes
Occupation fixed effects	Yes	Yes	Yes	Yes
Constant	−0.008	1329.093***	0.148*	1702.685***
	(0.04)	(342.30)	(0.06)	(415.22)
R-squared	0.430	0.107	0.272	0.126
N	40,009	4,238	10,284	2,212

*p < .05 **p < .01 ***p < 001

NOTES

1. The chapter draws on the Jordan Labor Force Survey 2019, which identifies Syrian refugees through self-reporting, using a definition that varies from the definition used for the 2021 Vulnerability Assessment Framework survey (up-to-date registration in proGres). For this chapter's main results, however, this divergence likely makes no difference.
2. The dependency ratio is the number of persons below 15 or above 64 in a population divided by the number of persons of working age (between 15 and 64 years old) in that same population.
3. The vast majority (90 percent) of Syrians are refugees or asylum seekers, but not all are (figure 5.1).
4. The survey includes refugees irrespective of their residence in camps or host communities and of their legal residency status: registered with national authorities and the United Nations High Commissioner for Refugees or undocumented.
5. Syrian refugees have been employed by nongovernmental organizations and development partners under cash for work (outside camps) or incentive-based (inside camps) volunteer schemes since 2018.
6. The minimum wage in Jordan was set at JD 260 as of January 2024.
7. In Jordan's construction and accommodation and food services sectors, close to one in three workers is Syrian.

REFERENCES

Attanasio, Orazio P., and Miguel Székely. 2001. *Portrait of the Poor: An Assets-Based Approach.* Washington, DC: Inter-American Development Bank.

Bussolo, Maurizio, and Luis F. López-Calva. 2014. *Shared Prosperity: Paving the Way in Europe and Central Asia.* Washington, DC: World Bank.

Carter, Michael R., and Christopher B. Barrett. 2006. "The Economics of Poverty Traps and Persistent Poverty: An Asset-Based Approach." *Journal of Development Studies* 42 (2): 178–99.

ILO (International Labour Organization). 2015. "Work Permits for Syrian Refugees in Jordan ." ILO Regional Office for Arab States, Amman. https://www.ilo.org/wcmsp5/groups/public /---arabstates/---ro-beirut/documents/publication/wcms_422478.pdf.

Jordan Department of Statistics. 2019. "Labor Force Survey 2019." Department of Statistics, Hashemite Kingdom of Jordan, Amman.

Jordan Ministry of Labor. 2023. "Foreign_Workers_EN" (data file). Accessed December 2023. https://mol.gov.jo/EN/Pages/Foreign_Workers_EN.

López-Calva, Luis F., and Carlos Rodríguez-Castelán. 2016. "Pro-growth Equity: A Policy Framework for the Twin Goals." Policy Research Working Paper WPS7897, World Bank, Washington, DC.

Stark, Oded. 2004. "On the Economics of Refugee Flows." *Review of Development Economics* 8 (2): 325–29.

World Bank. 2022. *Syria Economic Monitor—Spring 2022: Lost Generation of Syrians.* Washington, DC: World Bank. https://openknowledge.worldbank.org/entities/publication /82c50366-fb28-5ae9-8fda-d5ab9bff51f0.

6 Budgetary Benefits of Refugee Economic Participation

JOHANNES HOOGEVEEN, ERWIN KNIPPENBERG, AND CHINEDU OBI

MAIN MESSAGES

This chapter estimates a monetary value for the global public good that the government of Jordan provides to the international community: the reduced need for assistance that results from refugees' ability to earn incomes themselves. It explores the cost of hosting refugees in Jordan under three scenarios of labor market participation—exclusion, partial inclusion, and full participation—and finds that the need for assistance falls as the degree of labor market integration increases. By implication, Jordan's contribution to hosting refugees rises with their degree of participation in the country's labor market.

The results reveal a substantial ongoing cost of hosting Syrian refugees: $465 million for their subsistence needs and $444 million for including them in public-services provision. Refugee economic participation is associated with large savings as well: relative to a baseline in which refugees earn no income at all, these savings amount to more than $860 million per year and could increase to more than $1.3 billion with further enhancement of refugees' financial autonomy. The budgetary benefits associated with refugee economic participation create scope for a triple-win bargain in which Jordan receives additional development assistance, international donors save on aid needed for refugees, and Syrian refugees gain in financial autonomy.

INTRODUCTION

The 2018 Global Compact on Refugees places enhanced sharing of the responsibilities associated with supporting refugees at the center of the international protection agenda. In a world in which low- and middle-income countries—countries with limited physical and financial means—host most refugees, the compact recognizes that international cooperation will enable countries to achieve a sustainable solution to refugee situations. Responsibility sharing has implications for donor countries, which should provide financial resources, and for host countries, which should provide cost-effective ways to meet refugee needs.

Implicit in the responsibility-sharing discussion is the understanding that any solution to the issue of refugee support must address refugee needs cost-effectively and avoid inefficiencies. Because most refugee crises are protracted, a consensus is growing that—after the immediate emergency phase—including refugees in national systems meets their needs more efficiently than serving them through parallel humanitarian systems. This chapter focuses on identifying the recurrent cost associated with, and potential savings from, accommodating refugees through national systems.

Reliance on national systems implies that refugees participate in local markets. They seek their own accommodations and purchase consumption goods in local shops, and depending on host country policies, they may also participate in labor markets. All of these things affect the net fiscal cost of hosting them. By purchasing locally, refugees contribute to the collection of sales and import taxes, for instance; they also benefit from universal subsidies on food and fuel. Refugees who participate in the formal labor market generate revenues in the form of contributions to social assistance and the payment of income taxes.

The debate on how best to support refugee needs generally makes a dominant assumption that refugees are a humanitarian subject, vulnerable and worthy of assistance. The government of Jordan, however, has taken a different approach, one that allows Syrian refugees to succeed and contribute economically rather than merely survive. Syrian refugees have access to public health and education, are allowed to work, have historically benefited from subsidized utilities,[1] and have freedom of movement. As previous chapters have demonstrated, Syrian refugees respond as expected: they send their children to Jordanian schools and are economically active, like anyone else in Jordan, even though their productive capabilities (limited human capital) and policy choices (like the possibility of working in selected sectors, as chapter 5 showed) constrain the degree to which they can contribute.

Host country contributions to sharing responsibility are not always fully recognized—at least not in a monetary sense. This underappreciation is behind the December 2017 United Nations resolution[2] inviting the United Nations High Commissioner for Refugees to "coordinate an effort to measure the impact arising from hosting, protecting and assisting refugees, with a view to assessing gaps in international cooperation and promoting burden- and responsibility-sharing that is more equitable, predictable and sustainable, and to begin reporting on the results to Member States in 2018." The underappreciation also contributed to the Measuring Impact initiative, which aims to identify at the global level the cost of hosting refugees in an inclusive manner.

This chapter operates within the context of this global work. Yet unlike the global program, which to date has published estimates only for the cost of inclusive refugee education (World Bank and UNHCR 2021; World Bank 2023), this chapter estimates all recurrent cost associated with hosting refugees: the cost of supporting their subsistence needs, as well as their use of public services (see figure 6.1). And it estimates how much refugees' participation in economic activities reduces this cost.

By identifying the monetary value of the recurrent resources needed to assist Syrian refugees in Jordan as well as the aid money saved as a result of refugee participation in Jordan's economy, this chapter advances the discussion on sharing responsibility for refugee support. The remainder of the chapter is organized as follows: the next section discusses the methodology for estimating the monetary cost associated with enabling refugees to attain an acceptable minimum standard of living: the cost of meeting their subsistence needs. The second

FIGURE 6.1

FIGURE 6.1

Decomposition of cost of refugee assistance

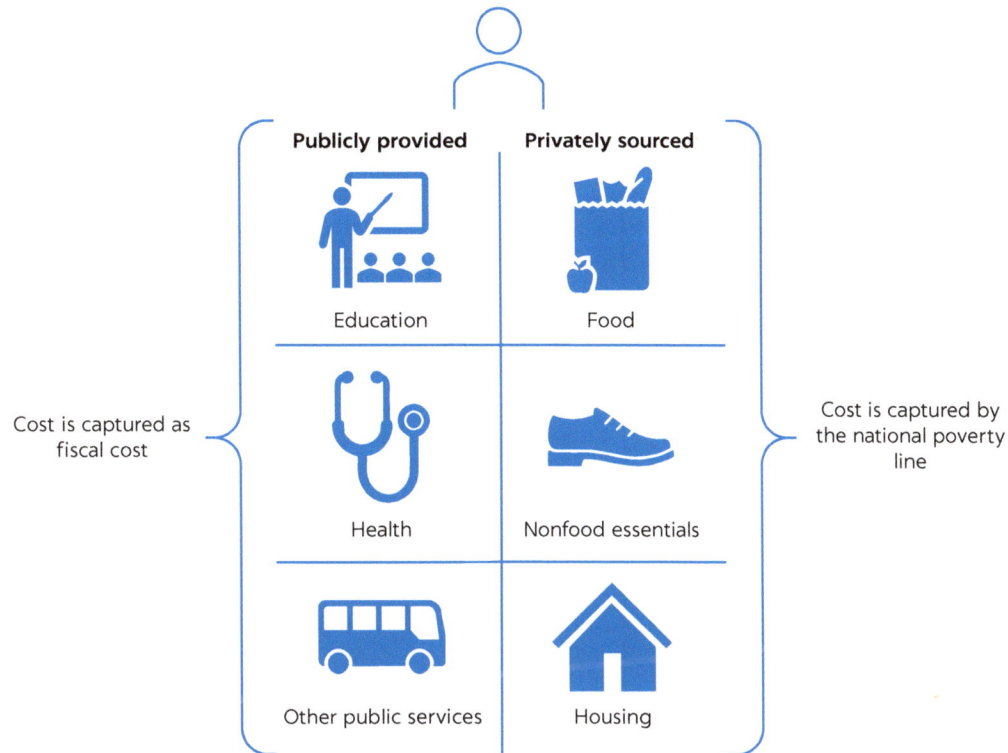

Source: Original figure for this publication.

section deals with estimating the fiscal cost of providing public services to refugees. The third section explores various cost implications of refugees living in and outside of camps. A final section concludes.

COST OF SUBSISTENCE NEEDS ASSISTANCE UNDER VARIOUS ECONOMIC PARTICIPATION SCENARIOS

Cost of subsistence needs versus fiscal cost

To estimate the cost of meeting refugees' subsistence needs, it is critical first to establish what constitutes an acceptable minimum standard of living. This volume has presented two possibilities for doing this: the minimum expenditure basket (discussed in chapter 4) and the poverty line (examined in chapter 3). Of these two approaches, the latter, employing the so-called cost-of-basic-needs approach, is more commonly used.[3] This approach starts by identifying the minimum cost of acquiring enough food for adequate nutrition (defined in terms of meeting the minimum daily caloric requirement), using a basket of goods consumed by households predetermined to be poor. To this cost is added the cost of satisfying basic nonfood needs (clothing, shelter, private expenditure on education and health), defined as the amount spent on nonfood items by households whose total consumption value equals the minimum cost for food.[4] The idea is that the items these households consume have to be essential, as their purchase comes at the expense of meeting the minimum caloric requirement (Ravallion 1998).

In line with the common use of the terminology, in this chapter, the "cost of subsistence needs" for refugee assistance reflects the private expenses refugees need to make to attain a minimum standard of living. Figure 6.1 shows these expenses in the "Privately sourced" column. They cover food, nonfood essentials, and housing. In addition to these private expenses, refugees also incur public expenses, such as those for health and education, reflected in the "Publicly provided" column in the figure. Public expenses are not included in the cost of subsistence needs, but they are identified separately as the *fiscal cost* for refugee participation; later in this chapter, the section "Estimating Savings from Refugee Participation in Public-Services Provision" looks at them in depth.

An illustration may clarify. If a household purchases a uniform for its school-going child or copays for seeing a doctor, these expenses are reflected in the cost of subsistence needs and captured in nonfood expenses. By contrast, government spending on the school or on public health care is captured under (education and health) cost.

Calculating the cost of subsistence needs assistance

This section determines the cost of subsistence needs assistance to Syrian refugees by multiplying Jordan's official monthly per capita poverty line for 2017/18,[5] based on Jordan's 2018 Household Income and Expenditure Survey, by the number of refugees it supports. The annual cost of providing sufficient assistance to enable refugees to exist at the poverty line can then be written as

$$CSN_0 = N \times 12 \times z, \tag{6.1}$$

in which z is the per capita (monthly) poverty line and N the total number of Syrian refugees in Jordan. This equation calculates the cost of meeting subsistence needs as an upper bound, because it assumes refugees earn no income (referred to here as the *no-income scenario*), as if they are fully excluded from the labor market and require aid to cover all their subsistence needs.

The no-income scenario, however, does not adequately reflect the situation in Jordan, where refugees do earn incomes. Some refugees earn more than the poverty line and do not need assistance. Others do not earn enough to reach the poverty line, but they do have income. Consequently, the no-income scenario overestimates the amount of aid needed to complement poor refugees' own earned income. Earned income and refugee assistance are communicating vessels, and more of one implies less of the other (figure 6.2).

To calculate how much refugees contribute to their own subsistence needs—the *current participation scenario*—requires an estimate of the income they earn (figure 6.3). Consumption, with reported assistance received netted out, can approximate this amount. The difference between the poverty line z and preassistance consumption y_i, summed over all refugees living below the poverty line H, is the *poverty gap*—grounding the analysis in the Foster, Greer, and Thorbecke (1984) welfare metric—which reflects the cost of assistance once refugees' earnings are taken into account.

$$CSN_1 = 12 \times \sum_{i=1}^{H} (z - y_i). \tag{6.2}$$

FIGURE 6.2

Ability to earn an income and need for assistance as communicating vessels

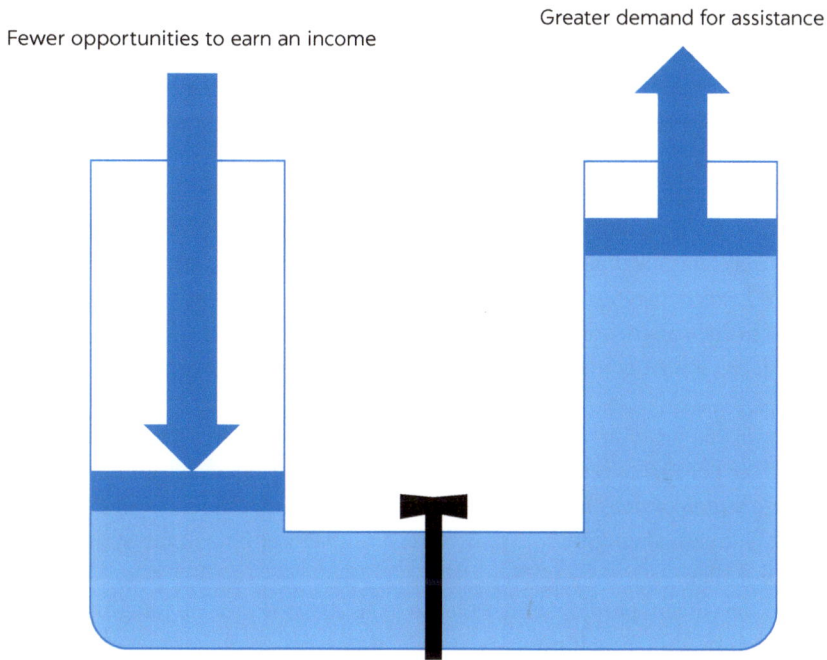

Source: Original figure for this publication.

FIGURE 6.3

Cost of basic needs, with refugee earnings accounted for

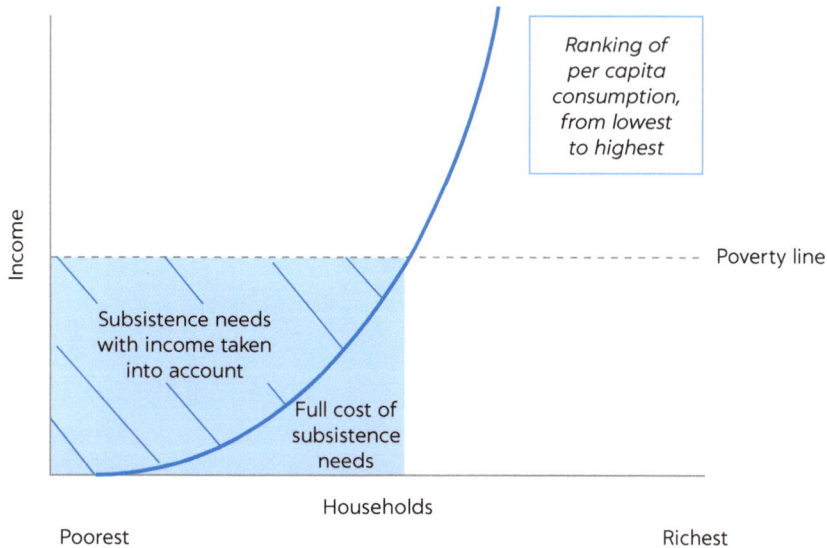

Source: Original figure for this publication.

Calculating the cost of basic and potential savings under different participation scenarios

As refugees' potential for earning an income depends on their access to the labor market, not only can the methodology just described be applied to the status quo, but it can also be used to estimate how much refugees would earn—and the change to the recurrent cost of meeting their basic needs—under different labor market participation scenarios, as figure 6.4 shows.

One notable implication illustrated in the figure is that the cost of assistance to meet refugee subsistence needs depends on host country policies as well as on refugee assets, education, and demographic profile. Host countries that do not allow refugees to work—the no-income scenario—have the highest cost for basic needs assistance. Allowing refugees to work but imposing restrictions—the current participation scenario in Jordan—reduces the cost, but the cost is still higher than when refugees are fully included in the host country's labor market.

Figure 6.4 also illustrates a second implication: as the cost of subsistence needs assistance declines with refugee integration in a host country's labor market, the host country's contribution to responsibility sharing increases. Refugees' ability to earn an income is a consequence of host country policies and can be considered a host country's contribution to sharing the cost of assistance to refugees.

Under the baseline scenario of no income, the annual cost of basic needs assistance per Syrian refugee in Jordan is calculated by multiplying the monthly poverty line amount by 12, after adjusting for inflation. The calculation allows for 13 percent annual administrative overhead ($1,948 per person for Syrian refugees in Jordan).[6]

For the current participation scenario in Jordan, the income refugees earn is estimated by assuming it goes toward meeting subsistence needs. Because the available data on incomes among Syrian refugees in Jordan are patchy, income earned is approximated by deducting assistance received from total consumption, as this is the share of consumption that refugee earnings fund.[7] The difference between the poverty line and preassistance consumption (referred to as the preassistance poverty gap) reflects, in the current scenario in Jordan, the cost of the assistance needed to bring all refugees up to the poverty line.[8] This poverty gap among Syrian refugees in Jordan is 36 percent;[9] the average per capita cost of meeting a refugee's subsistence needs is therefore 36 percent of the cost in the no-income scenario, or $704.

FIGURE 6.4

Cost and potential savings under different economic participation scenarios

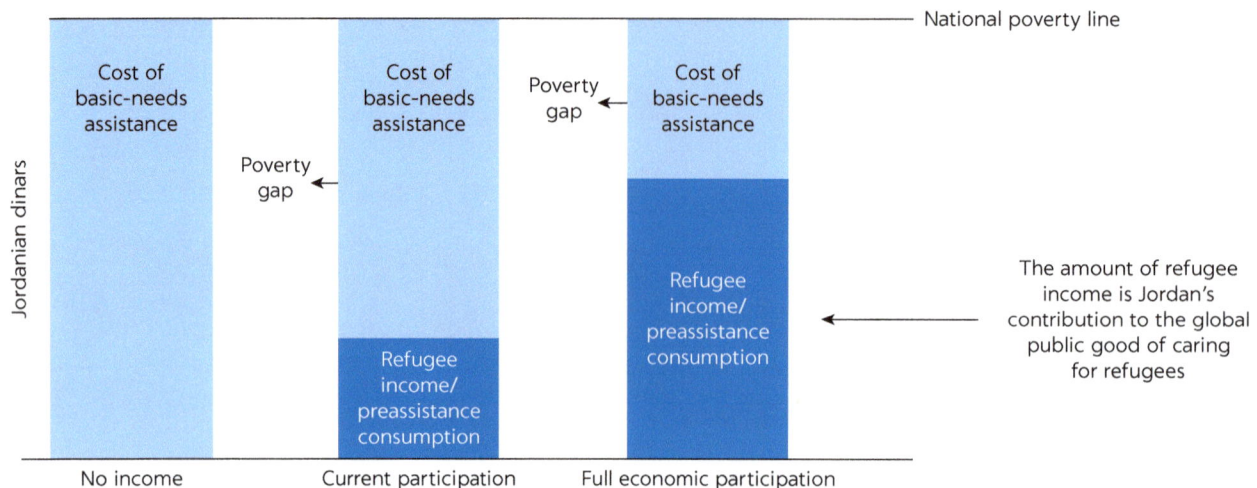

Source: Original figure for this publication.

Determining the fiscal cost of refugee support under a *full-participation scenario*—in which refugees participate fully in the host country's labor market—requires, in the case of Syrian refugees in Jordan, estimating how much refugees would earn if they faced the same restrictions in Jordan's labor market as Jordanians and foreigners other than Syrians: that is, it requires controlling for differences in personal characteristics (household composition; age; level of education). Here, how much Syrian refugees could earn in a full-participation scenario is calculated through a matching exercise.[10]

The refugee asset framework (presented in chapter 5) highlights how the loss of productive assets limits the possibilities for Syrian refugees in Jordan to earn incomes. Although the matching conducted here controls for differences in invariable personal characteristics, it does not account for differences in financial or productive assets needed to participate as equals in Jordan's labor market. Syrian refugees' projected income, as calculated here, is therefore based on an optimistic scenario in which asset disadvantages have been redressed.[11]

Chapter 5 showed that Jordan's labor market is composed of three groups of workers— Jordanians, other migrants, and Syrians—each with different labor market and socioeconomic characteristics. To account for this, two different participation scenarios are explored here: one in which Syrian refugees are matched with Jordanians, and one in which they are matched with other foreigners.

The poverty gap is then calculated, using predicted consumption. The average poverty gap is found to be 8 percent when Syrians are matched with other immigrants, and the per capita fiscal cost of meeting subsistence needs is therefore 8 percent of $1,948 (the subsistence needs amount in the no-income scenario), or $163.[12] The average poverty gap is lower, however—5 percent—when Syrians are matched with Jordanians, and the per capita fiscal cost of meeting subsistence needs drops to $107. Figure 6.5 illustrates all four scenarios.

The policy scenarios explored here illustrate four points in particular:

- The cost of subsistence needs assistance for refugees depends on the degree of their economic participation. Because Syrian refugees in Jordan can earn incomes, the need for assistance to meet their subsistence needs drops from $1,948 per refugee per year to $704. With about 660,000 registered refugees as of 2021, according to the United Nations High Commissioner for Refugees,

FIGURE 6.5

Cost of basic needs assistance under different participation scenarios

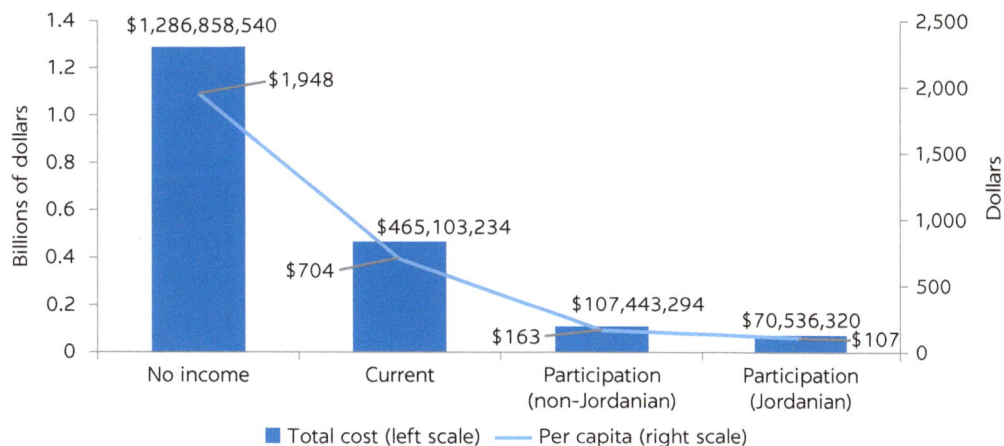

Source: Original figure for this publication using data from UNHCR 2021.

refugees' economic participation thus reduces the total cost for basic needs assistance in Jordan by $821 million per year, from $1.286 billion to $465 million annually.

- This reduction in assistance represents Jordan's contribution to global responsibility sharing for Syrian refugees, because it reduces the cost of subsistence needs assistance—by the $821 million annual reduction just noted.
- Greater integration of refugees into economic activities reduces the cost of subsistence needs assistance further. Jordan has scope for additional reductions from this source and could reduce the annual cost of subsistence needs assistance from the present $704 per refugee to between $107 and $163 by allowing Syrian refugees to participate fully in the labor market.
- Achieving the full potential reduction in cost would require restoring refugees' productive capacity and pursuing more-inclusive economic policies.

ESTIMATING SAVINGS FROM REFUGEE PARTICIPATION IN PUBLIC-SERVICES PROVISION

In Jordan, refugees can make use of public services, much as Jordanian nationals do. Refugees attend public schools, use the public health system, and benefit from subsidies. When subsidies lower input costs and thus indirectly reduce the costs of goods, refugees benefit from these lower costs just as others do. In return, refugees contribute to government revenue, as do nationals, through payment of income tax (very limited), sales and import taxes, and other levies.

This section outlines an approach for estimating the cost of including refugees in public-services provision and the savings that result when refugees become more financially autonomous (that is, when they are permitted to participate in the host country's economy, including the labor market). It assumes that refugees are treated in the same way as nationals, that is, they have comparable access to public services for which they are eligible and the same obligations when it comes to contributing to public revenues. Participation implies that refugees access national health and education services and benefit from subsidies when they purchase goods. When subsidies lower the price of bread or fuel for nationals, refugees pay these lower prices, too. And like nationals, refugees benefit from the use of public goods like infrastructure, security, and the presence of a public administration, among others. However, the approach employed here explicitly excludes benefits from direct cash transfers and other modalities that are targeted specifically to nationals.

One straightforward way to assess the total fiscal cost of providing services to refugees is to calculate per capita budgetary spending (by sector) and multiply this by the number of refugees. However, public spending does not affect everybody equally. Governments often consider it their mandate to limit inequality by redistributing resources from better-off households to the most vulnerable in society. Those at the bottom of the income distribution, such as refugees, therefore tend to benefit more from services provision and contribute less to the public coffers.

Analysis of how this kind of redistribution affects poverty and inequality in society is known as *fiscal incidence analysis*. Fiscal incidence analyses have been performed for many countries, including Jordan. The remainder of this section uses information from Jordan's most recent fiscal incidence analysis to estimate the (net) fiscal cost of allowing refugees to use public services.

Fiscal incidence analysis in Jordan

In 2021, Rodriguez and Wai-Poi published the most recent fiscal incidence analysis for Jordan. Their approach follows the Commitment to Equity Institute (CEQ) methodology, an internationally recognized fiscal incidence diagnostic method developed by the institute that applies standard incidence analysis to each tax and transfer in a country's fiscal accounts. Here, the taxes and transfers are allocated to Jordanian households based on the information available in the Household Income and Expenditure Survey, including information on household employment and income (which determines personal income tax and receipt of social assistance benefits) and expenditures (which determines indirect taxes and subsidies), as well as use of social services such as health and education. Dividing total values by the number of Jordanians yields per capita values.[13] To calculate the indirect effect of consumption taxes and subsidies, the analysis uses a 23-sector input-output table from 2010 that has been updated to 2016.

Figure 6.6 illustrates the results of the fiscal incidence analysis for Jordan by household income decile. It identifies contributions to revenue (direct and indirect taxes, below the horizontal line), as well as benefits to individuals from education and health services, transfers, and direct and indirect subsidies. As the figure illustrates, Jordan's fiscal system redistributes resources from wealthier individuals (for those in the tenth decile, the total net impact is negative) to poorer ones (for whom the net impact is positive). The impact is largest for those in the first and second deciles.

The figure also illustrates that all individuals in Jordan, even the poorest, contribute to revenue collection and that education, health, subsidies, and social transfers account for the majority of the benefits the poorest receive. The last of these are excluded from the analysis in this section, as refugees receive humanitarian assistance and are not eligible for social assistance programs. Rather than using social transfers to establish refugees' needs for assistance, the previous section calculated the cost of subsistence needs directly.

FIGURE 6.6

Taxes paid and benefits received in Jordan by household income decile

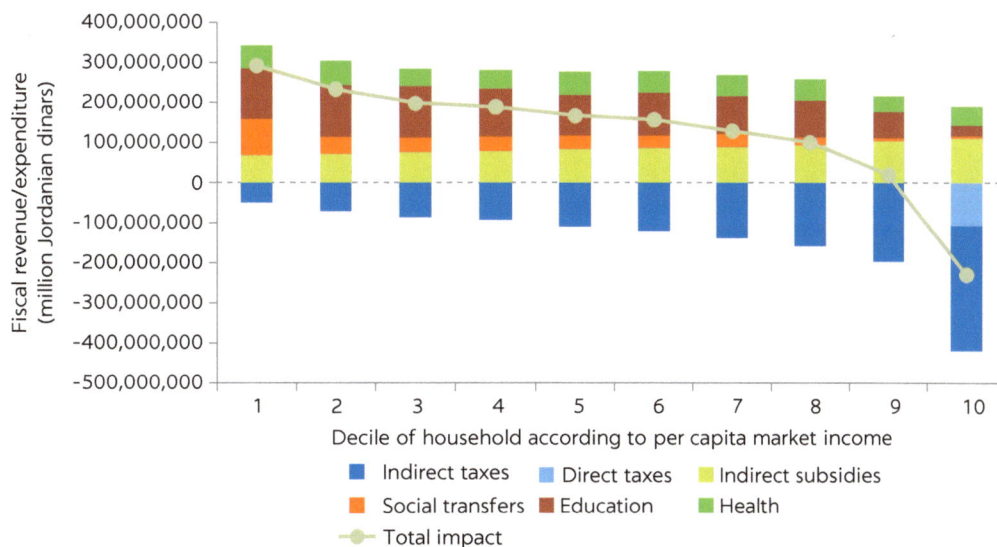

Source: Original figure for this publication using data from Rodriguez and Wai-Poi 2021.

Finally, note that the CEQ approach to fiscal incidence analysis intends to determine distributions within the entire budget. In practice, major elements of the budget (such as spending on defense, infrastructure, or interest) cannot be allocated, nor can grants received. This unallocated net balance is treated separately.

Savings from refugee participation in services provision

To calculate the fiscal cost of refugee participation in services provision, the approach here assumes that the cost of providing services equals that for providing services to nationals in the same consumption decile. Refugees are mapped to the decile corresponding to their income (figure 6.7).[14]

The fiscal cost for providing services in sector s is the sum across all 10 deciles d of the fiscal cost attributable to that decile, $C_{d,s}$, weighted by the proportion of refugee households in that decile, w_d.

$$C_s = \sum_{d=1}^{10} w_d \times C_{d,s} \tag{6.3}$$

To assess the cost of refugee participation in services provision, the same logic as that used for estimating the cost of subsistence needs is followed:[15]

- In the no-income scenario, refugees earn no income, and all are mapped into the first income decile.
- In the current participation scenario, refugees are mapped to the decile that corresponds to their consumption level with assistance excluded; although they remain concentrated in the lowest deciles, a few end up in higher income deciles.[16]
- In the two full-participation scenarios, counterfactual income (that is, potential earnings if refugees participated fully in Jordan's labor market) is used to determine how Syrian refugees would be distributed across income deciles if they were able to earn income in the same way as other immigrants or Jordanian nationals.

FIGURE 6.7

Distribution of refugees by consumption decile under various participation scenarios

(percent)

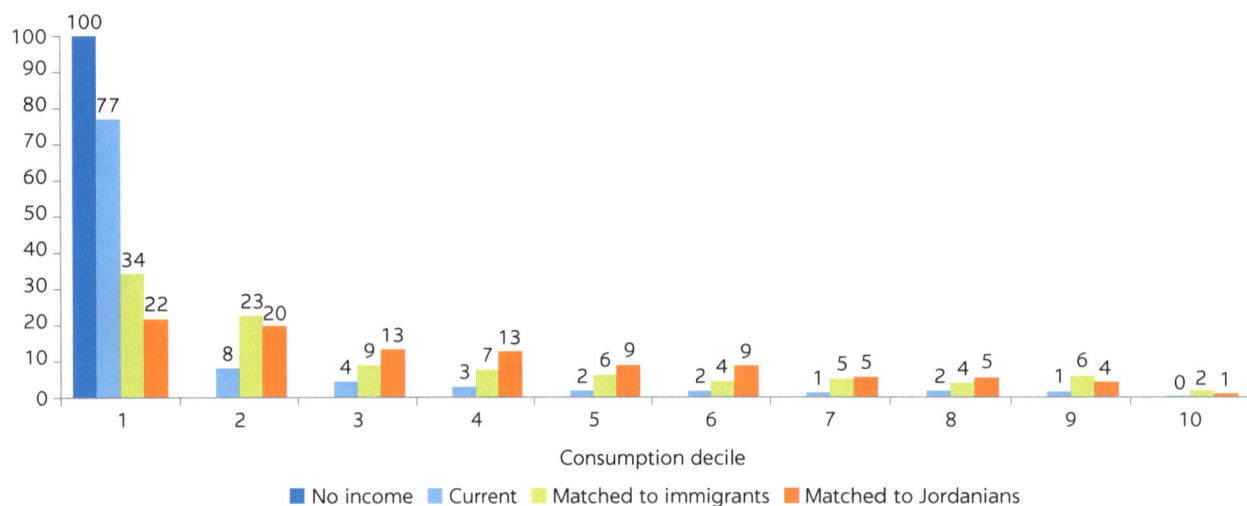

Source: Original figure for this publication using data from UNHCR 2021.

As the net cost of providing public services declines for higher income deciles, greater integration of refugees into a host country's labor market reduces the fiscal cost of protecting them. In the methodology employed here, once refugees are mapped into income deciles and the fiscal incidence is expressed in per capita terms, the net cost of public transfers to refugees can be determined through straightforward multiplication.

Table 6.1 presents the data needed to estimate the fiscal cost of providing services to Syrian refugees in Jordan. The first eight columns in the table present the distribution of refugees by income decile for the different scenarios; the last column shows the net fiscal cost captured in the CEQ (excluding social transfers). These include in-kind transfers for health and education, subsidies, and the indirect effect of subsidies, net of the contributions made to revenue collection.

As the table shows, net per capita cost declines with wealth and even becomes negative for those in the tenth decile.

Fiscal incidence analysis, aiming to identify the distributional aspects of spending and revenue collection, analyzes those revenue and spending categories that can be attributed to individual households and ignores categories that cannot. The implicit assumption is that the unanalyzed costs are uniformly spread across the population and hence distributionally irrelevant. For identifying the fiscal cost of hosting refugees, however, these omitted categories are not irrelevant. Refugees benefit from the justice system, from public waste and environmental management, and from the maintenance of roads and highways, as do nationals and other immigrants. Refugees also contribute to implicit revenues, such as profit taxes collected from firms and grants received from donors. To capture these benefits and contributions, an "unallocated attribution," the net (revenue-spending) portion of fiscal spending not analyzed by the CEQ methodology, is included here. This unallocated attribution is a uniform per capita amount and is thus proportional to the number of refugees in the country. In the

TABLE 6.1 Data needed to estimate fiscal incidence of participation in services provision

	NO-INCOME SCENARIO		CURRENT PARTICIPATION SCENARIO		FULL-PARTICIPATION SCENARIO				ALL SPENDING (EXCLUDING SOCIAL ASSISTANCE) MINUS REVENUES
					MATCHED WITH OTHER IMMIGRANTS		MATCHED WITH JORDANIANS		
	DISTRIBUTION (%)		DISTRIBUTION (%)		DISTRIBUTION (%)		DISTRIBUTION (%)		JD PER CAPITA PER YEAR
DECILE	CAMP	OUTSIDE	CAMP	OUTSIDE	CAMP	OUTSIDE	CAMP	OUTSIDE	
1	100	100	80.6	58.6	37.2	19.3	23.4	12.6	306
2	0	0	6.6	14.9	23.7	17.3	20.8	14.4	290
3	0	0	3.5	8.4	8.4	11.1	13.4	12.3	245
4	0	0	2.3	5.1	7.4	8.2	12.5	12.8	231
5	0	0	1.5	3.2	5.8	7.4	8.2	11.7	202
6	0	0	1.4	2.7	2.8	11.9	8.5	9.4	192
7	0	0	1.2	1.5	4.4	8.0	4.8	9.0	148
8	0	0	1.6	2.4	3.0	7.8	4.8	7.4	123
9	0	0	1.2	3.0	5.5	7.3	3.2	8.3	17
10	0	0	0.2	0.4	1.8	1.8	0.7	2.3	−358
	100	100	100	100	100	100	100	100	

Source: Original table for this publication using data in Rodriguez and Wai-Poi 2021.

FIGURE 6.8

Total and per refugee costs of services provision under different participation scenarios

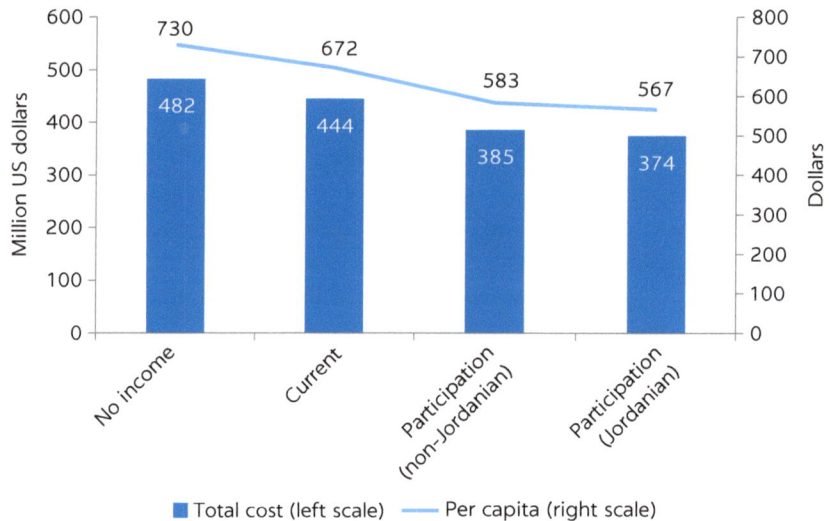

Source: Original figure for this publication using data from UNHCR 2021 and Rodriguez and Wai-Poi 2021.

Jordan CEQ methodology, the net amount not analyzed is JD 799 million, which translates into an unallocated attribution of $195 per capita per year.

For calculating the value of participation savings, this amount does not matter, as it is the same irrespective of a refugee household's decile in the income distribution. But for the determination of the fiscal cost of hosting refugees in an inclusive manner, it does matter.

The cost of hosting refugees and the value of refugee participation in basic services provision can now be calculated.[17] Figure 6.8 presents results for all refugees (no distinction is made between those living in and outside of refugee camps).

The total fiscal cost of services provision to Syrian refugees in Jordan is about $482 million per year in the no-income scenario and $444 million per year in the current participation scenario. The difference, $38 million per year, is another contribution Jordan makes to the fiscal cost of sharing responsibility for Syrian refugees.

The cost for services provision drops further once Syrian refugees are more integrated into Jordan's labor market, reaching a minimum of about $380 million annually (an annual saving of $92 million).

These policy scenarios thus illustrate that, like the fiscal cost of basic needs assistance, the fiscal cost for services drops with the degree of refugees' economic participation. Yet savings are much less than those due to the reduction in the cost of subsistence needs. Of the total cost savings of $860 million per year, $821 million is attributable to the reduction in subsistence assistance, whereas $38 million is related to public-services provision.

HUMANITARIAN COST SAVINGS AND SPILLOVER COSTS

As noted earlier, when the resulting cost savings in terms of subsistence needs assistance ($821 million per year) and from reduced fiscal expenditure ($38 million) are taken together, the current policies of the government of Jordan save the international community an estimated $860 million per year. The question is: to whom do these savings belong?

When there is a large influx of refugees and they are hosted in an inclusive manner, there will undoubtedly be negative spillover effects in the host country. The quality of services might decline, for instance, as more children attend school in the host country and as the demand for health care there increases. Some of these spillover effects will likely be economic. For example, prices of goods will rise when demand for them increases. Many of these spillover effects will be temporary, as people and governments respond to the new realities. For some goods and services, like food, a quick supply response usually follows the increase in demand, and prices return to normal after a short period. For others, like housing and medical services, the supply response takes longer, because making additional housing available takes time, as does recruiting new doctors and nurses. In the labor market, it takes time before the additional labor is productively absorbed,[18] even more so in a segmented economy like Jordan's, with low labor participation rates and high unemployment (see chapter 5). After some time, most of the negative spillover effects will have been absorbed (though not all), and what remains will be mostly positive contributions of refugees to jobs, gross domestic product (GDP), and economic growth.

Putting a monetary value on the cost of such spillover effects is challenging in respect to the situation in Jordan, as it is hard to disentangle the effects of the inflow of Syrian refugees from those from other events, such as the civil war in the Syrian Arab Republic that caused the inflow of refugees in the first place, or to establish a causal relationship between the arrival of refugees and other changes in Jordanian society. Figure 6.10 shows, for instance, that the inflow of refugees in 2012 and 2013 coincided with a rapid increase in Jordan's debt-to-GDP ratio, a decline in its GDP per capita, and rising unemployment. None of these events can be (solely) attributed to refugees: how much of the rising

FIGURE 6.9

Correlation between country contributions to cost savings and spillover cost

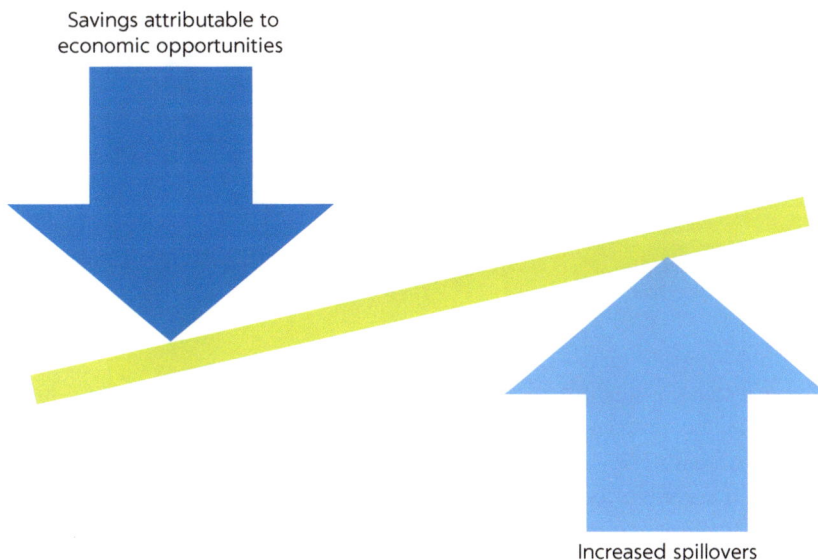

Source: Original figure for this publication.

FIGURE 6.10

Coincidence of inflow of Syrian refugees with economic changes

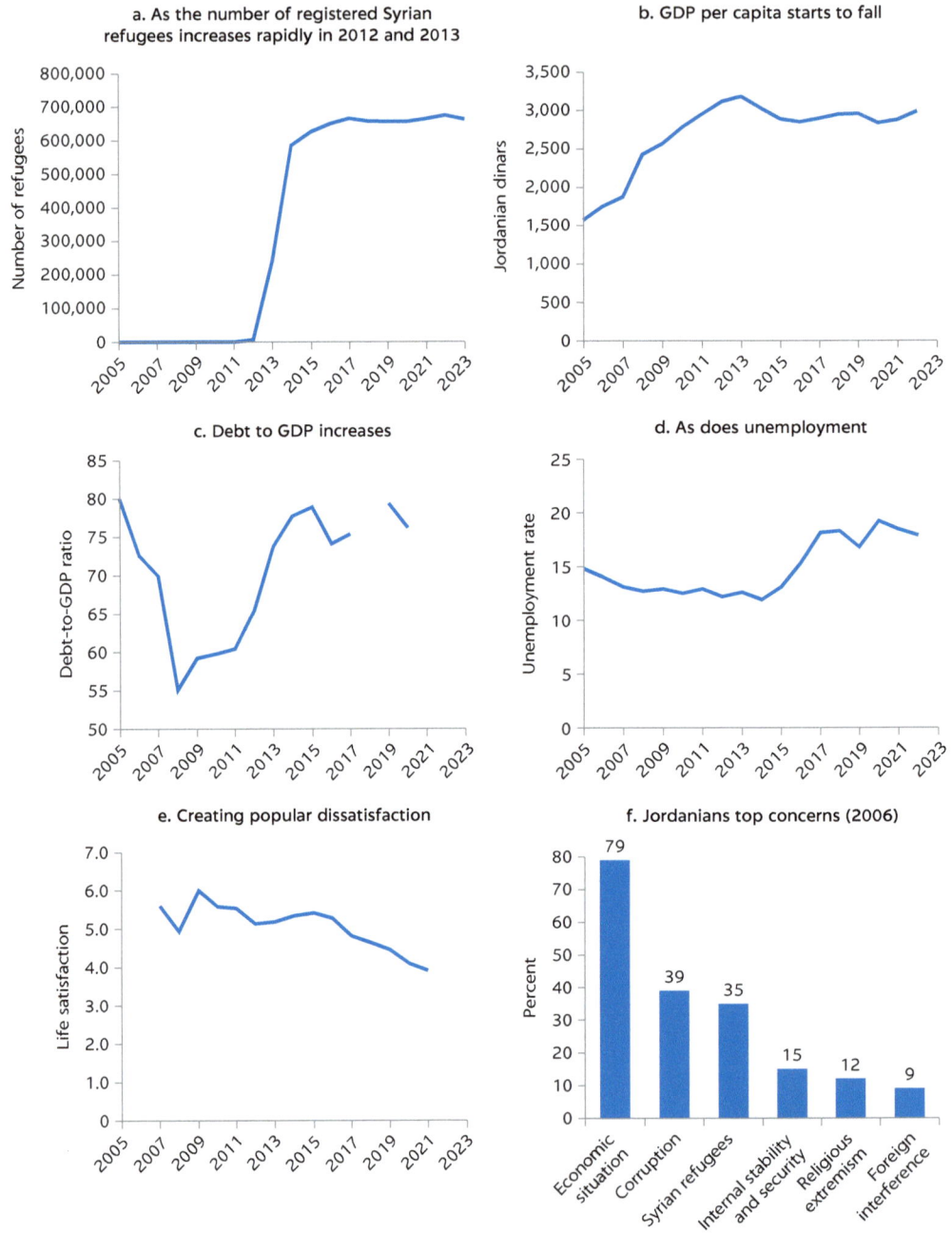

a. As the number of registered Syrian
refugees increases rapidly in 2012 and 2013

b. GDP per capita starts to fall

c. Debt to GDP increases

d. As does unemployment

e. Creating popular dissatisfaction

f. Jordanians top concerns (2006)

Sources: Ceyhun 2017; World Bank, World Development Indicators database (https://databank.worldbank
.org/source/world-development-indicators).
Note: GDP = gross domestic product.

unemployment is attributable to spillover effects from the war in Syria, how much to economic decision-making, and how much to the additional availability of refugee labor?

Even if certain effects can be attributed to the inflow of Syrian refugees into Jordan, it is not evident how to estimate their cost. For many impacts, it is hard to obtain counterfactuals, and even when there is evidence of a particular effect, such as that the influx of refugees increased rents, particularly for low-cost housing,[19] how should this effect be costed: as the additional spending paid by renters, or as the construction costs for additional social housing? And what if the policy response is a no-cost easing of construction permits for the private sector? Or how should the windfalls landlords experience and the associated increase in tax revenue be accounted for? In short, even when spillovers are evident, estimating their costs is challenging.

Even though the monetary costs of spillovers are hard to estimate with any degree of precision, citizens perceive them nonetheless. As long as they do, it makes less sense to expand on the nuances of estimating costs and whether these costs can be attributed to refugees. If citizens report a decline in their well-being and attribute this to the inflow of refugees, decision makers are forced to respond to avoid further discontent and a crumbling of support for hosting and including refugees in the economy. Thus, the drop in life satisfaction after 2012 in Jordan noted in panel e of figure 6.10 is of concern, as is the fact that when asked what their top concerns are, Jordanians frequently mention the presence of Syrian refugees (Ceyhun 2017).

Jordan's contribution to cost savings in regard to support for Syrian refugees is a global public good that currently benefits the international community, which otherwise would have borne additional cost for providing refugees with subsistence needs (had all refugees remained in camps or if no refugees had been allowed to work in Jordan). Yet these savings are intrinsically related to impacts felt in Jordan's society (see figure 6.10), and using part of these savings to help Jordan build continued support for refugee participation would make sense—both the current savings, which would need to be sustained, as well as any additional savings that could be realized if Jordan integrates Syrian refugees more deeply into its economy.

Bills are potentially being left on the sidewalk, as there is scope for a mutually beneficial bargain. As noted earlier in the chapter, savings on humanitarian assistance to Syrian refugees could rise from $860 million to $1.3 billion with further participation of refugees in Jordan's economy and services provision. But Jordan's decision makers are significantly and understandably reluctant to take the next step. They worry about competition with Jordanian workers; currently refugees mostly compete with immigrant labor (Malaeb and Wahba 2023), but the next generation of refugees is better educated and might compete with Jordanians, especially if the labor market is opened to them. They also worry about unpredictable funding, the lack of multiyear commitments to funding, and financing modalities that are ill-suited for financing recurrent costs related to health, education or—maybe one day—social protection.

CONCLUSION: A TRIPLE WIN

This chapter has presented an approach for identifying the fiscal cost of hosting Syrian refugees in Jordan inclusively and the savings associated with including refugees in Jordan's economy. It builds on the idea that the cost of hosting refugees varies with the degree of their integration into Jordan's labor market and estimates the cost of hosting them under three scenarios: a baseline with no economic participation, a scenario that reflects the current situation, and a scenario that sketches what full economic participation might look like.

Empirical application of the approach identifies significant savings associated with labor market integration. The cost of hosting a Syrian refugee in Jordan drops from $2,678 per refugee per year in the no-income scenario to $1,148 in the current participation scenario and to $543 in a full-participation scenario.

The chapter also discusses spillover effects associated with including Syrian refugees in the Jordanian economy. These spillovers affect Jordan's citizens through their impact on prices and the labor and housing markets. Any substantial refugee influx, like the one resulting from the Syrian conflict, will have substantial impacts, particularly in sectors of the host economy in which a supply response takes time: rental prices may temporarily rise in the housing market, for example, and the quality of services provision may be affected. These impacts are hard to quantify. Yet politically these hard-to-quantify effects matter greatly, and through careful analytics, they can be assessed.

Sharing responsibility for refugee support requires a dynamic and continuous interaction between host and donor countries and a readiness to find solutions to emerging challenges. Jordan's experience with the Jordan Compact can inspire in this regard. The compact offers nonfiscal compensation for the country's willingness to host refugees, such as increased access to the European market, which may have helped offset adverse labor market impacts of the refugees' presence.

The $860 million in cost savings identified in the chapter and the possibility for an additional $400 million with further economic participation of refugees make a strong case for continuing down the path of refugee economic participation. It would be a triple win: for the government of Jordan, which would receive funding for development projects that would make refugee participation more palatable to its own population; for the donor community, which would save on the amount of aid it needs to provide; and last but not least, for refugees, who would gain increased (financial) autonomy.

ANNEX 6A. ADDITIONAL TABLE

TABLE 6A.1 **Poverty incidence and poverty gaps under different scenarios (using national poverty line)**
(percent)

SCENARIO		TOTAL	CAMPS	OUTSIDE OF CAMPS
Arrival / baseline	Poverty incidence	100	100	100
	Poverty gap	100	100	100
Current	Poverty incidence	72	85	70
	Poverty gap	36	55	32
Participation (matched with other immigrants)	Poverty incidence	37	58	33
	Poverty gap	8	16	7
Participation (matched with Jordanians)	Poverty incidence	25	37	22
	Poverty gap	5	9	5

Source: Original table for this publication based on data in UNHCR 2021.

NOTES

1. Subsidized electricity for refugees was abolished in 2021.
2. United Nations General Assembly Resolution A/RES/72/150, "Resolution Adopted by the General Assembly on 19 December 2017" (https://www.un.org/en/ga/72/resolutions .shtml).
3. Chapter 4 pointed out that both the poverty line and the minimum expenditure basket have shortcomings in regard to estimating the amount needed for assistance. Those of the minimum expenditure basket (inconsistency, nonconformity with revealed preferences of refugees, and an arbitrary maximum household size of seven, among others) are particularly concerning. Yet the poverty line also has limitations (it does not account for adult equivalence or economies of scale at the household level).
4. There are variations on this approach, for example, one in which instead of total consumption value, the value of food consumption is equated to the cost of a minimum basket of food. In essence these approaches are comparable in that they determine a minimum cost for basic needs without predefining which goods need to be purchased.
5. Jordan's national poverty line exceeds the refugee poverty line of JD 81 (for 2021) presented in chapter 3, which is calculated based on the United Nations High Commissioner for Refugees' Vulnerability Assessment Framework survey. The consumption module used in the Vulnerability Assessment Framework survey is an abbreviated version of the Household Income and Expenditure Survey consumption module, and shorter consumption modules typically bias consumption downward. Moreover, poverty lines, even those measuring extreme poverty, are relative and tend to increase with income (Joliffe et al. 2022; Ravallion and Chen 2011), as reflected in lower international poverty lines for lower-income ($2.15 at purchasing-power parity) than for lower-middle-income ($3.65 at purchasing power parity) and upper-middle-income ($6.85 at purchasing-power parity) countries. For Syrian refugees, whose consumption is less than that of their hosts, a similar phenomenon is observed, as refugees' food consumption is composed of cheaper calories, and their nonfood consumption is lower.
6. Administering assistance comes with significant cost—for program design, planning, and coordination; eligibility determination and recertification activities; information to clients, public relations, and appeals; payment of benefits; maintenance of beneficiary databases; and audits, monitoring, and evaluation—that depend on program characteristics. To account for this cost, the equation uses a coefficient for the cost of basic needs to apply an 8 percent markup to account for administrative cost (Grosh et al. 2022; Tesliuc et al. 2014) and an additional 5 percent top-up to capture the cost of refugee registration and protection.
7. No savings are assumed, which seems reasonable in view of the high degree of destitution among refugees.
8. Consumption before assistance is determined using the Vulnerability Assessment Framework survey (see chapter 4). Since that framework's shorter consumption module underestimates consumption relative to the longer module in the Household Income and Expenditure Survey, and as the poverty line is based on the latter, the calculations here adjust Vulnerability Assessment Framework survey consumption for underreporting, using the approach presented in chapter 3.
9. The analysis presented here is derived from the Vulnerability Assessment Framework survey, as it allows identification of the assistance refugees have received. The Household Income and Expenditure Survey consumption module is more detailed than that in the Vulnerability Assessment Framework survey, so the former records higher levels of consumption. Where both are used, as is the case here, the difference must therefore be accounted for. To make the necessary adjustments, the chapter follows the same approach as that in chapter 3 for long- and short-form consumption modules.
10. In the matching approach, a logit regression is first estimated, with nationality as the left-hand variable and personal characteristics and region as independent variables. Next, using predicted odds ratios, Syrian refugees are matched with other immigrants and Jordanians, respectively, using the nearest-neighbor method, in which each refugee is matched with the two nearest neighbors and the refugee's consumption is predicted using the average of the two nearest neighbors' consumption.

11. The ability to increase Jordan's contribution to refugee burden sharing thus depends on policies allowing refugees to be included fully in the labor market *and* on livelihood support to restore refugees' productive asset base.

12. The consumption of matched Jordanians includes direct transfers. To account for this, these direct transfers are added to the fiscal cost of assistance calculated using matched consumption.

13. Non-Jordanians are not covered by the CEQ methodology for Jordan.

14. To facilitate comparison, all amounts are reported in 2023 dollars, adjusted for inflation at an exchange rate of 1.41 dollars to 1 Jordanian dinar.

15. For countries like Jordan where the consumption survey comprises a refugee stratum, the fiscal cost of participation can also be calculated directly. In the absence of access to Household Income and Expenditure Survey data, estimating the fiscal cost by mapping refugees into existing income deciles offers a reasonable alternative.

16. The national poverty line in Jordan falls in the second income decile.

17. To account for differences in the unit cost of providing certain services, an overhead of 25 percent is assumed for health and education. This number is informed by the range of refugee coefficients included in the World Bank and United Nations High Commissioner for Refugees (2021) global education costing exercise. For water, education, and collection of revenues, a coefficient of zero is assumed, as there is no reason to assume that the cost of providing electricity or water to refugees differs from that for providing it to nationals.

18. Winkler and Gonzalez (2019) report that an increase in the relative wages of unskilled labor accompanied the increase in the supply of unskilled workers driven by Syrian refugees, suggesting that the demand for unskilled workers grew faster than the rising supply.

19. See Alhawarin, Assaad, and Elsayed (2018) for evidence of the disruption to housing markets. These authors note that the influx of Syrian refugees in Jordan hurt housing quality; increased rental prices, particularly among poorer and less-educated households; and induced locals to move to other localities. Their analysis suggests that poorer Jordanians are in direct competition with refugees for access to affordable housing, and the authors argue that more inclusive housing finance or greater incentives to increase the supply of affordable rental housing could mitigate this effect.

REFERENCES

Alhawarin, Ibrahim, Ragui Assaad, and Ahmed Elsayed 2021. "Migration Shocks and Housing: Short-Run Impact of the Syrian Refugee Crisis in Jordan." *Journal of Housing Economics* 53: 101761. https://doi.org/10.1016/j.jhe.2021.101761.

Ceyhun, Huseyin Emre. 2017. *Jordan Five Years after the Uprising: Findings from the Arab Barometer.* Jordan Wave 4 Country Report. Princeton, NJ: Arab Barometer. https://www.arabbarometer.org/wp-content/uploads/Jordan_Public_Opinion_Survey_2016.pdf.

Foster, James, Joel Greer, and Erik Thorbecke. 1984. "A Class of Decomposable Poverty Measures." *Econometrica* 52 (3): 761–66. https://doi.org/10.2307/1913475.

Grosh, Margaret, Phillippe Leite, Matthew Wai-Poi, and Emil Tesliuc, eds. 2022. *Revisiting Targeting in Social Assistance: A New Look at Old Dilemmas.* Washington, DC: World Bank. https://doi.org/10.1596/978-1-1814-1.

Joliffe, Dean Mitchell, Daniel Gerszon Mahler, Christoph Lakner, Aziz Atamanov, and Samuel Kofi Tetteh Baah. 2022. "Assessing the Impact of the 2017 PPPs on the International Poverty Line and Global Poverty." Policy Research Working Paper 9941, World Bank Group, Washington, DC. http://documents.worldbank.org/curated/en/353811645450974574/Assessing-the-Impact-of-the-2017-PPPs-on-the-International-Poverty-Line-and-Global-Poverty.

Malaeb, Bilal, and Jackline Wahba. 2023. "Impact of Syrian Refugees on Male Immigrants' Labor Market Outcomes in Jordan." *International Migration Review* 58 (1): 1–32. https://doi.org/10.1177/01979183221149015.

Ravallion, Martin. 1998. "Poverty Lines in Theory and in Practice." Living Standards Measurement Study Working Paper 133, World Bank Group, Washington, DC. http://documents.worldbank.org/curated/en/916871468766156239/Poverty-lines-in-theory-and-practice.

7 Takeaways on Refugee Economic Participation and Steps toward a Triple Win

JOHANNES HOOGEVEEN

MAIN MESSAGES

Refugee participation in a host country's economy creates a triple win: it improves refugee financial autonomy and generates savings on humanitarian assistance; these savings can, in turn, be invested in measures to offset negative spillovers associated with refugee participation and in development of the host economy. Realizing this triple win, in the case of Syrian refugees in Jordan, requires commitments from international financial donors, humanitarian agencies, and the government of Jordan. The large amounts involved—$860 million per year is on the table and an additional $400 million per year within reach—should generate interest in achieving a successful bargain.

With the monetary amount at stake clarified in chapter 6, this chapter outlines what each of the institutional partners needs to do to realize the bargain. The government of Jordan needs to remove obstacles to labor market integration of Syrian refugees. International financial donors need to commit to providing funding for the recurrent fiscal expenses associated with hosting refugees inclusively, as well as resources for additional investments in Jordan's economic development. Humanitarian agencies need to improve the efficiency of their delivery models and focus on the most vulnerable while aligning the provision of assistance with refugee financial autonomy.

Realizing the bargain will not be easy, but Jordan's refugee response has a history of embracing innovative solutions. The chapter outlines four measures partners can take to facilitate a bargain: more research on refugee participation; greater transparency on financing, costs, and spending; a strategy for investing in the host economy; and a regular dialogue.

RECAP OF KEY RESULTS

This book set out to do two things: to shed light on the welfare of Syrian refugees in Jordan, with deep dives into poverty, cash assistance, and the labor market, and to contribute to the discussion on sharing the burden of hosting refugees by putting a monetary value on the cost of doing so and on the savings in humanitarian aid that can be realized by embracing refugees' economic participation. The main findings can be summarized as follows.

Syrian refugees are not passive subjects in need of assistance. Like everybody else, they seek autonomy and are ready to work. Given the opportunity, they will do so, but opportunities in Jordan are constrained. Still, the government of Jordan has made noteworthy efforts to host, accommodate, and include refugees in Jordan's economy and service provision. Refugees are allowed to use public services, especially those related to education and health, and are at liberty to stay where they want: 80 percent of Syrian refugees in Jordan live in host communities, outside the refugee camps established for them.

Syrian refugees are also allowed to work. Yet unlike what is the case for education and health, Jordan's economic hospitality comes with restrictions with respect to the kind of professions and the sectors that are open to refugees. Limited opportunities in the labor market, in combination with personal constraints such as low levels of human, financial, and physical capital and high dependency ratios, relegate Syrians to low-paying jobs typically taken by immigrant labor from the Arab Republic of Egypt (Betts 2021; Malaeb and Wahba 2023).

Low wages and limited labor market participation constrain refugees' financial autonomy and explain why, 13 years after arriving in Jordan, Syrian refugees remain dependent on humanitarian aid. Fortunately, like the government of Jordan, the international community has played its part and generously provided financing to assist these refugees. The aid has barely been enough, though, as evidenced by the high level of poverty among refugees: 58 percent. Still, in the absence of assistance, poverty would have been much higher, and 80 percent of refugees would have fallen below the national poverty line.

Although the lowering of the poverty rate among Syrian refugees in Jordan underscores the importance of aid in reducing poverty, the largest contributor to poverty reduction among these refugees remains the labor market. Despite limited labor market access, 28 percent of Syrian refugees are financially autonomous and not dependent on any assistance. For the remaining 72 percent, whose consumption is below the poverty line, incomes earned in the labor market cover 50 percent of the minimum standard for consumption (that is, the national poverty line). Humanitarian assistance covers an additional 21 percent.[1] The remaining consumption gap (29 percent) reflects the deprivation poor refugees face.

The cost of hosting refugees, and the savings generated by allowing refugees to work, also reflect the importance of refugees' earnings. Hosting an estimated 660,000 registered Syrian refugees costs about $909 million per year, split almost equally between expenses for providing basic needs assistance and the cost of refugee access to public services. Calculations in chapter 6 show that these costs would have been twice as high ($1.8 billion per year) had the refugees not been allowed to work. Allowing refugees to work generates substantial savings: $860 million per year.

The findings of this volume also imply that whereas eliminating poverty among Syrian refugees would require $465 million annually in basic needs assistance, poor Syrian refugees receive considerably less than this amount. This explains the continued high levels of poverty among Syrian refugees in Jordan.

It would be easy (and correct) to state that more money is needed for humanitarian assistance to Syrian refugees in Jordan, but such an appeal is unlikely to fall on willing ears in the current context. More-promising avenues for alleviating poverty among refugees would be to increase the efficiency of humanitarian aid provided (chapter 4 suggests that there is scope to do so) and to further promote refugees' economic participation.

A TRIPLE WIN

Additional economic participation holds the promise of delivering a triple win (figure 7.1) that increases refugees' financial autonomy and reduces the amount of aid the international community needs to provide to cover the cost of hosting refugees, thus freeing up resources for developmental investments in host communities, from which refugees would benefit as well, as long as they are integrated into these communities.

As straightforward and obvious as a triple win seems on paper (after all, it could save some $400 million per year), it is hard to realize in practice. Even the existing savings on assistance that stem from Syrian refugees' current level of economic participation are far from given, and the government of Jordan and international donors engage in constant negotiation about benefits granted to refugees and the financing available. In this tug of war, refugees have already lost access to subsidized electricity (since 2021, available only to Jordanians) and soon may have to pay fees for their work permits.

Two issues seem particularly pressing: limited clarity on how much financing is provided and concerns about the economic consequences of a fuller integration of Syrian refugees into Jordan's economy. On the financing issue, this volume has little to add, other than that data on the matter are not readily accessible and are inconsistent. The second issue is discussed on the next page.

FIGURE 7.1

Increased economic participation by refugees: A triple win

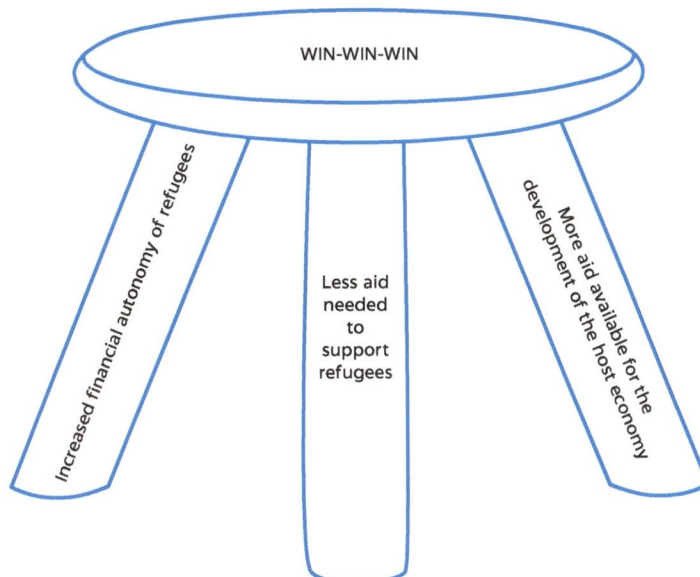

Source: World Bank.

Refugee economic participation often comes with spillover effects. Depending on how these effects are distributed, they may be perceived as positive—for instance, employers who benefit from cheap labor or landlords who increase rents as the demand for housing increases—but they can also be negative, as in the case of, for instance, unskilled Jordanians who face additional competition in the job market or poor Jordanians who face higher rents. Many of these effects are temporary and diminish as economies adjust to refugees' presence, but the temporary welfare losses some citizens may experience because of refugees' participation require policy attention. Precisely because of the existence of negative spillovers, the monetary savings associated with refugee participation need to be considered in combination with additional aid to address these spillovers and to create a dynamic economy that can absorb additional refugee labor and demand for goods.

The size of the existing and potential savings and the possibility of a bargain that is mutually beneficial should motivate discussions among the donor community, humanitarian agencies, and the government of Jordan. Such a bargain should comprise three elements:

- *Consolidating existing achievements.* Refugees' economic participation increases their financial autonomy, and it currently reduces the cost of humanitarian assistance to Syrian refugees in Jordan by as much as $860 million per year. These are noteworthy achievements worthy of protection, requiring commitments from the government of Jordan to continue its support and from international donors to provide predictable (recurrent) funding to share the burden of hosting refugees.
- *Promoting greater economic participation of refugees.* Further integrating refugees into Jordan's economy would give the 72 percent of refugees who remain dependent on aid a shot at financial autonomy. It could also offer an additional $400 million in savings on humanitarian assistance per year that would free up resources for investments in development priorities for host communities and the country in general. Further integration would require easing labor market restrictions on refugees, facilitating refugees' efforts to find work, and investing in restoring refugees' human capital.
- *Aligning humanitarian assistance with the promotion of financial self-reliance.* As long as humanitarian assistance continues to be provided, its delivery mechanisms should favor refugees' financial autonomy. They currently do not: assistance is unconditional, refugee camps are located in isolated areas with few economic opportunities, and those residing in camps are privileged in the receipt of assistance. It is important to scrutinize the aid delivery model with a focus on ways to increase the cost-effectiveness and targeting efficiency of delivery models and a better alignment between assistance and self-reliance. The adoption of measurable targets with respect to cost-effectiveness, efficiency, and self-reliance would be welcome.

Eventually, the incorporation of more and more refugees into the labor market and public services provision should open a pathway toward the dissolution of refugee camps. Refugees who continue to remain dependent on assistance need to be transferred to national social protection systems, with international donors providing credible commitments to bear the cost.

HOW TO GET THERE

Obviously attaining the triple win will be challenging. All institutional partners involved in the bargain will need to make important concessions and changes in the way business is done. None of the proposed measures is straightforward or easy to achieve. A number of confidence-building measures may promote progress:

- *Strengthening the evidence base for refugee participation.* The discussion on burden sharing for refugees deserves to move from deliberations about principles to discussions about numbers. This volume puts a monetary value on the cost of hosting refugees and the savings attributable to refugee participation. More research could further inform the debate.[2] Preferably researchers familiar with Jordan will carry out the necessary research using Jordanian data, requiring investments in data collection and local research capacity.

- *Developing a strategy for investing in Jordan's economy.* Absorbing additional refugee labor in Jordan's economy will require an investment strategy that identifies opportunities and bottlenecks. The Jordan Compact, which has been a political success but has had limited economic impact (Betts 2021), underscores the importance of a well-developed strategy. The investment strategy should build on the evidence mentioned in the first bullet and will help assure financial donors that reallocating humanitarian savings toward development activities is good economics.

- *Creating an active dialogue based on evidence.* The three objectives of the triple win can be realized only in conjunction with dialogue between the international community and Jordanian authorities. This dialogue can take many shapes. One option is to create an annual moment of reflection, for instance, through a high-level conference regarding the results of policy research on Jordan's economic progress and refugee participation. As this is not the first time that there has been a focus on realizing a triple win—the Jordan Compact also aimed to do so—a first conference might want to assess the successes and failures of the compact, the main obstacles to further refugee participation, and the gains to be realized if these obstacles were removed.

- *Aligning the delivery of humanitarian assistance with the promotion of refugee financial self-reliance.* As refugees transition to fuller economic participation, the existing provision of humanitarian aid should be made more conducive to their financial autonomy. Currently assistance is unconditional, and the continuation of camps far away from economic opportunities is an obstacle to economic integration, as is the privileging of assistance to refugees residing in camps. With aid budgets under strain and allocations for support to refugees split across ever-increasing refugee numbers, scrutiny of the aid delivery model is needed to identify ways to increase the cost-effectiveness and targeting efficiency of delivery models and to align assistance better with refugee self-reliance. The adoption of measurable targets with respect to cost-effectiveness, efficiency, and self-reliance would be welcome, and a program of research to develop and test different approaches could support it.

- *Committing to transparency.* Any collaboration is strengthened by trust, requiring a commitment to transparency and information sharing. Trust and understanding are strengthened when there is a common appreciation of the facts. Regrettably much information relevant to collaboration remains inaccessible. Data from critical surveys collected at great expense by Jordan's Department of Statistics remain unavailable for public analysis. Lack of information on overhead and the share of funding that reaches beneficiaries makes it extremely hard to assess the efficiency of services provided by humanitarian agencies. Financial donors need to be more transparent about the financing they make available for refugees, along with the conditions attached to it. All institutional partners with a stake in realizing the triple win face challenges only they can address. Improving transparency does not require collaboration; each institution can accomplish it independent of the others, providing the government of Jordan, financial donors, and humanitarian agencies active in Jordan each with an opportunity to demonstrate their commitment to realizing the triple win.

NOTES

1. As chapter 6 notes, the preassistance poverty gap is 36 percent, and the preassistance poverty incidence is 72 percent. If preassistance consumption is taken as a proxy for income, then poor refugees finance 50 percent (0.36/0.72) of the poverty line through self-earned income. Once assistance is included in consumption, the poverty incidence and poverty gap become 59 percent and 17 percent, respectively, implying an average poverty gap for poor refugees of 29 percent (0.17/0.59). It follows that 21 percent (50–29) is the average assistance offered to poor refugees.
2. What can be learned from the implementation of the Jordan Compact, how large the negative spillovers associated with additional refugee participation are, what options are available to address negative spillovers, how much these solutions would cost, how much financing is made available for refugees and hosts, what the regulatory and other barriers to further refugee participation are, and how humanitarian assistance can be aligned with refugee participation are just some of the issues that research could address.

REFERENCES

Betts, Alexander. 2021. *The Wealth of Refugees: How Displaced People Can Build Economies.* Oxford, UK: Oxford University Press.

Malaeb, Bilal, and Jackline Wahba. 2023. "Impact of Syrian Refugees on Male Immigrants' Labor Market Outcomes in Jordan." *International Migration Review* 58 (1): 1–32. https://doi.org/10.1177/01979183221149015.

Ravallion, Martin, and Shaohua Chen. 2011. "Weak Relative Poverty." *Review of Economics and Statistics* 93 (4): 1251–61.

Rodriguez, Laura, and Matthew Wai-Poi. 2021. *Fiscal Policy, Poverty and Inequality in Jordan: The Role of Taxes and Public Spending.* Washington, DC: World Bank.

Tesliuc, Emil, Lucian Pop, Margaret Grosh, and Ruslan Yemtsov. 2014. *Income Support for the Poorest: A Review of Experience in Eastern Europe and Central Asia.* Directions in Development. World Bank. https://doi.org/10.1596/978-1-4648-0237-9.

UNHCR (United Nations High Commissioner for Refugees). 2021. "Vulnerability Assessment Framework Population Survey for Refugees in Host Communities: Jordan, 2021" (data set). UNHCR, Geneva.

Winkler, Hernan Jorge, and Alvaro S. Gonzalez. 2019. "Jordan Jobs Diagnostic." World Bank, Washington, DC.

World Bank and UNHCR (United Nations High Commissioner for Refugees). 2021. *The Global Cost of Inclusive Refugee Education.* Washington, DC: World Bank.

World Bank. 2023. "Developing a Methodology for Measuring the Impact of Hosting, Protecting and Assisting Refugees (Phase II)—The Global Cost of Inclusive Refugee Education: 2023 Update." World Bank, Washington, DC. http://documents.worldbank.org/curated/en/099121323075047346/P179836067c4a9080bf7e0835f119a1da0.